"It is very easy and certainly less scary to read about Jan Broberg's story and pass judgement on her parents. Nobody wants to believe that the relentless saga of abuse Jan suffered at the hands of Robert Berchtold, could be happening right under their noses. After all they were loving and involved parents raising the children within a community that they assumed was safe. With bravery and humility Mary Ann Broberg takes responsibility for every single "wrong" choice she and her husband made over many years. Nothing can undo the harm done to Jan. But this breathtaking and unflinchingly honest book could be the reason that countless other children don't suffer similar fates."

        -Anna Paquin, Academy-Award Winning Actress

"The Broberg family's story is terrifying and tragic, but it's also one of dignity and healing. Jan and MaryAnn have written a haunting, unforgettable book that will not leave my mind. In *The Jan Broberg Story*, they detail the complete account of their family's years under the spell of a charismatic, psychopathic predator — and they tell it with candor, guts, and somehow even a great sense of humor."

        -Nick Antosca, TV Writer & Executive Producer

"Jan's true life story is unbelievably captivating and heartbreaking. I admire her ability to overcome so much trauma and abuse and then use her experiences to raise awareness and help other victims."

        -Mckenna Grace, Actress and Singer

"*The Jan Broberg Story* isn't *just* a story, it's an experience; an experience everyone should be aware of. It is the heart-gripping account of stolen innocence, offender mentality and tactics, and how trauma at its deepest levels can be survived and victims can thrive. This is a life-changing must read."

      -Det. Dave Markel, Ret., Sexual Assault Investigation and
            Trauma-Informed Interview Consultant

"Not only is *The Jan Broberg Story* completely engrossing, it exposes the ruthlessness of 'friendly' predators like Robert Berchtold, who will stop at nothing to satisfy their depraved urges. MaryAnn and Jan Broberg's courage to tell the unvarnished truth makes for a thought-provoking, jaw-dropping, cautionary tale of how predators groom their victims—and the victim's protectors—with friendship, flirtation, gifts, and twisted lies."

-**Merrie Campbell-Lee**, Writer, Editor, and Victims' Advocate

"Jan and her mother's courage to overcome such difficulty in their lives is already to be applauded, but to be able to share such a raw story with the world… that's a rare gift. What Jan went through was horrific, but her story can enlighten and teach others about the true dangers of those we think we know, trust, and love. Jan and MaryAnn are a true inspiration in overcoming the unthinkable. You won't be able to put this book down."

-**Michael Mazzella**, Emmy-nominated Producer

THE JAN BROBERG STORY

The True Crime Story of a Young Girl Abducted and
Brainwashed by a Friend of the Family

Jan & MaryAnn
Broberg

Fedd Books

P.O. Box 341973

Austin, TX 78734

www.thefeddagency.com

Published in association with The Fedd Agency, Inc., a literary agency.
Cover Design: The Fedd Agency

ISBN: 978-1-957616-11-7
EISBN: 978-1-957616-12-4

Library of Congress Number: 2022910474
Printed in the United States of America
First Edition 22 23 24 25 /6 5 4 3 2

This book is dedicated to:

Bobby, my love, my rock, and my best friend. Love forever, MaryAnn

My Dad, from whom I learned gratitude and that everyone matters!
The one who taught me that our highest calling is to practice unconditional love, to see the good, to be kind, and to laugh every day. You are
my Hero.

ACKNOWLEDGEMENTS

from MaryAnn and Jan

Deep loving thanks goes to:

My forever patient and supportive son, my rock who has battled life's ups and downs alongside me. You teach me open-mindedness and curiosity, fueling the fire that keeps me going, Austen.

To my incredible and resilient family, you are why I survived and thrived. You've been the best parents on the planet, Mom and Dad. Karen, you are my example and teacher. Susan, you are my defender and life coach.

My forever best friend who makes me talk and always listens. You're my cheerleader Caroline.

"The Girls" McKenzie, Tess, Melissa, Faith. You show me that blood is not as important as love.

To our many inspirational, close and enduring friends who constantly have encouraged us and who were there for us at the crossroads of life: Catherine, Jan, Tode, Gwyn, Merrie, Valerie, Dan, Stephanie, Emily, Tiffini, Anna, Michael, Travis, Chris, Dave, Alex, Nick, John, Nathan, Matt, Duke, Luigi, Eric, and Larry. Our families of friends, including the Tanners, Felts, Gardners, Campbells, Hofmans, Paynes, and Myers.

To our large extended family, the Brobergs and the Bucks, we are so lucky to have in our lives Grandchildren, Great Grandchildren, and incredible Aunts, Uncles, and Cousins that give our lives so much meaning. We appreciate your love so profoundly Matt, Eric, Kauren, Allison, Joel, Dane, Ashley, Nathan, Jasmin, Paige, Blake, Nevaeh, RJ, Tristan, Mason, Cora, Raynee, the Twins, and more.

Special thanks to the Fedd Agency, Funk Studios, Collective Speakers, Eat The Cat Productions, Top Knot Films, Talent Management Group, and Cohen Entertainment.

FOREWORD

By Jan Broberg
Reclaiming the Happiness of Childhood at Any Age

It's 2022, twenty years since my dear mom, MaryAnn Broberg, with my input, memories, interviews, and diary entries, completed the original self-published manuscript, *Stolen Innocence.* This tells the story of how I was twice abducted, brainwashed, and sexually abused at the hands of my captor, Robert Berchtold. It wasn't until long after I returned home that I finally opened up and told the whole truth about my full experience. She included my voice (along with my diary entries) alongside hers to provide a clearer picture of what was happening in real time.

I am Jan Broberg. This is the story of how I lived through some of the worst childhood experiences a vulnerable, developing teenager ever could. It is also an uplifting story of how experiences that could have ruined my life and the lives of my family members didn't! This is the story of what my mother experienced, what happened to me, and what we as a family endured… and then learned from. It's my hope to inspire readers to learn from our mistakes and, most importantly, to believe it is possible to reclaim their childhood and overcome their trauma to live full, happy lives no matter what age they may be.

Grooming—Influencing Through Fear

I was abducted and sexually abused by a close family friend, Robert Berchtold, who, over the years before the kidnapping, groomed, and manipulated my parents, my siblings, and me into trusting him, using underhanded tactics to get what he wanted from us all. When I could finally look back with adult eyes, I understood how insidiously he worked to instill fear in every choice I made. This is how he brainwashed me.

Soon after our families became friends, Berchtold started to tell stories of alien abductions and UFO sightings, not just as entertainment (because they definitely were) but as cautionary tales. He told them as though he believed aliens were real. We thought they were spooky and intriguing.

UFO sightings and the suspicion of alien invasions were a semi-obsession in the US, which started in the late 50s, as evidenced by the hundreds of popular television shows and movies on the subject at the time. The Broberg sisters and Berchtold children loved to talk about the stories B shared with us. He was a master storyteller and remembered intricate details from films like *2001: A Space Odyssey*, Orson Welles' novel, "War of the Worlds," and TV and radio series like *The Twilight Zone*, not to mention the Roswell, New Mexico alien conspiracy. His stories had an effect on our imaginations, and we also gravitated to the popular shows of the time, like *Lost in Space* and *Star Trek*.

Berchtold's wife Gail would occasionally recount the story of her own dad's famous UFO sightings along the Utah-Idaho border in the early 50s. Though I was kidnapped in the mid-seventies, the time period for Gail's father's "sightings" coincides with the national obsession with UFOs and alien life forms. As the story goes, after picking up farm supplies in Brigham City, Utah, her father had been driving home along a deserted, bumpy road when a group of lights appeared in the sky. He noticed they formed a clear and obvious circle. On another occasion, Gail's dad said dozens of people had reported seeing these objects flying around at night. Berchtold latched onto the story, and when he retold it, he would ominously add, "The government is saying they are weather balloons. It's obviously a cover-up."

Berchtold repeated his alien stories to the point of annoying my dad so much that he finally told him, "I don't want you alarming my kids with all this talk of aliens and spaceships. You do a good job of keeping them stirred up. In my opinion, it's one of the mysteries of the universe I don't have time to think about."

"Well, Broberg," he responded, "I have my own thoughts about it, but I would never frighten your girls. What's the big deal? They're getting a big kick out of it," he said sarcastically, downplaying my dad's concerns. It didn't seem like much, but looking back, we recognized his sci-fi storytelling as a simple, innocuous way to plant ideas in our minds, the idea that aliens were real. By the time Berchtold kidnapped me, he had spent months launching his elaborate con. His stories made me receptive to ideas that would ultimately provide him intimate access to me, his well-groomed, innocent victim.

When Berchtold finally kidnapped me, he used all of the popular stories from the news, movies, and television, and even his wife's family history to carefully implant the possibility of lies about aliens being real in a child's mind. His fantastical, supposed, communications with aliens ordered me to partner with him in following "their mission". He made me believe it would be through our obedience to everything they asked of us that we would be able to help them save their dying planet. The fear I experienced from their communication utterly brainwashed me into believing without question all of this was true. If either of us were to betray the aliens' commands, my family, the community, and church members would be at risk of total destruction. I was being fed messages over and again by the aliens. I later found out this was a series of recorded cassette tapes Berchtold had made and rigged so they could be played from secret hiding places wherever I was. He made the voices sound like aliens. In the aliens' words, the world and those I loved would be "vaporized" if I didn't obey their instructions.

In general, predators try to be as discreet and subtle as possible when grooming their victims (their goal is to go unnoticed); but few predators' tactics were quite as elaborate or fantastical as Berchtold's. He used all sorts of other means to groom our family, but it was the alien story in particular that conditioned me to be fearful, passive, and secretive, allowing him to gain prolonged, private access to me. This tactic was so highly unusual at the time that when the FBI eventually found the "alien" recordings on cassette tapes, they didn't know what they were listening to and dismissed them as irrelevant. He was clever enough to ensure the tapes were vague so no one would be alerted to their purpose. Berchtold influenced the minds and hearts of those who were supposed to know better and protect me from people like him. With the benefit of all this hindsight, I was finally able to identify his schemes as clear grooming tactics and describe them in detail.

Were We Clueless?

Events, as they unfolded in my life, were surreal. My mom was groomed every bit as much as I was for three years by our seeming family friend. Communities of trust can sometimes be the easiest grounds for not asking questions. We were taught that leadership knows best, and we should not question but respect those in authority. The 1970s were a different time. There was more trusting, less reporting, and in many cases, much more covering up, saving face, blaming, and disbelieving to preserve the institutions and family name to the detriment of the victim. We were told to protect the child but to forgive the sinner. This mentality is confusing and painful for a child. There needs to be better information, resources, and support for the victims. Trauma is not reversible, but there are proven methods to cope with psychophysiological harm. The prevailing wisdom toward change and healing is encouraging if we can make access to these modalities easy and affordable.

In my family's case, we were all predisposed to believe that people, in general, are helpful, kind, loving, and honest. We were surrounded by people like this and had little exposure to their darker sides. Robert Berchtold was a cruel, remorseless, serial pedophile. He was also charming and fun, a husband and father of five, a successful businessman, a church leader, and we trusted him. The fun he and his family brought to our lives made it easy for us to dismiss any tiny concerns that may have ever so briefly crossed our minds.

I need to make it clear for all who read this book: as a prepubescent child who was regularly hearing messages from aliens, reinforced by a man my whole family trusted, I was too young and afraid to even question whether this could possibly be made up, let alone suspect Berchtold was a pedophile intent on harming me. I say this because, for so many years, people have reacted with utter disbelief that I could have been so gullible. Trust me, any child at this stage of brain development would be susceptible to believing crazy things if they were hearing messages and were then sworn to keep it all a secret or someone might die.

Robert Berchtold was a master manipulator. He went to clever and elaborate lengths to gain access to me. His bag of tricks was seemingly endless. He created a sense of safety with everyone through his charming ways. He would sow confusion, fear, and chaos on those he wanted to cast suspicion. He would play favorites and create power plays for the children who wanted to feel special in his eyes. He cleverly created misguidance through scary stories or surprise visits. The lengths he went to in stirring up chaos and guilt which would be used to manipulate both of my parents—separately—were cunning and disgusting. His tactics to divide and conquer were effective on them both for a long time.

Berchtold always had excuses and answers for everything he did which might seem confusing, nonsensical, or outlandish. But if anyone pushed back, he would gaslight, deny, blame, deflect, and feign disbelief. This is a key defense pattern for predators. However, if he ever sensed he was crossing too far over a line or losing someone's trust, he would become instantly remorseful and beg for forgiveness. Berchtold was hard to **not** like.

In the end, we learned our lesson about extending trust too easily. Berchtold had destroyed our innocence.

Let's Talk Data

Information is powerful. When families discover the statistics of grooming and sexual abuse, they are empowered to recognize where they fall in
the stats and take action. Sexual abuse, molestation, incest, pedophilia,
and sexual assault in childhood are all traumatic events that change lives
forever. In my family, it was a close family friend who perpetrated the
crime. The Rape, Abuse, and Incest National Network (RAINN) tell us
that 93 percent of child victims of sexual assault are perpetrated by someone they know. Thirty-four percent are assaulted by a family member,
while 59 percent are assaulted by someone in the broader category of - a
social acquaintance. It is now widely known that perpetrators will often
spend just as much time, if not more, grooming the entire orbit of individuals around the intended victim, starting with the family.

The Jan Broberg Foundation—Strategy and Solutions

The year 2022 marks the launch of the Jan Broberg Foundation (JBF).
My story went viral for a reason. It was bizarre and strange enough that
the public was captivated. It helped me unwittingly become a beacon for
so many people. Everywhere I go, whenever I share my story, I see people's eyes fill with tears. I see expressions of pain and shame because many
of the people I talk to have stories so similar to my own. So many individuals are desperate to be heard, seen, believed, and understood. I can relate.
We were all groomed. We were all victims. But more importantly to me,
in my family's story, we are not only survivors, but we are thrivers—or as
I like to call those of us who make it through such horrors, "thrivivors"—
because we are so much more than just survivors, we thrive in spite of
what we've endured.

I was asked a long time ago by Charles Gill, an expert on pedophilia
as well as an advocate/ Juror for cases of abuse, how I was able to "come
back" from all of this. The answer I gave then remains true today: because
of the absolute love and support of my family and close friends —and a
lot of good counseling along the way. Today I would also add it is because

I truly believed I could heal, I could be happy, and I was worth it. I loved myself and my inner child enough to care for me/her. I needed to find my/her healing path—to spend the time, energy, and resources to make my life one of a "thrivivor." I took a very proactive approach. I stood up for myself, asking for and receiving the help I needed. Now it's my turn to be that support for others.

Helping Survivors Heal

Sadly, it is rare for a survivor to have the luxury of receiving unconditional love from their family. I was listened to. I was believed. I was never blamed. The majority of childhood sexual abuse survivors are not believed nor heard. They carry the suffocating burden of blame and shame. I call this the B.S. cycle. My choice to be in this space with sexual abuse survivors is because I want to create opportunities for each one to be heard (if they choose), believed (always), and to feel a sense of love and support from my foundation, similar to what I received. I want to do all I can to raise awareness, remove shame, and encourage forgiveness, understanding, and healing. There are proven science-based methods that deal with trauma and recovery that everyone should have access to, regardless of their ability to pay.

It goes without saying, the most deeply affected families and children need a village to help them thrive. To this end, in 2023, the JBF is launching an online village—a community to share our stories and support the two out of five children who are victims of sexual assault in the United States alone, not to mention their extended family members. The rates of assault vary from country to country, but my hope is that you will find healing and safety in our JBF online village, no matter where you are in the world.

Prevention Through Education: Spotting Grooming/ Stopping Predators in their Tracks

I also want the JBF to be part of the growing conversation that's been started as we collectively learn about grooming and how familiar and friendly most predators actually are. By sharing my story and educating the public on how to recognize the subtle, nearly imperceptible signs of grooming predators use to gain general trust and attain authoritative alone time with the intended victim(s), I hope the JBF helps to prevent abuse from ever happening in the first place. Our story has helped expose the truth: that contrary to most people's perceptions of predators as scary, dangerous strangers, they are much more likely to be people we know, trust, or even love. They are the "nice guys" hiding in plain sight. The truth is, most victims are sexually abused by someone they know—not a stranger—whether he or she is someone in our own home, our church, community center, sports team, school, neighborhood, or other institutions.

This is the ultimate reason my mother and I shared our story with such transparency and vulnerability. We want the mistakes we made to be part of the learning curve that helps all of us do better at **not** protecting predators because they are "good people," or a family member, etc., and instead intervene without hesitation and prevent predators from being able to gain access to a potential victim.

As we talk about and expose the grooming tactics predators use, the millions who have experienced this will recognize that they were groomed and also know they are not alone, and that it's not their fault. The JBF will provide helpful information and resources to the children and families who have been violated by this kind of trauma. We are here to help every person—whether it's the person who's been abused or the caregivers and others who are connected to the victim—to feel empowered! We will help you learn to speak up, act out, and stop predators from gaining access to the innocent. We want survivors to be free from shame, to be healthy and whole, to love themselves fully, and reclaim their happy childhood at any age!

The Jan Broberg Foundation is my way of making all of this happen. It allows me to share the story of how I've made it through the trauma of my youth, which makes it that much more "permissible" for others to share their stories. We will provide resources for individuals to forge their own path out of the secrecy and shame, out of the pain to live the full, rich lives they were always meant to live. Please join our JBF community through our newsletter and at thejanbrobergfoundation.org.

PROLOGUE

By MaryAnn Broberg
If Only

If only we had recognized the early signs that a sexual predator was targeting our daughter. If only we had acted earlier and with more intensity. If only we had understood where to get more help more quickly. The "if only" thoughts and regrets dominated my thinking as a mother for many years after the events described in this book.

Then it became clear to me that if our family had the courage to share our story, we could provide information that would prevent others from going through a similar experience. I came to understand that the greatest service we could give to other families was to tell the entire truth—the ugly truth, the tragic truth, the hopeful truth, even if it cast us in a less than ideal light. It was worth it to us.

Our family experienced a nightmare that was almost unendurable, yet somehow, we kept pulling together to put love before fear and creation above destruction. We were unaware and unwise, and our weaknesses were manipulated. Daring to see the complex reality took years. Healing took even more years—but we did it. We did it!

Shining a Light in the Dark

Child sexual abuse is widespread, but this doesn't have to be something we accept as inevitable. Together, as families and communities, we can evolve into societies that protect and nurture the innocence of our children. For years, abuse was such a deep secret that pedophiles flourished in the darkness, but the more light we shine on the issue and the more we focus on how to keep pedophiles away from our children in the first place, the less harm will be caused.

The chaos that unfolds in a family when abuse is present is hard to resolve. The shame and guilt I felt as a mother who had placed Jan in harm's way, along with the deep regret Jan's father experienced from his inability to protect her, could have torn our marriage apart. Instead, we recommitted ourselves to each other and pulled together in the same direction.

It is common for family members to feel such huge guilt and shame when they realize they provided a pedophile with access to their children that they become silent. Each member of the family suffers in his or her own way. Trauma often causes people to withdraw.

What is needed instead is awareness, prevention, early response, and deep healing. What is required is speaking up often, early, and completely. The current pattern is to treat harm and trauma after the fact rather than to prevent it. I think we as a society are ready to get to the root of it and prevent it.

What You Need to Know

What happened to our family is one example of the lengths to which a pedophile will go to have access to a child. We offer this book to families around the world as a warning. Some pedophiles are opportunistic and act quickly, while others plan carefully and move slowly. According to law enforcement in the United States, some pedophiles have access to between thirty and seventy children during their lifetimes. We often see examples of "stranger danger" in the media, so families have a false sense of security, imagining that the threat to their children is more likely to come from outside their immediate circle rather than from inside.

What is currently understood about child sexual abuse, as reported by the FBI, is that one in four girls and one in six boys will be raped or molested during their childhood. Of this shockingly high number, only 3 percent of the pedophiles are strangers to the family, while 97 percent are family members or people who are trusted by the family!

This doesn't mean that families must live in paranoia or on high alert, though. We don't have to constantly scan for threats to our children.

It is possible to create a safe and loving environment in which children thrive and in which healthy family members and friends are welcome in the inner circle. Real power comes when parents and grandparents are educated and are ready to act and know where to go for help.

To have a safe family, it is important to be close and attentive and to create an environment of communication and well-being. Once you know the early warning signs of the potential for abuse, you can act quickly to prevent it. It is better to stop it before it begins than to deal with the aftermath. Together we can deny predators access to children.

Our family learned that life is too precious to be lost to the darkness and that with support, the damage of abuse can be thoroughly healed over time. We are committed to helping educate and empower others, and we invite you to do so as well.

Sharing to Make a Difference

These events are shared with you in the order that they unfolded. There are many parts of Jan's story that may strike you as surreal. Everything you are about to read in this book is true and was well documented at the time it happened. As I polished the final draft of this book, I walked into the bedroom that was Jan's, sat down on her bed, and relived again the questions that nearly drove me mad when we realized Jan was missing:

• How could this happen to our "ideal" family?
• How could I have given permission for Jan to go with a man like Robert Berchtold—even for a few minutes?

- How could a man whose family members had become our best friends, who had been like a brother to my husband, and who had been so close to us and our children be a pedophile?
- How had our trust in him been so completely misplaced?

For three years, Robert Berchtold (whose nickname in our family was simply "B") said that he loved our children like his own. Surely, he couldn't; he wouldn't hurt Jan. But what kind of a man would disappear and take his friend's twelve-year-old daughter with him? How could our dearest friend become our worst enemy?

I understand the frustration that many of you will feel as you read this story. How could any parents be so duped as to allow their daughter to be taken advantage of over and over again in this way? After this man had kidnapped our daughter, how could we have ever let him back into our lives for even a moment? How could we have been so naive?

Due to our close-knit religious community and the trusting, loving nature of our then twelve-year-old daughter, Jan (who had the innocence of a seven-year-old at the time), we felt safe since our lives were surrounded by friends and family who all shared our high ideals, wholesome values, and spiritual goals.

All of us were unaware. All of us thought that any potential threat would come from the outside, not from within, our community. We simply couldn't imagine a wolf in sheep's clothing among us. Robert Berchtold was a master manipulator. Not all pedophiles are as sophisticated in plotting abuse. He had clearly been involved in abuse for years and knew just what he was doing by the time he preyed upon our family.

Because all of us—including our entire community and Berchtold's own wife and children—assumed and believed he was as harmless and God-fearing as we were, he used our trust in him to get what he wanted. He was calculating and patient and knew every facet of our lives, and because he was a trusted friend, he was able to exploit all of us.

It is also important for readers to understand that we cannot look at the past through the lens of the present. So much has changed since the

1970s. Growing up in my generation, there was not much talk about the subject of child sexual abuse. If something bad happened, it was covered up as quickly as possible and was whispered about in ways that children would not be able to understand. It was as if it didn't exist, although we now know that it did exist then and always has.

At least now, we have the language for it, along with specific tools to deal more effectively with it in families, schools, and churches. In some (but not all) parts of the world, people are now trained to recognize and deal with abuse more skillfully, especially in medical, legal, and law enforcement arenas.

Laws are changing, but that takes time. The laws against child abuse were not yet established in the state of Idaho during the years of Jan's kidnappings. Congress approved the Child Abuse Prevention Act in 1974, but every state in the union had to establish its own set of laws before prosecuting and sentencing an abuser. It would be several years before the Idaho legislature addressed the act. It would take decades more to train law enforcement and to update the legal system. It would take many years for the healing of trauma to be studied and for the arrival of professionals who were equipped to deal with the aftermath of child sexual abuse.

Chapter 1
NEW NEIGHBORS

October 17, 1974, 11:00 a.m.

That fateful morning, I picked up the phone and dialed our family business, a flower shop, where my husband, Bob, was working. When Bob answered, I asked, "B wants to take Jan horseback riding after school today. What do you think?"

"He already talked to me," Bob said. "He's visiting a customer in American Falls, and the guy invited B to bring his kids to ride horses. The man has done some professional training, and B thinks he should see Jan's talent for riding, but I said no."

Surprised, I asked, "Why?"

"MaryAnn, it's time for him to back off. I know he is trying to help give our kids opportunities that I haven't been able to, but I'm still in charge of my family, whether he likes it or not."

I was irritated. This seemed like a power struggle between Bob and B, and I thought it was starting to take its toll on their friendship.

When I picked up Jan from school, she excitedly talked about going horseback riding again—until I burst her bubble. "Your father said you couldn't go."

"Why?" she asked, surprised.

"You have piano today, gymnastics on Saturday, and you also have drill team practice. There's just a lot going on."

Jan quickly understood that my feeble excuse was a cover-up for her father's stubbornness. "Dad needs to quit feeling guilty just because he can't do all the things B can do. I know Dad's allergic to horses, and if B hadn't taken me out to Uncle Keith's, I still wouldn't know how to ride. Please, Mom, call Dad and ask him again."

My brother owned several horses, but we had never taken advantage of his offer to teach our girls to ride. With B having grown up on a farm and with our permission, he arranged with Keith to take Jan and his son Jerry for Jan's first riding experience. Keith had been pleasantly surprised at Jan's ease at riding, and he had encouraged her to come whenever possible.

Before I had a chance to call Bob again, B popped his head in the back door and enthusiastically hollered, "Hey, Jan, are you ready to go?"

Jan looked at me, and I shook my head. "Her dad said no. Besides, she has piano."

With his lower lip protruding, he scowled. "Come on! Let me do this. I have to go all the way out there, and it's a fantastic opportunity for her." Quickly reversing his frown into a broad grin, he continued, "And look at this gorgeous fall day. It's Jan's last chance since she's training every day for her gymnastics competition." I shrugged and sighed as B persisted. "I've made the appointment. It's already set. Let me drop her off at piano lessons and pick her up when she's finished." Still protesting, he said, "Bob will be okay. It's his pride, you know. I need to quit ribbing him about his allergy to horses. Besides, having company will be nice. Don't you trust me?"

"Well, of course," I responded.

Jan interlaced her fingers and shook them at me in a pleading way. "Please, Mom, please! I don't have any homework tonight, and I promise I'll practice piano when I get home." With her eyes wide and her head tilted adorably, she waited.

Weary of the coaxing, I heaved a defeated sigh, "Okay, you two win, but I'm the one who has to explain it to your father." Glaring at B, I asked, "How is it that you always get your way?"

"Must be my good looks," he said, chuckling. "Come on, Jan. Tell your teacher to make your lesson short because you have important things to do."

As Jan ran in to pick up her books from the piano, B hollered, "Hey, Jan, have you had your vitamins today?"

Rolling her eyes, Jan looked at me. I answered for her. "No, she hasn't."

B opened the door to the cupboard, reached for the top shelf, and retrieved a bottle of vitamins. The day he had brought them, he put them in our cupboard and said, "Your girls are sick so often, and these are better vitamins than those cheap ones you buy. Try them. Do you ever see my kids get sick?"

Grabbing a glass from the cupboard, he filled it with water and handed it to Jan. "Open wide," he said, popping the vitamin into her mouth. "Just what Dr. B ordered."

"Would you get out of here before you make Jan late for her lesson?" I said, irritated.

Jan gave me a quick kiss before dashing out the door with her piano books in hand.

Trailing behind her, B shouted, "Tell Bob I made you do it. Besides, I'll have Jan back before he gets home from work."

"Please do. Dinner will be ready," I said, watching them dash to his car.

"Stop worrying. I'll take good care of her, and she won't get hurt." He flashed a winning smile and saluted as he jumped into the driver's seat.

Bob arrived home around six o' clock, and I sheepishly admitted to letting Jan go horseback riding. Irritated, he said, "I'm not upset with you, honey. I know how persuasive he can be. How many times has he talked me into things I had no intention of doing? I only want him to stop defying me and ignoring what I say. I am the head of this home, and I am responsible for being sure they are safe and sound. It is my responsibility, not his."

Bob picked up the newspaper and headed for his recliner as I finished making dinner.

ening wore on, Bob's frustration turned into concern. "Do
y~   guy's name where they were going?"

I had no details. "All I know is it was one of his better-heeled customers."

"Call Gail," he demanded.

Growing increasingly edgy, I snapped back, "I've already talked to her
twice. B told her that he and Jan were going to ride horses and would be
home before dark. Gail assumed they were going to my brother's place.
They'll be here soon."

Helping Karen and Susan finish their homework overshadowed my
concern. After exchanging hugs and goodnight kisses, they went to their
rooms. It was a family bedtime ritual for Bob to kneel with each one of
our three sweet girls while they said their prayers, and then he would tuck
them into bed. Having a few minutes to myself, I used the time to think
back on the Berchtold's and how our friendship with them had grown so
much recently.

Just Call Me B

My mind wandered back to June 1972, when I had first seen B; that's
what we started calling him almost immediately because he asked us
to, and to avoid confusion because he was Robert, and my husband was
Bob. He was standing in the church foyer observing a group of teenage
boys. He had an annoyed look on his face because of their boisterous
laughter as they roughhoused down the hall. He had pursed lips, and
a furrowed brow as the boys noisily made their way outside the church
into the warm summer air. By his side stood a thin, willowy woman who
was holding a baby while a toddler twisted himself around the woman's
skirt.

As friendly members of the congregation stopped for introductions,
his stern look dissipated, and he relaxed. He flashed a broad smile at them
and vigorously returned handshakes while he and his wife pleasantly responded to the welcoming adults. Shortly after, a group of young children

who were in Sunday School raced down the hallway as an older woman—the teacher—briskly followed after them.

"I'm Robert Berchtold," the man said to the aging teacher, thrusting his hand forward to shake hers. "So, you've met my tribe of boys bounding alongside the rest of these loud-mouthed warriors, eh? Hope they didn't cause any problems. I warned them to be good, but I know what a handful Joey can be, even on his best behavior."

The teacher smiled and assured the gentleman that his three boys had behaved well. As the man was about to rejoin his family, a small group of chattering girls made their way down the steps.

Admiring them, he smiled broadly and then remarked enthusiastically to the woman, "I finally got one."

Uncertain of his comment, the teacher said, "Excuse me?"

Mr. Berchtold replied, "Oh, I mean after four boys, our baby's a girl."

The teacher chuckled and nodded her head. "How nice," she said.

My eavesdropping had been unintentional. I had been standing at the library window returning materials I had used for a lesson. As the new family headed out into the warm morning, my friend Zola asked if I had met them.

I shook my head, and Zola exclaimed, "Oh, they're a nice family. I knew Robert Berchtold in college. Remember Zada, my twin sister? Well, she was engaged to his roommate, and we double-dated. Isn't that something?"

Grabbing my arm, Zola accompanied me out to the parking lot while my daughters rushed through the doors ahead of us.

"They're practically your neighbors," she added.

The Berchtold's were walking toward their car when Zola shouted, "Yoo-hoo," and waved them down. Robert Berchtold was exuberant as introductions were made. He shook my hand vigorously. "It's a pleasure to meet you," he said, "and you're a very impressive chorister as well. I've never heard 'Onward, Christian Soldiers' sung with more conviction."

"Oh, thank you," I said, flattered and slightly embarrassed. His infectious grin and friendly personality were captivating. His wife, standing slightly behind him, had smiled pleasantly and nodded her head in agreement. As we stood chatting, my three daughters were focused on the baby she was cuddling in her arms.

"Robert and Gail opened a discount furniture store called Freight Outlet, and their home is two blocks from yours," Zola explained.

"Bring your family over, and we'll give you a tour," Mr. Berchtold said.

He reminded me of Merle Haggard, the Country Western singer. He stood about five foot eight and had a short, pointed nose, wavy sandy-blond hair, a full bottom lip that protruded slightly, and glasses that covered his blue-gray eyes that crinkled at the corners when he smiled. More impressive than his boyish good looks was his friendly, charismatic personality.

Gail Berchtold was dressed in a simple red peasant blouse and a colorful gathered skirt that was somewhat wrinkled from wrestling a baby. Her thin body reminded me of Twiggy, a 1960s model, and I thought how a little makeup would pink up her cheeks and enhance her blue eyes, which were framed by dark-rimmed glasses.

After exchanging friendly chitchat, I again welcomed them as I began to leave.

"Wait—you can't go," Mr. Berchtold said, his eyes dancing with delight. "We haven't met your beautiful daughters."

Zola pointed her finger at my oldest. "Well, that's Jan. She's nine and is a great little actress. Last summer, she played Gretel in *The Sound of Music*. But you have to run fast to keep up with her. She's a real live wire."

Enjoying the notoriety, Jan's beaming smile reflected approval. "I'm almost ten and will be in the fifth grade," she added, fluttering her long dark eyelashes that outlined her piercing blue eyes. A petite strawberry blonde whose tiny, freckled nose crinkled when she flashed a grin, Jan was a vivacious, spirited, people pleaser of a child who had a drive for stuffing more into life than I thought humanly possible.

Mr. Berchtold extended his hand and gripped hers. "Hello, Jan. I'm pleased to meet you."

Gail said softly, "Our oldest son is ten."

Jan turned to look at the boys. "Yeah, I met Jerry in Sunday school."

Earlier, we had watched Jerry, a handsome, sturdily built boy, wrestle one of his younger brothers to the ground.

Zola continued her introductions as the parking lot emptied. "You haven't met Bob, but take a good look. Karen looks just like her father. She's nearly eight, the same age as your Jimmy."

Feeling conspicuous, Karen blushed. Paternal genetics served her well. She inherited a creamy-tan complexion, blond hair, a short straight nose, and large penetrating sky-blue eyes. Karen was taller and statelier than her older sister, Jan, and claimed a quieter disposition. Content with less exhaustive projects, she nurtured with explicit kindness anything that purred, barked, chirped, or crawled. "And this cutie is Susan," Zola announced, pointing at my youngest. "She'll be in first grade this fall."

Susan presented a shy, unenthusiastic smile. Dark-haired like me, she was fair-skinned and hazel-eyed and sported a big freckle on her perfectly small button nose. "It's a genuine pleasure to meet such lovely young ladies," Mr. Berchtold said. Bending down, he viewed each girl intently, his eyes narrowing while flashing a big smile. "You girls bring your parents and come over for a visit."

Nodding their heads, Susan pulled on my arm while the other two dashed to the car.

As I followed after them, Mr. Berchtold called out, "Remember, the invitation is wide open, and I want to meet your husband."

"We'd love to come," I said, getting into my car as the girls waved at their new friends.

I hadn't purposefully shrugged off the invitation, but busy schedules kept our association limited to church events. Our lives revolved around church, family, and our business—a quaint, well-established flower shop Bob had purchased before we were married. Born and raised in Pocatello,

Idaho, he had deep roots here and was a well-respected young business owner. His activity with the Chamber of Commerce, the Rotary Club, and other business organizations had expanded his circle of associates, and he seemed to know everyone in the community. Bob's gracious personality and sincere empathy for customers had been the right fit for a business centered on emotions.

Our city of Pocatello had a small-town vibe. It was peaceful, quiet, and had little crime. It was considered a safe environment in which to raise a family. As active members of our church, we maintained a strong devotion to family and strongly believed in caring for the needs of others. Our friends, neighbors, and associates throughout the community had our respect, and it didn't matter if they were of a different faith, culture, or ethnicity. We accepted them openly. We considered everyone we met to be a friend.

Our home was adjacent to Idaho State University and was a block from the local hospital. Several physicians, university professors, and elected public officials were our neighbors, contributing to a fairly eclectic culture of religious views, race, politics, and opinions. It was a civil group of smart, peace-loving neighbors, a few of whom we went to church with. We knew each other by first names. We enjoyed annual neighborhood block parties, sporting events at the indoor Idaho State University Mini-Dome, and community musical theater events, providing us further appreciation for our great community.

Our faith community was highly focused on the importance of families and the important role parents and religion played in their children's upbringing. When the school system planned to teach sex education in grade school, I joined with the opposition and worked to stop it from being implemented. I believed my children should hear about sensitive subjects from us, and we would decide when it was time for the birds-and-bees conversation. Our girls were innocent and happy, enjoying their neighborhood, playing kick the can, making clubhouses with their friends, and reading the Boxcar Children books by flashlight in the big, oversized closet downstairs together. My thought was that as long as they were playing school and singing Dr. Seuss songs, they didn't need to be concerned about such grown-up things. Bob and I had discussed that a good time to approach that conversation with our children was when they were around age eleven—when they were in sixth grade and before junior high school.

I fit the image of the stay-at-home mom perfectly, and I happily accepted the supportive-nurturing-mom and father-in-charge culture of our church, where love and service were of paramount importance and where community involvement and contribution were highly valued. I went jogging with friends, I participated in the PTA, civic affairs, book clubs, music groups, and county elections, and I was the Miss Pocatello Scholarship Pageant director. I considered my life idyllic.

It was not until late fall, right after Halloween, that Bob and I decided to visit Freight Outlet to shop for a new kitchen dining set. Seemingly pleased that we would choose his business, Mr. Berchtold had been anxious to make us a "screaming deal" while entertaining us with friendly jokes and delightful chatter.

After the delivery was made, the doorbell rang, and Mr. Berchtold shoved a large fruit basket into my hands as a token of appreciation.

"I needed to see if the dinette set arrived in good order and how you like it," Robert said.

"Come in and see for yourself. But this too?" I said, admiring the gift.

"Only for special people like you," he said, smiling broadly. "You haven't come to our home yet, and we feel slighted, so I refuse to leave unless you promise to come over Monday and have dinner with us."

"That sounds great, but I need to check with Bob when he gets home. What can I bring?"

He excitedly replied, "Your husband and beautiful daughters."

From the crackling fireplace and the aroma of freshly baked bread to a very enthusiastic reception by all, there was a cozy feeling as we entered the Berchtold home. We were directed to find a place on the floor around a big red-and-white-checkered tablecloth that had been spread out on the braided living-room rug.

"Since we missed having you over for a summer picnic, we decided to move it indoors. It's a bit off-the-wall, but that's how we are. So, pull up a pillow while I grill the burgers," Robert said.

The unique setting had brought a relaxed, friendly atmosphere that contributed to an engaging interaction between both families.

Following dinner, Jan announced that the kids had prepared a talent show for the evening's entertainment. The program varied from a silly skit and group singing to square dancing and piano solos. At the conclusion of their presentation, the performers disappeared to the family room to watch their favorite TV show, *The Brady Bunch*.

Robert then asked, "What did you do to produce such adorable children? I've watched Jan at school and at church functions, and she's not only smart, but she's also creative and has lots of talent."

"Oh, Jan's been performing since the day she was born. As a baby, she would wake up in the middle of the night and peer through the slats of her crib and would hum, babble, bounce, and grin from ear to ear while we were trying to sleep. She has never changed," Bob said.

"When I first saw her at church, I thought she was seven or eight," Robert said.

Bob responded, "She's a little squirt, but she's such a wide-eyed, trusting little girl. If only we could bottle her innocence until her teen years have passed."

"When you know the magic formula, will you share it?" Gail asked.

The evening was delightful, and we committed to having more events together. It was evident from our visit that we had similar interests and shared common goals, family values, and personalities.

Soon after our evening together, Robert Berchtold suggested, "Just call me B. It's easier and better than Berchtold—and I mean the kids as well."

With each adult agreeing, the discussion ended. As a matter of respect, my husband felt that our girls should address him as B.

Within days, B had come to our home and asked if he could transport our girls, along with his boys, to school. Feeling it to be an imposition, I had fumbled in giving an answer, and I suggested carpooling.

"No way! It's on my way to work, and you don't need to get out on these cold mornings. It's being a good neighbor, for heaven's sake."

The only complaint we heard from our children about B during 1972–1973 was about having to listen to him sing "Kiss an Angel Good Mornin'" every morning from his Charley Pride 8-track tape.

The summer of 1974 brought new excitement for Jan and Karen when B had offered to divide their large bedroom in our basement into two separate rooms. It had been on our agenda for a couple of years, but lack of funds had put it on hold.

"Let me do it," B said. "Bring the girls down to my store, and they can pick out their own bedroom furniture. I'll get it wholesale. You buy the needed materials, and the labor will be a freebie. Where could you get a better deal?"

The opening ceremonies began with a bang as Jan, Karen, Susan, and B's three boys (Jerry, Jimmy, and Joey) congregated in the hall with hammers in hand to make their mark where the new door would be installed to Jan's new room. They had a blast hammering down the wall.

Each member of the family agreed to accept assignments in order to get the rooms done within a two-week time span. Bob accepted the job of providing refreshments and giving out compliments, which he did profusely since he had no building skills. The girls ran errands and brought the right tools to B, handing him nails, boards, or whatever he needed as he meticulously measured, sawed, and hammered. My job was cleaning up, taping seams, and painting.

B's patience was commendable, and I often heard laughter from him, and our kids as B told funny incidents about when he was young and added wild stories about aliens visiting earth from other planets.

At the completion of the construction, Bob enthusiastically thanked B for his great work and tried to pay him. "There are things you do for those you love, and it comes without a price," B kindly remarked. "You can't put a price on friendship or love."

So many good memories flooded my mind that night as I awaited Jan's return. It was like a movie taking me from one exciting place in time to another. As I tried to bring myself back to the gravity of the present, my stomach was churning. Where were my little girl and B? Were they still horseback riding? Were they okay? Wandering into Jan's room, I longed to hug and kiss her goodnight like normal. But nothing was normal. I eyed the little diary on her new bedside table. Picking it up to feel close to her, it fell open to an entry she had made a couple of months earlier:

Jan's Diary, August 4, 1974:

Today B called. My furniture came. Mom's still painting. I get my own room. Mom did wallpaper and is making a bedspread to match, and I got a blue velvet hanging chair. I practiced piano. Dad and I saw my furniture. I went babysitting and got a dollar. B stopped in. We all had a tickling fight.

Laying her diary aside, I walked back to the living room and nudged Bob's arm. "I'm sure they are having car problems. Jan has a gymnastics competition Saturday, and they will be showing up. I know we will hear as soon as B can get to a phone."

Chapter 2
THE MOTORHOME DISAPPEARANCE

Bob, MaryAnn, and Gail:
October 17, 1974, 9:00 p.m.

Gail appeared around nine o'clock, admitting that she, too, was concerned. Bob was pacing the floor while I watched every passing car with anticipation. We wondered, "Did the car break down? They must be stranded and can't get to a phone. Should we call the police to see if they have news?"

Gail's face paled while she nervously fingered her car keys. "I don't know how to tell you this, but last week I went looking for Bob." Her long pause had our full attention. "I found him working on a motorhome." Staring at Gail, Bob probed for more information.

Dropping her eyes, she drew a deep breath and then exhaled slowly. "For the last two weeks, he's been leaving home after dinner and hasn't returned until after I'm asleep. He never explained where he was going, so I followed him one night. I found him at the storage unit where we keep our boat for winter." Swallowing, she raised her eyes. "The door to our unit was open, and I could see him working on a motorhome."

Apprehensive, Bob questioned, "Who does it belong to?"

Gail shook her head. "I have no idea. Probably a friend he's helping out."

Trying to absorb what Gail said, I remained silent, but new fears filled my brain. Six weeks earlier, B talked to me about his unfulfilling relationship with her. He had given me "permission" to try to "help her be more attractive, sexy, you know—more like you." I had blushed and told him I was not going to make her feel bad since Gail was already a pretty woman, although thin and not as voluptuous as he had hoped for apparently. I pointed out that she was talented and sweet and was a great cook and was so good with their kids and with our girls too. But he insisted he couldn't really talk to her anymore and was contemplating divorce.

Bob was angry and said, "Let's call the sheriff's office and give them a description of your car. Where is that guy's ranch?"

Gail shook her head. "I don't know, but I'm going out to the storage unit." Handing a slip of paper to Bob, she said, "I've been trying to call B's salesman, but he isn't home. If that ranch guy is a customer, Jim probably knows him. Here's his number. Will you try to reach him while we go check the storage unit?"

Seeing the anxiety on Bob's face, I felt responsible. I assured him we would hurry. Ironically, I still felt calm, assuring myself that my daughter was in safe hands. After all, wasn't B one of our best friends in the entire universe?

I reassured myself that there was a good reason they hadn't returned. Gail wasn't overly concerned, which helped relieve my uneasiness. "Maybe the motorhome belongs to the rancher who has the horses," I suggested. Gail shrugged and remained silent.

I began to probe. "B seems to be so happy lately. That's a big change from the past few months. His medication must be helping."

Gail nodded. "It might be, but you generally see him at his best. He's always happy when the Brobergs are around! His depression has been an issue at times, but he really knows how to put on a happy face when he's out of the house. Maybe it's just me who makes him unhappy. One doctor told us it is manic depression when you have big highs and then really deep lows. It's a strange thing."

Admitting my ignorance, I remarked, "I know nothing about depression. Is it like baby blues?"

Gail shrugged, her voice quivering. "I only know he's irritable and doesn't talk to me. What on earth would I do if he left me and the kids?"

With no answer, I shook my head.

Gail stopped the car at the gate of the storage units. She got out and tried several keys before finding one that fit.

Driving around the storage units, we strained our eyes to look for Gail's new '74 Maverick, which B had been driving when he picked up Jan.

Finding their storage unit, Gail tried each key on the ring, but found no match. A new pang of fear pierced my stomach. Coming back to the car, Gail stared at me and asked, "Now what?"

I had no answer.

As we drove out of the lot, Gail took one final desperate look. "I'll call in the morning and find someone who will let me in."

We drove home in silence. I wanted to say something comforting, but I had no words, no assurances. Finally, for the sake of conversation, I asked, "Is B really selling your business?"

Gail sighed deeply. "I don't know. He's been talking about it for a few months."

"He told us he was thinking of opening a sports business. Think he will?" I asked.

"I suppose. Why not? His gift with people has served him well, and it's the reason he's done so well. The first time I met him, I fell flat on my face because of his charm, and he has a way with words; of course, I was only fourteen, and he was older, but he still has it."

Her positive response opened the door for me to continue. "When he disappeared earlier this year, it was a mystery, but we never knew about his depression."

"He didn't want anyone to know. He's disappeared for a day or two before. It was his California counselor who told him to get rid of self-pity and do something positive for someone else, to make a difference. His high school buddy helped him decide to take a trip to Mexico, to the area where he served his mission for the church. I was shocked when he called and said that he found Maria, a little eight-year-old Mexican girl we could adopt. He told me to bring personal references from three people who would vouch for us. I was in a panic, but once I had the letters from Cor and Elaine Hofman, Bishop Meyers, and his brother Joe, I flew down to meet him."

With her voice warm and confident, she related the experience. "It was a family who lived in complete poverty, with several children but without a father. The mother knew there was no future for her daughter in Mexico, but with us, she would get an education, food every day, and nice clothes. But the mother wanted to meet me before she would let her daughter come. After we signed the papers and were ready to leave, Maria's mother burst into tears and couldn't let her go. I cried with her because I understood."

Gail's voice cracked, causing my own emotions to surface. Whispering, I said, "There is nothing you can compare to the love a mother has for her child. I'd crawl the earth for one of mine."

Our eyes glistened in the passing of streetlights. Only the hum of the engine broke the silence.

After gaining her composure, Gail reached over and patted my arm. I looked at her with tenderness. She remained silent and subdued. When she finally spoke, her voice was passionate. "Bob's a good man and a good father, but maybe I've tried too hard to make myself into what I perceived he wanted. Whatever I've done, it's probably all wrong."

I felt compassion for Gail. Her husband knew the art of capturing the hearts of women, and Gail was aware of his magnetism. She longed for his total devotion but knew it had faded. Even I felt exhilarated each time B told me I was extraordinary. His flattering remarks and complimentary words would swell my head, and tiny sensations would prickle my spine. I tried to shrug off his comments by telling him it was foolish talk and that he was embarrassing me.

After we arrived back home, Bob told us that he had no news and hadn't been able to reach B's employee. Later that evening, Gail contacted the salesman, who said that her husband was going to meet a customer but hadn't given a name or told him where he was going.

We finally called the local police and asked if there had been any report of a car stalled on the highway between Pocatello and American Falls or if there had been any reported accidents. The dispatcher took our number and said he would call if he heard anything.

Far into the night, Bob and I went back over recent conversations with B, but nothing came to mind except his talk of divorce and his restlessness regarding his business. I couldn't go to sleep with my mind questioning past conversations and wondering if B and Jan were stranded on some desolate country road with a broken-down car and no way to let us know. I told myself to go to sleep, and that everything would all be resolved in the morning.

Chapter 3
DOLLY

Bob once asked B why he called Jan Dolly. B replied, "Well, Broberg, you have such fun names for your girls—Blue Eyes, Freckle, Precious Jewel, Woman of Destiny, and Doll Love Sweet. It is silly for sure, but I admired your humor and wanted to get in on the fun. The day after Christmas last year, your girls were all playing 'boat' on Karen's bed with the big stuffed dolls MaryAnn made for them. Jan was braiding her doll's thick yarn hair to keep it from getting wet in the 'water.' I thought it was cute, so I said, 'Dolly, don't let that hair get wet.' She laughed, and that was that! It stuck."

Jan and B:
October 17, 1974, 4:00 p.m.

B dropped Jan off at her piano lesson and said, "I'll be back in half an hour, Dolly. Do your best, and then we'll go riding."

Jan tried keeping her mind on the piano pieces she had prepared for Mrs. Brink, but she kept looking at the clock. Mrs. Brink counted out the measures with exact precision while Jan repeated the drill over and over. Her lack of interest didn't deter Mrs. Brink's methodical instructions for the coming week as she urged Jan to spend more time on her piano studies. Jan peered around her teacher, impatiently watching for B's car.

At last, she saw it pulling up. Gathering up her books, she acknowledged her teacher's last-minute advice and issued a hasty goodbye. She bounced out the door and skipped down the front walk. B grinned happily as Jan opened the car door and jumped in.

"Whew! That lesson seemed to be extra-long today. I don't know why, but I feel edgy."

"Oh, you're just excited," B replied.

Jan chatted exuberantly about school and the upcoming gymnastics meet. However, the hum of the motor and the movement of the car soon had a tranquilizing effect on Jan, who began fighting drowsiness. "Wow! I don't know why I'm so tired," she remarked.

"It will be a while before we get there. This ranch is about a half-hour drive. Just put your seat back and relax." B's voice was soothing. "You need to be refreshed to ride that stallion."

Jan moved the seat into a reclining position, took a deep breath, curled up, and quickly fell fast asleep.

Strapped Down, Drugged, and Terrified

When Jan awoke, she felt dazed and heavy, as though a weight were crushing her body. Her eyes refused to focus. Her thoughts were muddled and disjointed. She knew she was riding in a car; she felt the motion and heard the hum of an engine, yet it seemed to her as if she were lying on a bed in a dark and unfamiliar room. Trying to gain control of her senses, she moved her body. She was startled to find her hands strapped to something. Terrified, she tried to pull herself up, only to find her feet restrained in the same manner. A scream stuck in her dry, parched throat.

A strange, high-pitched voice began speaking: "Female companion. Female companion." The phrase was repeated several times.

Horrified and overwhelmed by the eerie atmosphere, Jan cautiously scanned the darkened room with wide eyes. Unable to find anyone attached to the mysterious voice, she gasped for air, thinking hysterically, *What is going on?*

She frantically tried to free herself from the restraints around her wrists and legs that confined her. A cold sweat engulfed her entire body as the realization sank in, she was a prisoner!

She heard the unearthly voice again: "Female companion. Female companion." Another shiver of fear shot through her. Still dazed, Jan felt out of touch with reality. Unable to fight consciousness, she slipped back into an unsettling sleep.

Unaware of the passage of time, Jan stirred again and slowly opened her eyes. As she moved her tiny body, she became conscious of the reality that she was strapped to a bed. The room was dark and deathly quiet. Trying to gain a sense of why she would be there and what was happening, she tried to recall the message of the voice she had heard earlier. As she licked her dry lips and attempted to moisten her mouth, she remembered leaving her piano lesson with B, but was unable to recall anything after getting into his car.

A sliver of light flickered faintly around the edges of what appeared to be a door. In a panic, Jan watched the door and waited for her abductor to appear, but the ominous silence still hung heavy in the air. Agonizing over her vulnerable position, Jan thought, *Where's B? Who's talking to me?* As she struggled to move, the silence was broken by the same high-pitched, monotone voice repeating words in a short staccato tone. Alarmed, she listened to the weird utterance from this unidentified spokesman: "Female companion. My people die. You special. Like us. It is time for your mission to begin. You help save planet."

Moving her head toward the voice, she could see from the corner of her eye a small ivory box situated near her head. The message was repeated several times before silence invaded the room. Terrorized by the message and unable to move, Jan felt as if she were being swallowed into a deep, dark hole. Shuddering with fright, her agonizing thoughts continued. All the stories B had related about flying saucers, spaceships, and aliens came back in a frightening flurry. Her mind raced as she reflected on the news special they had watched on UFOs and Area 21, as well as the newspaper stories of sightings with the black-and-white pictures of flying discs. Instantly, she knew she had been taken by aliens, but she could not see them. She could only hear their eerie, other-worldly voices. She couldn't understand why they would take her or what was coming next. *Where was B?*

Thoughts about her impending fate worked her into a frenzy. Her heart raced, and her breathing was labored. She couldn't stop the tears from running off her face and onto her shirt. Several minutes later, a voice crackled again: "Female companion—companion. Help us. You very special. You chosen. Important to planet—planet. You save us. Cannot fail."

Jan's thoughts raced wildly, and she was overcome with horror. *Me? Why did they choose me? Save their planet? I don't understand what they expect me to do.*

The alarming message continued to repeat itself over and over again in that high, unearthly staccato voice. Terrified by the senseless repetition and emphatic demands, Jan struggled to keep her emotions under control. Unable to bear the sound any longer, she burst into sobs.

Jan was sick to her stomach. She felt extremely groggy and kept thinking she might throw up. Unable to move from the uncomfortable position, due to the restraints, she continued to struggle until exhaustion replaced nausea. The darkness in the room made it impossible for her to distinguish night from day. Shutting out the voice proved to be impossible as she strained to cover her ears with her shoulders, but the restraints limited her mobility.

Over and over again, the voice repeated the haunting refrain. Several hours passed. Jan agonized. *Why are they doing this?* Exhausted, horrified, and longing for some comfort, she closed her eyes. Ever since she had woken up hours ago, she had been fighting heavy drowsiness. Now she welcomed sleep as an escape from her unexplained circumstance. At last, sleep brought her some relief.

Waking to light filtering softly through a closed blind that was hanging over the window, she panicked again. The room was semi-dark, yet she still heard an engine humming.

Startled by her surroundings, she moved suddenly and discovered that she was no longer confined by the straps at her ankles and wrists. She remained still. She searched the room with her eyes and was barely able to see the outlines of objects. She realized she was lying on the floor next to a bed. A partition, which she had previously imagined to be a door, blocked the view of anything beyond. She felt certain that things had been rearranged from her earlier recollection and that there was more light than before.

A small ivory box was tucked into the corner of the bed. A door to her left was partially open; she saw it was a bathroom. As she sat up, a sharp pain shot through her head and caused a dizzy sensation. She groaned, cradling her head between her hands. Her limbs felt lifeless, and they tingled when she moved them. As Jan rose on unsteady legs, thinking they might buckle under her, she squinted as her eyes became more accustomed to the light. She moved carefully and quietly into the small bathroom compartment for relief. As she returned to her confined quarters, her solitude was abruptly interrupted by the same eerie, high-pitched staccato voice. Jan's worst nightmare was a reality. The sounds came from the little ivory box.

Apprehensively, she listened, "Female companion. Female companion. I Zada. Listen!" Overwhelmed by the ghastly sound of the voice, Jan didn't move.

"Female companion. Female companion. Do what we say! You fail, you vaporize!"

The ivory box crackled and remained silent. Minutes ticked away. A wave of anxiety swept over her as she assessed her situation. Jan sat motionless and felt sweaty. Tears welled up again. For hours, she had not uttered one word. She dared not speak to a faceless voice. Vaporize? What's that? *I just want to go home*, she thought.

For a long time, Jan cringed in fright on the bed and stared at the walls. As much as she hated the messenger's voice, the silence was almost worse. *Where am I?* she thought, and *If that person is watching me, why doesn't it say something?*

45

Afraid to venture from her confinement, Jan watched the closed blind sway on the window. Quick snatches of sunlight let her know that it was daytime. Minutes seemed like hours. Hours turned into excruciating agony. After a lengthy period of silence, the repetitious messages again described the intended mission for Jan. Listening to an inhuman voice that insisted that she was special and chosen and that she would save a dying planet was incomprehensible to her young twelve-year-old mind. Save a dying planet? How would she do that? Why did they keep calling her "female companion?" Could they see her? It was impossible for her to even begin to understand, and it turned the small room into a torture chamber.

Jan couldn't understand why this was happening to her. She didn't know what to say or how to beg for mercy from the concealed person, or the "alien." She cried continually until she used the last of the toilet paper to blow her nose. She was convinced that all her tears had been shed—until she began hearing a new message, repeated again and again, of the devastating harm that would come to her family if she didn't do as she was instructed. The thought of Karen going blind, her dad dying, or Susan being taken next if she failed to follow their instructions was incomprehensible. *Why would they do that? No, no! Not my family*, she thought, tearing up again and crying softly. *What happened to B? Where am I going?*

Confined to the small room, Jan felt as if she were losing her mind. Nearing hysteria, she pondered what type of retribution she would face if she went beyond the partition, but fear kept her a prisoner. Finally, unable to stand her confinement any longer, Jan pushed against the partition that was separating the back part of the motorhome from the front half, but she was unable to move it. Determined, she pushed harder. She pounded on the solid wall, crying desperately. She screamed in panic, "Help me! Somebody get me out! Help me! Help me!" There was no response. *Where is my family?* she wondered. *Will I ever see them again? Will they rescue me? Who is driving?* In desperation, Jan slumped to the floor and cried despondently. Her agonizing, mournful lamentations continued until her energy was completely drained. She fell into another deep sleep.

Later that day, another voice startled Jan to consciousness. The voice, identifying herself as "Zethra," commanded Jan to eat. Zethra directed her to a small metal refrigeration box where she would find food. Zethra said they had been watching her since she was born, and that they knew everything about her. Obedient to the order, Jan found a small cooler full of Almond Joy candy bars, tuna fish sandwiches, pickles, apples, oranges, and Cheez-It crackers. They were all Jan's favorites. She quietly opened the crackers with anxiety, wondering if they were safe to eat. *Will they make me sick? What if they are poisoned?* Hesitantly, she placed one under her nose and smelled it, and then she licked it with her tongue. Laying it down, she took an Almond Joy bar and slowly unwrapped it. After one bite, emotions overpowered her and the half-chewed lump got stuck in her throat. Throwing herself on the bed, she sobbed.

The tiny rays of sunlight Jan could see through the blind were now fading, and she knew the night was approaching. Not feeling strong enough to face another lonely, helpless night, she curled up into a ball and begged again, "Please help me. I'll do what you ask, but don't hurt my family." She burst into an agonizing wail and pulled the cover over her head. Alas, the commands of the undisclosed stranger were finally obeyed.

"Female companion. Mission cannot fail!" the voice proclaimed. Followed by silence. Only Jan's tormented moans and sobs were heard. The mysterious voice didn't respond to her proclamation. She was once again feeling groggy and was fighting sleep. There was no doubt in her mind that she had truly encountered beings from another world and had no choice but to comply. Was she really like them? Were they always watching her? Have they really been watching her since she was born? Could they read her mind too?

Jan could hear nothing except the mournful hum of the engine. Lying on the bed for a seemingly long time, she anxiously feared the next blast of instructions from the supernatural voice, but the box remained silent. Jan's mournful cries were the only sounds in the quiet darkness as she begged her captors to let her go. She secretly prayed for someone to hear her.

Am I going to die? she wondered. She cried until she could cry no more. Her head throbbed as she fought to stay awake. Closing her eyes to ease the pain brought her some relief. Exhausted and drained, she eventually fell asleep.

Chapter 4
MISSING AND HELPLESS

October 19, 1974

It had been two days since B had taken Jan horseback riding and failed to return with her. Waking abruptly that morning, I frantically thought, *Jan is gone! She's really gone!* Anxiety overwhelmed me and a hard, painful knot pierced my gut.

Feeling smothered, I threw back the sheets from the bed and rushed wildly into the living room. Crazy thoughts ran incoherently through my numb brain. *Where is Jan? Where is B? Where did he go? What happened? I have to know what's going on! Any minute now, he'll drive up, laughing his head off, and have some wild story.* A hard lump that I couldn't swallow lodged in my throat.

Dashing back to the bedroom, I painfully cried and said, "Oh, Bob. I can't stand feeling so helpless."

Bob threw his arms around me, "I've been praying all night too, but what should we do?" Bob attempted to stifle his emotions, but the words choked in his throat. Sitting on the edge of the bed, we held each other and cried like babies.

"Why did I let her go?" I blurted out.

Karen and Susan came running into the bedroom and jumped onto the middle of our bed. "What's the matter? Do you know where Jan is? What's happened?"

"Oh, we are just trying to figure out where she is and are having a bawling session. Do you want to join us?" I attempted to smile, through my tears, at the two of them.

Bob questioned, "Do you have any ideas? Has Jerry or Jimmy said anything about their dad going somewhere?"

The girls shook their heads solemnly. "What should we do?" he asked.

"Dad, you always tell me to pray when I'm sad," Karen replied.

Bob put his arm around Karen. "You're right. Let's kneel down and ask our Heavenly Father to bless Jan and bring her home safe."

"And B too," Susan replied.

"Right, Susie Q." I choked back a sob and then muttered, "He better."

After intense prayer, we shed more tears, hugged each other, and re-treated to the kitchen for breakfast. Eight-year-old Susan consumed Cheerios before escaping to the family room for cartoons and puzzle enjoyment. Ten-year-old Karen stayed close by, listening intently to our conversation.

"We have to decide what to do," I said.

"I've been thinking about driving to different towns and places he used to go to or where he and Gail lived," Bob said, before adding, "But first, I have to run to the store and get the crew going on some funeral flowers. I'll be home in a bit." Bob gave me a kiss and bent across the table to kiss Karen. Trying to be reassuring, he said, "I'm sure Jan is fine. Your job is to keep your mom happy until I get back."

Clearing the table, I got consumed into my own thoughts and ignored Karen. After a matter of minutes, she said, "Mom, it's really hard not knowing where Jan is. Do you think B will bring her home today?"

"We hope so, but we don't know what happened to them." My statement expressed enough uncertainty that Karen looked at me with worried eyes.

I dialed the Berchtold home. "Any news, Gail?"

"Not a word. I called the owner of the storage unit, and he will be there at eight. I told him my husband was out of town, and I needed to get something out of it," Gail said.

An hour later, Gail brought disconcerting news: the motorhome was gone; only the boat remained in the unit. She begged us to have patience while she tried to locate him, "Let me call his family and see if anyone has talked to him."

Unfortunately, her contacts had no information regarding his whereabouts, but she knew he had purchased the motorhome from a relative in Wyoming about a month earlier. With this news, a wave of anxiety shuddered through my body. *What is going on? Has he flipped out, or is he just trying to let Gail know their marriage is over? Did he have to put Jan in the middle of their conflict?*

Staring into space, I tried to piece the details together. I was an emotional wreck, and the more I thought about it, the angrier I became. *How dare he do this? Who does he think he is? He needs to get Jan back and take care of his family!*

Gail waited for Bob to come home from the store, but she couldn't offer much help. She gave a few details about their situation when they had lived in Brigham City, but she couldn't think about why he would go there. From the phone calls to family members, she had learned that none of them had seen or talked to B for weeks. Desperate to do something, Bob took Karen and headed to Brigham City to see if they could find any sign of B, Jan, or the car.

I tried to do housework but couldn't stay focused. I went down and looked through Jan's room, noting that everything was in place.

Jan's Diary, October 7, 1973:

Mom and Dad are gone. We're sleeping over at the Berchtold's. B did my hair for church. B took us to the grocery store and said to get any-

thing that looks good, and we did, even though it was Sunday! We got home and listened to The Partridge Family.

I wandered aimlessly from one task to another, unable to concentrate. Hours later, Bob and Karen returned with no answers. After we called Gail, she came over and pleaded with us to not to call the police until she had exhausted every lead. "Just give me a little more time. I'm waiting for his brother to call me back. I know they will show up soon!"

Gail's pathetic voice was desperate. I stared at Bob for an answer. "I don't know, Gail," he said. "If there was an accident, we should have heard by now."

As Gail was crying, she said, "And I'm concerned about my kids too. What will they think? How can I explain it? I know he'll be back. He hasn't done this to hurt any of us. Please wait."

"You've been asking us this for two days now, but, we can't go through another night not knowing. Something has happened, and we need help," Bob said angrily.

I put my arms around Gail's frail body and let her sob on my shoulder. Bob's shoulders slumped as he listened to Gail's heart-wrenching wailing. Then he breathed deeply and walked away.

It felt as if a golf ball were stuck in my throat. The only thing I seemed capable of doing was crying. Determined to keep my own emotions under control, I tried to comfort Gail. I knew B would not hurt Jan. He had always talked about our girls being like his own, and he had always treated them with extreme kindness.

Call the FBI

Later that day, I picked up the phone book and found the number of the local FBI. I dialed, but I felt I was betraying Gail by making the call. As the phone rang, I frantically attempted to put my confused mind into a sensible order. A recording relieved my dilemma. If the call was an emergency, I was to call the main office in Butte, Montana. The Pocatello office would be open Monday morning at 8:00.

How could we endure another night of uncertainty?

Three Days Gone
October 20, 1974

All hell broke loose when the FBI answered the phone. The statement, "My daughter's been taken!" brought Agent Peter Welsh and a senior agent to our door within minutes of the call.

Agent Welsh's first question was, "Why did you wait so long to contact us?"

After I explained that I had called Butte, Montana, but hadn't left a message, the agent said, "But this is considered an emergency."

Trying to answer that question and many others took most of the morning as Bob, and I related the close and endearing friendship we had with the Berchtold family.

We explained to the agents how our children had brought the Berchtold boys into their circle and that we had a close relationship, almost like family. We related how B had frequently commented, "Your husband is just like a brother to me." Jimmy was Karen's best friend, and Jan and Jerry had a positive friendship as well.

Jan's Diary, March 12, 1973:

Today my parents are going out of town. We're staying at the Berchtold's. I went down to B's shop. Down there I answered the phone, and we went on break too! For supper, we fondued. It was fun. That night we showed films. Jerry held my hand and put his arm around me. It was good. It was a very fun day!

Smiling, the agents nodded and gathered more relevant information before going to the Berchtold home. Two hours later, they returned, probing for more details. Agent Welsh questioned whether Berchtold had ever given Jan drugs.

Surprised, I said, "No, only vitamins." Presenting the bottle of vitamins, I related the scene about B having Jan take a vitamin before she left for her piano lesson.

Agent Welsh explained, "Mrs. Berchtold walked in on her husband recently and saw him dumping contents from capsules into the toilet. When she asked what he was doing, he became angry and told her it was none of her business. She said he flushed the toilet, gathered the empty capsules, and left without any explanation. She thought they were vitamins but didn't know why he was destroying them."

Agent Welsh took the bottle of vitamins from the Berchtold home and sent them off to be tested at an FBI lab. Days later, he would report, "They were vitamins, but that doesn't mean he didn't drug her."

The agent explained our next hurdle, "Your daughter's abduction will be a big news story. You need to prepare yourselves because your life will never be the same."

Welsh called the phone company and arranged for the installation of a second phone line, explaining that all phone calls would be recorded in the hope that a call would come from either Jan or B.

Hauling in a large reel-to-reel tape recorder, Senior Agent Probst said, "This was used by a family in Montana whose daughter was missing for more than a year and a half before the abductor finally called, was caught, and was eventually convicted."

That evening, my sister and brother-in-law came to our home with news. Looking at their faces, I tried to remain calm. Leonard said, "Rulon [their brother-in-law and the Power County Sheriff] called an hour ago, and one of his officers found an abandoned green-and-white car at Massacre Rocks. It was registered to Berchtold. The driver's side of the car had a broken window, but other than that, Rulon had nothing else to tell us. His deputy found it after receiving an APB. Rulon said they impounded the car and were contacting the FBI, so ask your agent. See what he knows."

The following morning, Agent Welsh reported, "The car was found in a secluded spot, twelve miles south of American Falls, near the Snake River. Are you familiar with Massacre Rocks?"

I nodded my head. I remembered picking potatoes as a youth near the infamous landmark, where more than 240 Shoshone men, women, and children were killed and left exposed.

The agent continued, "The car is being transported to the Pocatello police station, where an investigation will be done. Right now, we have no answers. I've been out there with other law enforcement trying to piece things together." Agent Welsh paused as he viewed our questioning, alarmed faces. "It's assumed that Jan had been in the car. A stocking cap was on the seat. We also found a blue nylon jacket and two piano books. We're holding them as evidence."

A lump lodged in my throat as I looked at Bob. Panic rushed through my weakened body. Bob quietly whispered, "Those would belong to Jan."

The agent continued, "It appears that the day Berchtold disappeared, he left the store after telling his sales clerk that he was meeting a man who was giving him cash in exchange for gold bars. He said Berchtold carried two large, heavy cases out to his car, assuming they held the bars. Also, the car's passenger window was broken. It had bloodstains on it, and we found a few traces of blood inside the car, but we haven't been able to identify whose it is."

Immediately I thought the worst, and I gasped while tearing up. "Do you think Jan is dead?" I asked with a quivering voice.

Agent Welsh cautioned, "Don't jump to conclusions. Mrs. Berchtold never heard about any gold bars, so we don't have answers yet."

Whispering, I mumbled, "They could be in the river." My emotions gave way as I dabbed my eyes with a tissue.

"Don't think the worst," Agent Welsh said. "I have no answers yet, but there appeared to be only one set of footprints around the car. A set of tire tracks nearby measured wider than a car, which possibly could have been a motorhome. Right now, we're still gathering information, but be assured that all law enforcement agencies around this area are involved in the investigation."

I had tears in my eyes. Bob grabbed my hand and squeezed it tightly.

"I know this is very difficult for you," Agent Welsh said kindly.

Nodding my head, I tearfully responded, "I know Jan isn't dead!"

Agent Welsh nodded his head as he stood up to leave. "Until we know more, don't think the worst. I'll be in touch tomorrow."

There was nothing reassuring on the evening news as Berchtold's car was shown on a trailer being pulled by the police. The news station reported, "The Power County Sheriff's Office is engaged in a vigilant search along the banks of the Snake River in the disappearance of Jan Broberg and Robert Berchtold. Officers haven't determined whether foul play is a factor or if their bodies have been dumped into the river."

The distress of the unknown was earth-shattering as we faced the uncertainty of Jan's fate.

Chapter 5
THE MISSION

October 20, 1974

When Jan awoke, the heavy, dizzy feeling had lessened. A ray of light was beaming into the room, but it was hot and stuffy, and the partition was gone. Now what? Alarmed, she nervously peered through the doorway. A motionless figure was lying lopsidedly on a couch, with one arm hurled over the back of a cushion. Observing the figure made Jan gulp and draw back, terrified.

Confused, Jan tried to make sense out of this unreasonable situation. Carefully peering back into the room, she studied the still form before screaming in terror, "B!" Her plea was somewhat garbled as if a wad of cotton had been stuffed into her dry mouth. Hurriedly, she ran over to him.

When she saw his blood-smeared face and a bloody cut on his right hand, Jan began to bawl while screaming, "B! Wake up! B!" She shook him until he began to move, although he was moaning in pain.

Opening his eyes, he looked at her and cried out, "Jan? Oh, Jan! Are you alright?" He dramatically groaned, "Ow! My head!" Grasping his hand, he flinched. "Ouch! I hope it isn't broken!" he said, examining it carefully.

"B! You're bleeding," Jan wailed. "What happened to—?"

Cutting her off, he blurted out, "Oh, Dolly! You're alive! These guys! They wanted you!" Grabbing her tightly, he continued his display of emotion. "I thought they took you."

"Who? What are you talking about?" she shrieked. Slowly gaining control of his emotions, he began giving her a clear picture of what he had witnessed. "Uh, I . . . I, uh . . . aliens, they were, uh—oh, I can't believe it—from another planet. We had an encounter—with a spaceship."

Pale and shaken, Jan looked at him wide-eyed, nodding her head in agreement while he continued to hold his forehead and moan. Grabbing a dishrag off the counter, Jan dabbed at his bloody face and arm. B swallowed hard and burst out, "Ouch! That hurts."

Not sure what to do, she continued to cry while holding the rag in her hand.

"This is crazy. I can't believe it. Where are we?" B asked.

"I don't know," she desperately replied.

B pulled the shade back from the window. "Oh, my hell! Look at this!" His voice was loud and excited.

Terrified, Jan looked out the window. She expected to see another planet or thought they would be surrounded by aliens. Instead, she observed a desolate, weed-covered desert. "Where are we?" she whimpered apprehensively.

"I don't know, but I'm scared. I . . . I don't know what to think," B said. "I was driving to that ranch and got lost. It started getting dark when suddenly the car began doing strange, crazy things. I had no control. The car went crazy, and no matter what I did to steer it, I couldn't make it go where I wanted. It was awful. I stopped and got out, and that's when I saw them."

"Saw who?" Jan asked frantically.

"Lights. Several lights in a round circle hovering over the car—and then a group of people—aliens! I was scared to death and tried to get back in but was overpowered," he replied, his voice quivering.

"No! Don't say that!" Jan replied, stunned.

"I asked them what they wanted, and they said you! I tried to fight them off," he said, choking on the words as tears filled his eyes. He then pointed to his bloodied hand and bruised face. "And this is what happened. They pounded on me fiercely, but I couldn't stand the thought of them taking you." He snorted loudly and cleared his throat before gathering Jan in his arms. "I'm so thankful you're okay." His body trembled as he held on to her. "If anything ever happened to you, I don't know what I would do." Choking back the words, he rested his chin on the top of her head, with his arms still wrapped securely around her. He blubbered, "You mean so much to me. I would die for you if I had to. I love you so much!"

Jan was shaking her head as she thought about the stories B had convincingly told during the past two years about UFOs, along with the movies they had watched. Her mind raced furiously. At the time, she had sort of believed some of it, but now there was no doubt. "But how did we get here? And what's going to happen to us?"

B's answers were vague. "Dolly, I don't know where my car is, but the best thing we can do is get out of here."

"Are we going home?" she asked anxiously.

"They told me to drive South until they contact me again. Until then, I don't know what to tell you."

"But where's your car, and where did you get this motorhome?" Jan asked.

B explained, "That's what's so crazy. I bought it to take on buying trips, and it was—well, it was going to be a surprise for my family. But for the life of me, I don't know how it got out here. Hearing you scream woke me up. I guess I've been unconscious since I got beat up." He paused, staring off in space. Slowly he released Jan from his hold, looked around, and then moved up to the front of the motorhome.

Jan cautiously watched him, wondering what else was going to happen. She was relieved when he exclaimed, "Well, I'll be damned. The key's in the ignition. Who put it there?"

Jan started to cry. "B, I'm scared. They tied me up and said lots of weird things."

"Oh, Dolly, I know. They talked to me too. What did they say?"

"Crazy things. They said I have a mission, but I don't understand what they mean. I don't want to talk about it. I'm just scared and want to get out of here," she said, crying. "I want to go home."

"Jan, be careful what you say. They might be close by, and I think they can hear everything we say," he cautioned.

Hearing that announcement, Jan looked around nervously.

"Was it somebody with a funny-sounding voice?" B asked.

"Yes, two of them, and they said their names were Zethra and Zada," Jan anxiously reported. "I never saw them, but we should go home before they come back."

"Jan, tell me what they said to you," B demanded.

Walking over to her, he pulled her shoulders around toward him. "I can't believe what they told me, too, but we've got to be extremely careful. They said I'm to be the father of a special child, and, well . . ." He briefly paused as she looked at him, wide-eyed and frightened. "They said you're to be the mother." B shook his head and looked bewildered.

Jan shrieked. "They told you that? Why did they say that?" Her voice quivered with emotion. "I don't want to!"

"I know. But it's not for now. It's for later, when you're older. But they warned me to complete my mission or . . ." He paused.

Jan waited for B to finish his sentence. Urging him to reveal what they told him, she said, "Or what? What will happen?"

"There are lots of people who want me dead. Even now, I'm being hunted down and accused of terrible things. You have to believe in me, Jan. No matter what the cost, I want to live."

"Why do they want you dead?" she asked, alarmed.

"Because of the plan—the mission we've been given," he said.

"But what about me?" Jan asked, bewildered.

"They said you were chosen before this life because of your strong belief in God," B said. "You've remained pure and innocent and have proven yourself. Before some young guy comes along and ruins it, your mission needs to be completed."

"I don't understand," Jan cried.

"There are a lot of things that don't make any sense. If you think about Mary, the mother of Christ, it must have been very hard for her to hear what she had to do! But she listened to the angel and did what she was told. You're a very noble young lady. You've been chosen, and only God knows why."

"Do you think they are angels? When will they come back?" Jan asked as tears rolled down her cheeks.

"Oh, my precious Dolly." B reached for a tissue and dabbed at Jan's tear-stained face. "I know they were here and did this to me," he said as he gripped his bloodied hand. "These people, aliens, or whatever they are, really exist, and we can't ignore what they say. We don't know for sure who they are—maybe they are angels. They meant no harm. I wouldn't have gotten hurt if I had listened to what they were trying to tell me. But I was so afraid you were going to be taken away that I reacted and started fighting. They were trying to subdue me when I started swinging."

"But they don't sound like us. They talk funny. What did they look like—those people?" Jan asked anxiously.

"Just like us. They weren't strange or funny looking—in fact, they look just like regular people," B said. "They kept telling me they were just trying to save their world, and they need a special child."

"But we've got to tell someone!"

"No!"

"Why not?"

B answered, "Can you imagine what people would do if we told them? They would say we are crazy or are making it up!"

"But I don't understand what she meant that if I didn't do the mission, I would be vaporized! What does that mean?"

Shaking his head, he responded, "It means we need to do what they say."

"But it's my family too! What about them?"

Perplexed, B sighed, ignored her question, walked to the kitchen sink, and turned on the faucet. "Well, look at this. Water! The last time I worked on this motorhome, I couldn't get the water to pump."

Taking a hand towel from under the cabinet, he soaked it in the running water, squeezing out the excess before placing the towel on his face and wiping off the dried blood. When he blotted the bruise on his forehead, he shuddered, "Ouch! That's tender."

Looking at Jan, who had a look of fear on her face, he said, "Dolly, don't look so scared. This is something we both have to do, and for whatever reason, we'll have to make the best of it. In time, we'll understand it all."

Walking over to her, he sat down and took her hands in his. He held them to his lips and kissed them passionately. "Trust me, Jan. They will not hurt you. When they speak to you again, listen to them. They have a message we can't deny. I believe there are other worlds that are populated and are much farther advanced than ours. They have greater power and knowledge than we do, and they know our destiny. These people make visits to this planet in order to help us further our work, but there are so few who accept them or are in tune with what they have to say that they never get their message delivered. I know you are a special person who has a great mission—whatever it might be. Promise me that you will do everything they say. You have so much to give, and we have so much to live for."

B's solemn statement left Jan contemplating the uninvited voices. The messages had left her confused and frightened. No matter how she tried to ignore them, the hauntingly eerie words weighed heavily on her mind. Her only comfort was B. She knew that his assignment was difficult, too, and he understood her fear.

It seemed that B drove for hours over hot desert country. The roads they traveled were narrow and graveled instead of paved. She seldom saw other cars or trucks pass them on the two-lane road. Afraid to ask, she wondered if they would ever see any stores, people, animals, or farms—or anything that looked like America. Based on his facial expressions, Jan thought that B seemed very anxious.

When B realized Jan was growing restless, he turned and said, "They told me to go on this road, but it sure is long. I've been thinking about all that happened, and I can't believe what they did to you." He gave Jan a concerned look. "I'm still very angry about that."

Jan shrugged her shoulders without making a comment. A few minutes later, she asked, "B, do you know what day this is?"

B looked surprised. "Well, I'm not sure. I don't know how long I was knocked out. Maybe Friday. Why?"

"Oh, just wondering what everybody's doing at home," she said.

"I've been thinking the same thing. By the way, are you hungry?"

Jan nodded. "Thirsty," she said, "Can I get a drink?"

"Sure. Go back and see what's in the fridge. When did you last eat?" B asked.

"I don't know," said Jan. "They told me to get some food, and I did, but I went back to sleep, and, uh, I don't know."

"Well, go on back and find us something good. We can snack while I drive. I don't dare stop. Later we'll find something healthy."

It was late in the afternoon when they drove into a more populated area with better roads. After passing homes, gas stations, and stores, Jan had a feeling of relief. Earlier she had asked B if they were going to run out of gas. He had responded, "Zethra told me not to worry about it. If it becomes a problem, they will take care of it."

Crossing the Border

They continued to drive into the night when Jan saw blinking lights in the distance. Her first thought was that it was a spaceship. Frantically, she asked, "What's that, B?"

"I'm not sure. Go to the back and change your clothes. Some of Jerry's clothes are back there. Put on his ball cap. If we get stopped, I want them to think you're my son. Hurry!"

Jan rushed to the back and did what she was told. Her heart was beating rapidly as she threw on the oversize Levi's and shirt. Placing the cap on her head, she tucked her hair under the brim, swallowed hard, and then waited for more instructions.

"Now come up here and sit down in the seat. It's the Mexican border patrol. They might ask who you are. Tell them you are Jerry. Don't act nervous, and we'll be okay."

Jan did as B instructed. After giving the border patrol agents some papers and telling the officer that B and his son were on vacation, they were allowed to pass through.

B turned and winked, "Perfect, Dolly. They believed us."

Chapter 6
WHAT'S A PEDOPHILE?

October 22, 1974

On the evening of October 22, a tall, bearded man came to our door in a very distraught state. He introduced himself as Mr. King. He said he had been B's counselor and had referred him to the Clinic for Behavioral Therapy in Beverly Hills. The clinic had since closed because of questionable practices, and the FBI was looking for past personnel to interview. He had just learned of our daughter's disappearance and had requested a private audience with Agent Welsh.

After Mr. King left, Agent Welsh asked if we had heard the word "pedophile" before?

Bob and I both asked, "What's that?"

Realizing that we couldn't even pronounce the word, Agent Welsh educated us on pedophiles and their obsession with young children. We knew there were individuals who preyed on children, but we had never heard that word used to describe them.

Agent Welsh had become a close and trustworthy detective on the case. He was the father of three daughters, one of them the same age and grade at school as Jan. He had a similar religious and moral worldview as we did, and we trusted him, knowing that he was fully engaged in every angle of searching for her. He would say, "Berchtold is a clever criminal, and it appears he has planned every detail. He will slip up eventually."

We also had the faithful support of our longtime friends, Cor and Elaine Hofman. Bob continued to go to work most days, but I stayed home as much as possible. It was not healthy to be barraged with prying eyes everywhere I went with the girls. The Hoffmans fielded calls and visitors and started a campaign with flyers asking for anyone with any information to come forward. They believed in action, and they even organized a trip to Mexico with flyers in Spanish, but they returned defeated with no leads about Jan. By then, more than three weeks had passed with absolutely no word from Jan or any sign of her.

Mexico
October 25, 1974

While we searched for clues at home and any news of Jan and B in Mexico Jan on the other hand, was relieved when they finally arrived in Mexico City. Since Jan had no clothes except what she was wearing, their first priority was shopping. B insisted that she buy a pretty dress appropriate for dancing because he planned to escort her to a cantina. He told Jan that it would be an out-of-this-world event in the true atmosphere of authentic Mexico.

Jan found the Mexican people delightful and interesting. She loved the little street vendors and the unique gifts they peddled. She found trinkets for herself and her sisters, and she loaded up a few small sacks. When she asked B if he was going to buy anything for his kids, he shook his head and then persuaded her to go down to the beach with him and run through the water along the seashore. While there, they took a balloon ride that carried them high into the sky, whipping them over the ocean before they landed back on the sandy beach. These few days of fun helped Jan gain some distance from the recent traumatic experiences.

The first few nights of their journey, B was very compassionate in regard to Jan's expression of fear about the intended mission. He often pulled Jan close to him and whispered his affection for her. When they slept, they shared the double bed. Although it was awkward, his cuddling was comforting.

However, her comfort was short-lived. The voices from the box returned, and the messages from Zada and Zethra never stopped during the duration of her stay in Mexico. When B heard the voices, he would go into a trance and act very strangely. Knowing he was bothered by their messages, she watched him cringe, shake his fists, and moan. She felt absolutely helpless.

The Books

One of her first specific assignments came shortly after their arrival in Mazatlán. B had left early in the morning to find a part for the motorhome. Jan was awakened by one of the voices. She shuddered when Zada instructed her to find books in a cabinet. She was only to study the first one, which would help prepare her to make the baby. Jan located the books and took the first one out. Unaware of the contents, she opened the book. Gasping with shock, Jan felt her face flush as she stared at the first page. She quickly closed the book as a shiver pulsed through her body. Jan was shocked by what she had seen: graphic images of people in sexual positions.

When B returned to the motorhome, she breathlessly told him about the book and the graphic pictures.

B offered comfort, "I realize it has to be hard for you to see things like that, Dolly. You are so innocent. However, if there is anything you didn't understand, don't hesitate to confide in me and ask me whatever you'd like. It's my job to make you happy." Being obedient to their indoctrination, Jan found the courage to begin her study of the flagrant images.

A short time passed before Jan was instructed by the voices to take out a second book and look it over. Horrified, Jan swallowed hard as she observed pictures of naked children doing awful things with other kids and with grown men. Jan wondered, *Am I going to have to do things like that?*

The impressions of these images seared her mind. She would never forget them. They also increased her longing for home and the carefree life she had once known. She wondered what was happening to her family. *How were they getting along without her? Was Mom worried?*

The first "touching" experience happened soon after they arrived in Mexico. B exposed himself to her as he was getting into the shower. He gave a resigned chuckle, explaining he had nothing to hide if they were going to get married. Jan remembered, and her cheeks flushed as she turned away. As he moved his hands over her small body, she felt guilty and uncomfortable. The box had told her that she must allow the male companion to do what makes everyone happy. But she was not happy. She was scared. How could she tell him to stop? What if Zada and Zethra were watching?

She remembered the night the kids had slept out on the trampoline in the Berchtolds' yard. Karen, Jerry, Jimmy, Susan, Joey, and Jan each had their own sleeping bag. It had been fun laying on the trampoline and gazing at the stars while B told stories about flying saucers, other worlds, planets, and the people who lived there—aliens. Everyone shrieked with fright. It had been so scary, but in the end it was perfectly harmless.

Sometime during the night, Jan was awakened by something moving around her. Startled, she opened her eyes and saw B next to her. "What are you doing?" she cried out.

"Just tucking you in."

Jan laid still for a moment and realized that something was different. She felt uncovered, bare. Moving her body, she discovered her underpants at her feet.

She pointedly whispered, "What are you doing?" and jumped up from the bag. She dashed through the basement door, scared and nervous, and ran up the stairs. Gail was awakened by the sound of the door slamming and the noise of frantic feet running up the stairs. Jan began to bawl and tried to explain what had happened, but she couldn't. B darted into the room behind her.

Attempting to redeem himself to his wife, B said, "I didn't do anything. I was watching the kids from the bedroom window, and Jan seemed to be very restless. I wondered what was wrong, so I went down to see—and she woke up. I think she must have worked her panties off from thrashing around so much. I didn't touch you and would never do anything to hurt you. You have to believe that."

Jan scrunched next to Gail and remained silent. Gail quietly said, "Jan, come in and sleep with me since you are so upset." Glaring at her husband, Gail icily remarked, "I wish you would quit telling those horrible nightmare tales. Don't you think you should go down and sleep in one of the boys' beds?"

Jan's memory of that experience remained vivid in her mind. She did not believe that B had taken her panties off; he would never do anything to her that she didn't feel good about. She hadn't been able to tell her parents or Karen about it—even Caroline, her best friend in the whole world, didn't know.

No Escape

Now far from home, in a country where she didn't even speak the language, there was no one to turn to. There was nowhere to go to get away from the bad feelings. There was no way to hide from it. There was no way to pretend that B would never do anything she didn't feel good about. Ironically, her thoughts kept turning the finger of blame back to herself. *It was my fault these things happened*, she thought. *If only I could get sick and die, but what good would that do? I have to do this for them—for their planet. If I don't do everything they tell me, I won't be able to live, anyway, and terrible things will happen to my family. What can I do? I know—I will count. I will count the lines in the ceiling. I will count the leaves I see through the fan. Yes, just look at the leaves and count. Count until it's over.*

B stayed in each city for only a few days. Weary of traveling from town to town, Jan asked all too often where they were going and when they would be there. B's common response had been, "I don't know. They will tell me when to stop, and they will tell me when it is time to move on. We have no choice." There had been no TV to watch, no American movies to see, no books to read, and only Mexican music. Growing bored with nothing to do, Jan enjoyed watching the street vendors, and asked B to take her to the shops. Annoyed by her begging, B often gave in to her pleas. Trying to be diplomatic, he would entice her to the beach with rented snorkeling gear or surfboards.

B hadn't taken Jan to tourist attractions because he told her that it wasn't safe. The voices had told Jan that her male companion's life was in danger. If she was going to complete her mission, it was critical for him to remain with her. She was to be loyal to him because the alien council had chosen him to father her 'special child.' The warning of her being vaporized, if she failed, weighed heavily on her mind. At seventy pounds and years away from puberty, Jan had learned enough from brief conversations with her sisters and best friend to know that she was not yet physically able to get pregnant the human way. Was her half-alien body subject to different rules regarding how a baby is made? She decided it must be.

Every day, B would give Jan a vitamin pill in the morning and a relaxing pill at night to help her sleep. Sometimes, the voices would awaken her during the night. Thinking they might not come if she were awake, she would resist sleeping. B worried about her health, so he offered his pills so she could rest. Jan would freeze with sheer panic each time she heard the creepy, inhuman voices. There was no escape, but what was coming next?

Chapter 7
MARRY HER?

November 19, 1974

It was the fifth week of Jan's abduction, and I was so beside myself that I contacted a psychic who had successfully worked with law enforcement.

Nothing helped. I was desperate. I could barely get out of bed. My only comfort came from reading thoughts Jan had recorded in her diary. I tried to understand what Pete and other law enforcement officers consistently relayed to us, but from all our dealings with B, we couldn't imagine that he had taken Jan because he wanted to hurt her or us.

Jan's Diary, July 25, 1973:

The Berchtold family is so close to me. B and Gail are just like second parents, and the kids are just great. I made Gail a little present and made a card saying how much I loved her. She cried and said that it was special. Neat!

The Phone Call

It was past six o' clock in the evening when I received a phone call from B's brother Joe, who worked at a car dealership in Ogden, Utah. When he announced who he was, I felt a surge of adrenaline and a cold shiver through my body.

"I had a phone call from B today," he said.

A wave of anxiety came over me. With a lump in my throat, I asked, "Where are they? How is Jan? Is she all right?"

Joe Berchtold's tone was slightly impatient. I immediately perceived him to be his brother's heartless accomplice. "He didn't tell me where they were, but he said Jan is fine and is driving him crazy. All I know is he's far away, and unless you do what he wants, he isn't coming back. If you don't cooperate, he says you will never see either of them again."

This terrifying threat took away my ability to think sensibly. I tried to stay calm. "Okay," I said, "What does he want? I'll do anything to get Jan home."

"He's refusing to come home if he's going to jail. He said it's your fault and that you've made it impossible for him to come back."

"What does that mean?" I asked, bewildered.

Joe was a bit snappy as he explained: "He would've been back weeks ago, but you called the FBI and charged him with kidnapping. He's been trying to figure out how to come back and not end up in prison for the rest of his life."

My voice began to tremble as I blurted out, "What are we supposed to do? And what would you call it? Does he have any idea what he's done? What in the hell is he thinking? All we want is Jan home."

"Okay, this is his proposal. Just listen, and don't freak out," Joe said firmly. "He wants you and Bob to give him permission to marry Jan."

I was stunned. My mind was in total confusion. Does B want to marry my twelve-year-old daughter? There was no logic to what he was saying. "Is he crazy?" I asked.

"I know it sounds bizarre," Joe continued, "but he said he needs protection from prosecution. I'm supposed to tell you he means every word he says because he's not spending the rest of his life in the slammer. He insists it's your only choice if you want to see Jan again."

My heart was pounding so furiously that I patted my chest in an effort to calm it. Attempting to assemble the staggering news into some kind of sense and deal with the impact, I mumbled, "He wants to marry Jan?"

"That's what he said," Joe's message was direct and blunt. Did this man realize the torture we had endured these past weeks because of his brother? Did he have any compassion for our daughter or for us? All of this confirmed my suspicion that Joe was somehow involved in this with his brother. "He said if you don't give him permission to marry her, then make him Jan's legal guardian. It's the only way he can come back without being charged with kidnapping. You really made it hard for him."

"What a gutless idiot," I retorted. "Does he have any conscience?"

Joe sensed the anger in my voice and softened his approach. "Don't get upset at me. I'm just the messenger. I suggest you find a lawyer who can draw up some kind of legal paper. He's going to call back in a couple of days, so let me know what you're going to do." Searching for words, I said, "We'll do something."

"I told B your phone was probably bugged." Joe waited for my response, but I didn't answer. He then cautiously asked, "Is there any way you can keep this from the FBI?"

"Go to hell!"

With that response, he gave his first hint of compassion, "I really am sorry. It's so stupid of him."

"I can't give you an answer until I talk to my husband," I said, still shaken.

My thoughts ran wild. I was so grateful to know she was alive, but where? What had happened to her during these past five weeks? The thought of his demands to bring her home was utterly ridiculous. Marry her? Let him be her legal guardian? I'd do almost anything to get her back. But that?

After Bob arrived home, I broke into tears as I related the disturbing demands from Joe. Bob vented his anger by swearing, calling B a son of a bitch, and slamming his fists on the kitchen counter. We told the FBI everything about Joe's call. The good news was the fact that Jan was alive somewhere in the world. We just didn't know where.

In Custody
November 23, 1974

It was five weeks after Jan had gone missing. Now, efficient and highly motivated, Richard McDaniel moved quickly. FBI agents in Utah installed a recording system at the auto dealership where B's brother worked, and they moved in to make sure he cooperated. Every message Joe received would be recorded. The FBI coached Joe on how to keep his brother on the line for as long as possible.

Near the noon hour on Saturday, an apprehensive Joe answered the phone and heard his brother's voice. Joe had been told to tell B that we were getting the legal papers ready, but he didn't have them yet.

"What are they doing? Giving their consent for marriage?" B asked.

"I don't know. MaryAnn called and said they would either do that or give you guardianship," Joe lied. "They want Jan home."

Joe asked for an address where he could send the papers. B refused to give him any information. Instead, he said he would call Joe back and give instructions when he knew the papers were in Joe's hands.

B demanded, "Call the Broberg's and tell them to send the papers to you immediately. I have to know exactly what they say before I'll come back."

At the urging of the agents, Joe tried to extend the conversation. He asked about the weather and Jan but received only guarded information. B revealed nothing that would lead to any information about their location.

Growing nervous, B told his brother he had to get off the phone. "I'll talk to you next week. Just tell the Brobergs to hurry up."

For the next hour, telephone personnel were under great pressure to trace the call. If one operator closed the exchange, the call would be lost. After connecting with several toll exchanges, they finally secured what they thought was the originating location: Mazatlán, Mexico. The call had been placed from a hotel.

As soon as Agent McDaniel received information from his counterparts in Utah, he shared the details. Trying to remain calm was out of the question. Even though we were relieved that the long, nightmarish experience was nearly over, there were still too many unanswered questions.

Preparing us for unforeseen situations, Agent McDaniel told us that they were currently orchestrating a plan of action in Mazatlán. "The FBI is moving cautiously and has contacted the American Embassy in Mazatlán. We have spoken with the American Ambassador and have explained the circumstances. The problem now is that Mazatlán is a large resort city, and the agents are discussing a plan with the local Mexican police about how to proceed and how to detain Berchtold without violence in order to protect Jan," Agent McDaniel said.

"Violence?" I asked.

Agent McDaniel turned to me with a caring yet resolute tone, "The FBI is demanding that certain precautions be taken to protect your daughter. No one knows Berchtold's present state of mind. He could become desperate or violent and perhaps hold Jan hostage for his own protection. We don't want to worry you, but we know he has a handgun, and they fear Mexican police might react if they feel threatened. Anything could happen at this point."

With that said, movie scenes of bloody shootouts between lawmen and criminals flashed through my mind. Almost six weeks had passed. I had to keep my mind on the positive outcome we wanted, so I dismissed any gruesome thoughts. All I could do was wait, worry, and pray.

Finally, in the early evening hours, the long-awaited news arrived from Agent McDaniel, "Both the kidnapper and Jan are in custody at a Mexican jail."

It had taken hours for the Mexican police to locate the motorhome, but they reported that Berchtold had surrendered peacefully.

We were overcome with gratitude, weeping tears of joy, and shouting praise and thanksgiving to a loving God. The prayers of hundreds of people had been answered. Jan was safe.

Gail had been in and out of our home throughout the day and had suffered intensely. On the one hand, she expressed gratitude that the ordeal was reaching a conclusion, but on the other hand, she realized what the end result would mean for her family. Needless to say, she was visibly upset when the news came about the arrest of her husband. With tears streaming down all of our faces, Bob and I embraced her.

I whispered, "I'm so sorry, Gail."

She responded, "So am I."

As she left our home, I could see the worry, despair, and extreme hurt from the weeks of hell on her face. What would she do now?

The operation had been successful. Berchtold and Jan were in police custody in Mazatlán. We were overjoyed. Agent McDaniel gave us the phone number of the Mexican jail. After two desperate attempts to call the jail, a male voice answered. He spoke no English but realized the call was for the "Señorita Americana." With the four of us clustered around the phone, the sound of Jan saying hello brought great emotion and opened a floodgate of tears.

In a desperate, shaky, trembling voice, Jan pleaded with us, "Come and get me! I'm scared and don't know what to do."

While we were trying to console her, the emotional outbursts of each one of us seemed to be unnerving Jan even more at first. Karen and Susan were ecstatic. Tears ran down their cheeks as they nearly shouted at Jan to come home.

"Be patient, Jan," her father said, trying to calm her. "We love you and will be there as soon as we can make flight arrangements."

We could hear her sobs as she said, "Please hurry!"

I could hardly contain myself, "Jan, are they treating you okay?"

Her reply was choked between sobs, but we heard, "Uh-huh! They're nice, but I can't understand them."

"Have you had anything to eat?"

"Huh?" she asked.

"Food," I said again. "Have you eaten?"

"Not since we were taken from the motorhome. I don't think they're going to feed me," Jan's voice was trembling with emotion.

"Well, you have to eat!" Bob declared.

As we talked, Karen and Susan seemed to have the most calming effect on their sister. When it seemed like Jan had her emotions under control, Bob told her that we needed to hang up. It was difficult saying goodbye, but after we had expressed our love over and over, there was little else to say. We ended the call by assuring Jan that we would come immediately.

Agent McDaniel told us to get visas, make plane reservations, and carry Jan's birth certificate. How could we get visas on a Saturday night? I thought there was little chance until Monday.

Bob was beside himself and mentioned the difficulty to Cor Hofman. Cor reminded him that Elaine, his wife, had excellent political connections. Sure enough, in answer to our prayers, she was able to make arrangements with the county clerk within an hour after they opened Monday morning.

Adrenaline flooded my body as I pulled the metal security box off the shelf to gather the required documents. I opened the folder and thumbed through the papers, but I couldn't find Jan's birth certificate! I looked again. Panicked, I screamed at Bob as I frantically searched a third time. "Jan's birth certificate isn't here! I found Karen's, but Susan's is gone too." Thinking hard about the last time I saw them, my mind flashed back to a scene last summer.

B had approached us about becoming the guardians of his children if anything ever happened to him and Gail. We had told him we would consider it but suggested he turn to his own family first.

"There isn't one member of my family I like well enough to entrust with the care of my children. We have no other options," he had replied.

Bob agreed but left the final decision in my hands. "Well, if you feel so strongly about us taking that huge responsibility, MaryAnn will have the final say." Raising his eyebrows, Bob's blue eyes met mine for an answer. This was a big favor to ask, even from his best friend.

"What does Gail want?" I asked.

"Gail thinks it would be ideal. Our kids are here almost more than at their own home."

It made sense to me. "Well, sure. Why not?"

Bob looked at me in amazement, astounded at my willingness. With humor in his voice, he had pointedly looked into B's eyes and said, "Just be sure we get your fortune so we can raise them."

B laughed, "Sure. You can have every penny of the five dollars I have hidden in my top drawer. What about your girls? Can we return the favor?"

"Being an identical twin has its advantages. My brother Dick and I have already agreed to raise each other's children, and our kids would never know the difference," Bob joked.

"Do you have any legal papers I can look at?"

"No! Why do all that work? Our wives didn't protest, so Dick and I didn't think it was necessary. Right?"

Bob's eyes met mine, seeking approval.

While going through the papers, B had seen our girls' birth certificates. Admiring the tiny footprints, he remarked, "Look at these little feet. Aren't they about the cutest things you've ever seen?" I admired B's sensitivity about matters of the heart.

Now, years later, as I was searching in vain for the birth certificates, it was suddenly clear to me. I looked helplessly at Bob, "Oh no! B took them!"

"What makes you think he took them?" Bob questioned.

"Who knows? But he knew they were here." I felt frantic. "What should we do?"

"Have you looked through everything?"

I nodded.

"Then bring her baptism records, and we'll see if that works. We need to go."

News of Jan's rescue traveled fast. Friends and family members stopped by to express gratitude and love, give us a tender embrace, and wish us well on our journey. We also received numerous phone calls. One call was from Las Vegas relatives who had heard about Jan's recovery while at a basketball game between Idaho State and Las Vegas. During halftime, the Pocatello sportscaster had made a special announcement for Idaho fans, "Tonight, twelve-year-old Jan Broberg was found safe and well in Mexico."

"You can't imagine the excitement that announcement caused," our aunt exclaimed. "The crowd from Idaho went wild, but we screamed the loudest."

Bob's uncle added, "Our Las Vegas group couldn't believe how crazy we went during halftime. We are ecstatic."

The house was finally growing quiet, and I was able to throw together a few items for our departure. Out of the corner of my eye, I caught a glimpse of Karen standing away from everyone while Susan was asleep on the couch.

At that moment, my overburdened brain was struck with the realization of Karen's emotional struggles. Karen and Susan had not been ignored intentionally, but because of our chaotic lives during the past five weeks, they had received very little attention. Although they deserved much more, their patient and calm personalities had allowed us to put all of our energy into this painful crisis.

Karen quietly watched as I placed some clothes into a suitcase. Without a word, her wishes were revealed by the look on her face. I laid the clothes aside and turned to her. "Oh, Karen, this has been so hard for you and Susan. I know you want to go so badly, but we don't know what we have to face when we get there."

Karen remained silent. Bob tried to cheer her up by telling her about the fun she would have with Uncle Dick and her cousins. When that didn't work, he gave her a big kiss on her forehead. "We'll call and let you know everything," he told her.

With tears in her eyes, Karen looked longingly at me as she asked, "Can't I stay with Jimmy Berchtold instead?"

Bob's eyes widened as he raised his eyebrows, waiting for me to respond.

"Oh Karen, Gail has too much on her plate. It isn't possible," I said, putting my arm around her. "I know you've suffered too, and Jimmy is your best friend. I'm sorry you and Susan haven't had more attention. Can you be patient with us for a few more days?"

Embracing Karen, I watched huge tears fall from her beautiful round blue eyes. Reluctantly, she resigned herself to the fact that she would not be going, but wanted to be awakened before we left so she could say goodbye.

How ironic is it that all three of my girls had seen Gail and B's home as a safe haven, as the place they would most like to be, second only to home. How could we explain that all this had changed?

I rested for a moment. I was exhausted. The worst was over. Jan was alive and safe. It had been thirty-nine horrible days. What was going to happen to B and Gail and their children? I couldn't think of that now. Jan would be back home, and that is what mattered. What had she been doing all this time? Did she know that B had wanted us to give our permission for him to marry her? Had he told her? Certainly, nothing bad had happened to her, had it? Was she scared? What if she had no place to sleep that night? Had she eaten?

There was nothing more I could do about it right now. Although I tried to convince myself that everything was okay, at some level, I knew it was not.

Chapter 8
JOYFUL REUNION

November 24, 1974

The world seemed to reflect our inexpressible joy by providing us a quiet, reverent morning on our early Sunday drive to Salt Lake City—the location of the closest International Airport. Counting our blessings was a recurring topic in our conversation.

As we boarded Mexicana Airlines, the anticipation of seeing Jan triggered dark thoughts and worries about her state. As we stepped off the plane, the warm humidity of the Mexican coastline enveloped me. Then, panic followed! Where would we go? How would we get there? How would we communicate? No one spoke English.

An airline hostess gave us limited information about procedures, and told us that our first stop should be at the foreign exchange booth so we could get Mexican currency. Bob became frustrated when he attempted to communicate with gate personnel. Then someone appeared who spoke broken English. We followed him to the baggage area to pick up our luggage. He waited for us to exchange our American Dollars before taking us to parked taxicabs. He hollered in Spanish to one of the drivers, who immediately broke into a big grin and said, "Cómo está? Habla español?"

Bob replied, "Uh, no." The cab driver stood nodding his head, still smiling. We smiled back, shaking our heads, "No, we don't speak Spanish."

Our escort again spoke to the driver and told him where we needed to go. The driver sat in his taxi and waited for us to get in. Bob tipped our courteous escort, thanking him profusely. We loaded our luggage into the back seat and climbed into the cab. We didn't even manage to fully close the door before the enthusiastic driver sped away from the curb.

Our driver was anything but cautious. I braced myself each time he pulled behind a vehicle, which he would then quickly swerve around. He often honked at animals or people crossing the road. He rarely used his brakes, and he only seemed to be driving at one speed: fast. He careened over the bumpy road and took corners and curves without slowing down, tossing us from one side of the seat to the another like unfastened luggage. He seemed to hit every pothole on the road. However, he got us to where we needed to go.

Our taxi ride continued as it began to grow dusk, and I took in the unfamiliar surroundings. As we passed through the streets, I observed the open doorways of the small, antiquated shacks, and I felt compassion for those who lived there, as well as guilt for taking my comfortable surroundings at home for granted.

Jan in Jail

The driver stopped at the entrance of town square and pointed towards a gray sandstone building that was clearly the jail. With suitcases in hand, we walked towards the foreboding door. Upon opening the door, we instantly heard a familiar shriek of delight and saw Jan leaping toward us as if she were airborne. Kneeling in the courtyard with Jan in our arms, we wept openly, laughing through tears, and we hugged as curious onlookers chattered.

Police officers encircled us. They kept repeating, "La mamá! El papá! La mamá! El papá!" The officer in charge thumped his chest, smiling broadly, and said, "Me—papá!" indicating his own role as a father. I gathered he was relating to our joy at being reunited with our daughter.

We were escorted by four officers into a small, shabby room that contained a few wooden chairs.

Bob said, "Let's do what we need to do and go home." Conversing with the Mexican officers was difficult, and our attempts to explain that we wanted to take our daughter with us to the hotel turned into a comical charade. Laughter seemed to be the best solution when no one knew what the other was saying.

Pointing, Jan said, "This is my father, and this is my mother. I love them, and I want to go with them."

Her animated gestures brought about laughter from the men. They nodded their heads, which we took as permission to leave. As we began to leave, one officer frowned and shook his head. "No," he said.

Jan repeated her words again—with the same results. Bob then realized that they wanted some proof of who we were. So, he took the legal documents from the envelope, and the officer escorted my husband into a little four-by-five-foot cubical around the corner. Jan and I remained in the outer room with the three other policemen.

Jan hadn't slept since the police had brought her to the jail, and she was beginning to look haggard.

B Would Die for Me

Waiting in the dirty room, we watched a hungry mouse run back and forth as it searched for a morsel of food. I tried to ignore it, but Jan said, "There's more than one in here. I watched them all night."

"My poor girl," I said.

I asked where they were keeping B, and Jan pointed to a large wooden door behind us. I felt an immediate surge of uneasiness knowing he was so close. There was a sizable gap between the door and the wall which made me feel unsettled. He was more than likely watching us and listening to us, and I knew he couldn't be happy with the current circumstances. *But he deserves this*, I thought to myself.

Jan sat rigidly on the rickety chair. Her eyes widened with a look of fear. "B's in there and we have to get him out. They are really mean to him, and he's scared they are going to kill him. We've got to take him with us."

Her shoulders sagged against the back of her chair as she concluded, "I'm afraid something bad is going to happen to him."

"I'm sorry, Jan, but we can't get him out. The FBI will have to do that," I explained.

Jan raised her head, narrowed her eyes, and asked, "Why did you tell the FBI that I had been kidnapped?" Her words were sharp. "It made things so hard. B said that if we went back, he would be sent to prison for a long, long time."

With my mouth agape, I responded, "Jan, we had no choice. We didn't know what happened to either of you."

"Mom, you know B loves me. He wouldn't let anything bad happen. We've just been having fun. I wanted to come home a long time ago, but B said we couldn't. He was afraid something bad would happen to me." Jan nervously picked at the hangnails on her fingers and avoided eye contact.

I looked at her intently, "Why would something happen to you? You haven't done anything wrong. He never, ever, should have taken you."

Jan sat mute. Her silence bothered me.

Wanting answers, I continued to probe. "Tell me what happened the day you left with B? Where did you go after your piano lesson?"

"We went to ride horses, but he got lost and couldn't find the guy's ranch. I got tired and fell asleep. I don't remember."

"Well, it must have taken a very long time to drive here," I said. "Do you remember crossing the border into Mexico?"

"No."

"Well, what did B tell you when you found out you were in Mexico?"

"He said it was a vacation," Jan turned and stared at me with innocent eyes, seeking assurance. "You said I could go."

I shook my head. "No, Jan. That is not true. I never told him that."

Jan grew uneasy and looked down at the dirty floor. "I don't want to talk about it anymore." She kept her eyes on the wooden door as she continued to bite her fingernails. She ended my interrogation. "I'm really starving. I haven't eaten anything since last night."

"Oh, so you did get to eat last night. What a relief," I said.

"Two young missionaries brought me a hamburger and an orange pop. Did it ever taste good!"

"What did they say?"

"Not much. They were really nice and just asked how I was doing. They said they might come back today."

I felt such gratitude for this network of support.

"Wow! Your dad called the mission president and he said he would send some missionaries by," I said.

She paused with her eyebrows raised and eyes wide open. I waited to hear more. Shaking her head and with a sad look plastered on her face, she explained, "I was going to save some food for B, but I didn't see him."

Taken by surprise, I asked, "Have you seen him since you've been here?"

"Yeah, today before you came." She looked at the officers who were standing in the outer doorway. She leaned forward and quietly said, "He had to give one of the policemen his diamond ring so he could talk to me."

"What did he say?" I prompted.

Jan dropped her voice to a whisper as if she were afraid the officers would hear.

"He was worried about me, but told me not to worry about him. He said he would die for me if he had to and said that I should go home with you guys."

Growing fidgety, she began shifting from one position to another. Her bottom lip quivered, "They already beat him up once, and he's afraid they'll kill him after we leave."

Jan clenched her hands together and drew them to her lips. Seconds passed before she spoke, "He told me they won't do anything bad to him while I'm here, but he doesn't care if he dies because everything good in his life is over and he's going to prison for a long time." Massive tears welled up in her eyes. "Mom, we have to help him."

The rage I felt toward B raced through me. How could a mature man put his burden of guilt on my little girl as if his life depended on her?

Jan slipped out of her chair and peered around the corner into the small office where her father had disappeared. "What's going on, Dad?"

"I guess I'm about through," he said. "The police officer has taken our visas and we can't leave Mexico without them. He kept saying 'mañana,' so we'll come back tomorrow." Bob grimaced, placing the remaining papers back into the envelope, and shoving his driver's license into his wallet. "Let's go now," he said cautiously.

Waving good-bye and smiling, the three of us left. The friendly officers shouted things that sounded encouraging.

Entering the courtyard, Bob shrugged his shoulders and sighed deeply. "What if someone steals our visas? That guy just stuck them in his desk." I could see the anxiety on his face.

Uninformed about the city, we hailed a taxi, and the driver took us to a hotel. Pleased to find air-conditioning, we agreed to stay the night. Since there was no restaurant in the hotel, we ventured a few blocks down the street and found a place to eat. We ordered things that looked somewhat familiar, and we found the food appetizing. Jan chatted cheerfully, expressing her relief at our arrival and giving us a few details about her time in Mazatlán.

Returning to the hotel, we made the promised call to Karen and Susan. "When are you coming home?" Karen asked.

"Pray we can get our visas back and we'll be on our way tomorrow," Bob said.

Jan's conversation with her sisters seemed normal. There were no empty words or avoidance of feelings. Jan focused her attention on her sisters, her friends, and school. This was a time for rejoicing.

When she got off the phone, we shared the news that her grandfather had died during her time away. However, she was indifferent. Her only response was, "Oh, I'm sorry. How's Grandma Buck?"

She had little concept of the legal implications of what she would face upon her return. She chattered about one experience after another.

Concerned about the confiscated visas, Bob paid little attention to her chatter until she asked, "Why did you tell the FBI that B kidnapped me? He can't go to prison. He loves me and would never let anybody hurt me. We have to get him out of jail. Tomorrow, you have to tell the police that he didn't do anything wrong and that he has to go back with us."

I swallowed and glanced at Bob, knowing he was having a hard time with Jan's present mindset.

"It's late, honey. Let's talk about it tomorrow. What's important is the fact that you are safe and well," he stated.

It was unfair to expect Jan to know what we had suffered. But what about her? Certainly, B's arrest and her night in jail had been traumatizing, yet she had brushed it all aside. Was avoidance a way for her to cope with her own torment?

[From A Torn-Out Diary Entry Discovered Years Later]

Jan's Diary, November 24, 1974:

Last night was the worst night of my life. The Mexican police broke down the door to the motorhome while B and I were sleeping. I started bawling because they had guns and they hit B and knocked him down. I think there were about ten policemen who were hollering and waving their guns around. When they pushed us out the door and shoved us into that little car and all of them got in, I was squished in the middle of those three policemen who put me on the hump in the front seat. They kept talking in Spanish, and every time B tried to say anything to me, that one guy would hit him. I just kept thinking that I didn't want B to talk anymore and get punched again. I just kept bawling because I was so scared. When they put him in jail, I stayed in a dirty room that only had a broken-down chair. I had to tuck my feet under me so the mice wouldn't get on me. I wondered if the policemen were going to feed me. I was starving.

I'm really glad Mom and Dad came to get me. I couldn't wait to get home. I was really homesick for everybody. It was boring there with nothing to do. I wish Mom and Dad hadn't called the police. It isn't B's fault. If something happens to him, I'll get another male companion. That would be bad. Sometimes I get real scared. I think Zada might come and take me. What if I get vaporized like they said? B said it was like I wouldn't have a spirit anymore. I wouldn't even be anything. It's worse than being dead!

As Jan dressed in her familiar night gown from home, she thought about her unbelievable final day in Mexico. She didn't want to remember being in jail for two days with no food and no one to talk to as she watched the mice run around, but she couldn't keep the thoughts out of her mind. It was like watching a movie. She saw herself going back and forth to the door and looking out at the people in the courtyard, but every time she got to the door, a policeman would say something and wave her back while she said, "I'm not going anywhere. I'm just looking for Mom and Dad."

When one of the guards had opened the door to where they had thrown B, she saw him standing with a bunch of Mexican men. They pointed at her, talking fast. His cell was dark and dirty, with hanging plaster and small barred windows near the ceiling. The guard motioned at her to go in. Timidly, she walked past the other prisoners and stood close to him. The guard waved his gun at the others, yelling at them in Spanish, and they all moved back.

Jan began crying, "Are you okay? It smells like rotten water."

"One of the guards beat the crap out of me this morning, and I'm afraid they might kill me if I have to stay in here very long."

His words only made Jan feel worse and she began sobbing, "When Dad gets here, I'll tell him you can't stay here."

The guard looked at the sobbing girl and moved his weapon. B said, "Dolly, don't cry, or you will have to leave. I gave him my wedding ring so I could see you. I don't know how long they will let you stay, so listen and do everything I tell you."

Jan blinked her eyes and tried hard to push her emotions away. Swallowing hard, she nodded as teardrops trickled down her face.

B said, "Do you remember the private things you were told that you can never talk about?"

"I think so. They said a lot of things to me," she responded.

"Well, Dolly, remember four things. Number one, we can't tell anybody about 'them.' Nobody can ever know who they are. Number two is the mission. Don't talk about the baby that will save their planet. Three, never mention the pills for sleep. Fourthly, you can't tell anybody about you and me doing things to have a baby. Outsiders can never know about the plan of making a baby. Do you understand? Will you promise me?"

Jan nodded as she sniffled and fought back tears.

"Tell me what I just said," B remarked in an authoritarian voice.

Jan related the unbreakable rules that had been drilled into her head during the last five weeks. Squeezing her hand, B said, "Perfect! I know some people will say that I took you, but you know the truth."

"I know it! I can't talk about them, or I won't have a spirit," she said. "And they will take Susan!" With her eyes welling up with tears again, she bit her lip and silently wept.

"You'll be able to do this, Dolly. You're a strong spirit who has been given wonderful gifts. I just want to live so I can fulfill my part. Pray for me, Dolly. I need your faith to help me get through this. Trust in the Lord with all your heart, and He will answer our prayers."

"You have to get out of here," Jan declared. "I don't want another male companion."

B stroked Jan's hair and then wiped away her tears, "Be very strong. You're my only reason for living. Pray that I will live to see you again."

Back at the hotel, with her parents, Jan slipped into a fitful sleep, but B darted in and out of her dark dreams—she kept waking up wondering what would happen to him.

Going Home

Bob was up early the next morning. He complained about having a restless night, blaming it on the air-conditioning and humidity.

"I can't stand this," Bob said, as he fumbled around his wallet and pulled out a piece of paper from Agent McDaniel. "Conrado Batiz Canessi is the American Consulate. Maybe he can recover our visas."

Jan and I dressed while Bob went downstairs to find someone who spoke English. On his return, he seemed pleased. He had information about a good place for us to eat and had learned that the ambassador's office was nearby. Bob called and made an appointment.

It was midmorning by the time we located Señor Canessi's office. The American embassy was an impressive Spanish-tiled building with wide marble staircases and decorative wrought-iron railings around the mezzanine. A lovely Mexican woman who spoke English gave us directions.

Señor Canessi greeted us cordially. He spoke English well, but had a strong accent. He was large in stature and sported a bushy mustache. His thick black hair had been slicked back, and his cotton jacket needed pressing. After a few minutes of conversation, he asked to speak with Bob alone. Jan and I waited in the reception area. She asked, "Is Dad going to tell that man that B didn't kidnap me and that he needs to get out of jail?"

Hearing her question was aggravating. I wanted to shake some sense into her and tell her to wake up. The past five weeks had been unbearable for all of us. Why would she still want to protect him? Instead of giving her an empty answer, I shrugged my shoulders in disgust and turned away from her.

We walked around and looked at pictures on the wall and other artifacts that were on display. We wondered why it was taking so long. At last, the door opened. Bob looked pale and shaken. He thanked the man and told him we would be back in two hours. We followed after him, rushing down the marble staircase, out the door, and into the street without a word.

"Are you alright?" I asked. "What's the matter?"

"We have to come back and get our visas. He called the Police Chief while I was there and told him to bring the visas to his office."

"Was there anything else? You were in there a very long time."

"I can't talk about it." He choked back a sob.

We walked without any direction while Bob tried to get hold of his emotions. We found a small park and sat down.

I waited for Bob to speak. He searched for words that would not come. Silent tears rolled down his cheeks. It was several minutes before he blurted out in a painful cry, "Jan and B are legally married in Mexico!"

I was stunned. His next remarks were to Jan, "The ambassador said it looks to him like you and B were living as man and wife." Bob's cries were pitiful, and I tried to hold myself together.

"That's a lie!" Jan said, facing her father with her feet spread slightly apart and her eyes locked on his accusing face. "I never married B! That man is not telling you the truth!" The flush left her cheeks and her face turned pale. She placed both hands over her face to cover her sobs.

Bob pulled a document from his shirt pocket that looked very much like a marriage certificate. Although it didn't bear Jan's or B's signature, it had their names on it as husband and wife. It looked very legal. Jan was visibly upset and continued to deny it.

I tried to calm Jan and comfort Bob. It was excruciating. We all lapsed into a silence that was unnerving. Jan never asked again about B's plight or what was going to happen to him. Bob remained silent.

Returning to the Ambassador's Office, we retrieved our visas with great relief. We took a taxi to the airport and were able to book a flight that was leaving Mazatlán in a matter of hours.

Before changing flights in Los Angeles, Bob telephoned his brother and told him that we were scheduled to arrive at the Salt Lake City International Airport at six o' clock. Dick promised to bring Karen and Susan and meet us there.

Jan's excitement began to mount as we neared our destination. Informed about Jan's abduction, the airline personnel extended extra care and attention to our family. Bob told them we were emotionally drained and would appreciate keeping our arrival private. Television and newspaper reporters all over the intermountain West had requested an arrival time, but fortunately the airline honored our privacy.

After landing, we were invited to wait for our family in the private room where pilots and flight crew wait before departure. The anticipation of seeing her sisters was getting the best of Jan as she repeatedly opened the door and peeked out. Finally, she saw her siblings and greeted them ecstatically ("Karen! Susan!") while the sisters embraced. Tears of joy overwhelmed us all.

Chapter 9
HE WAS HERE

November 26, 1974

Jan's homecoming couldn't have been more gratifying. Cards, letters, phone calls, and personal visits all contributed to our joyous celebration—until Gail came to see Jan and broke into sobs. Our warm hugs and expressions of sympathy probably contrasted greatly with her own circumstances. B would certainly be convicted of kidnapping, which meant a prison term. How would she care for her children? Gail had such a grim future ahead; my heart ached for her.

The following day, Jan had an appointment with a gynecologist. Jan vocalized her dismay openly, even though the doctor did his best not to traumatize her. His report of finding no evidence of sexual abuse brought a huge relief. It was gratifying to know that our earlier assessment seemed to be true. B hadn't done anything to hurt her. Now we could push all those distasteful thoughts out of our minds forever.

Jan's refusal to discuss her kidnapping, however, was stressful on us. She denied being abducted and told everyone, "I wasn't kidnapped." Thinking she needed time, we didn't try to convince her otherwise. Restoring normality to her life seemed to be the best solution. Jan returned to school with her bubbly personality seemingly intact. Since she approached her life with exuberance and we could see no evidence of distress or withdrawal, Bob and I didn't feel any urgency to get her a counselor. The trouble was that we didn't have any idea about what was really going on in Jan's mind. She just wouldn't tell us.

The Marriage Certificate

In December, we met with Mr. Elliot, a Federal District Attorney from Boise. He was in the midst of preparing for the preliminary hearing, which was scheduled for January 3rd. As we discussed the supposed marriage between Jan and B, the attorney recognized that it was a tough situation for us, but he said it was an important piece of evidence to present at the trial. "I need the marriage certificate," he told us.

"But I don't have it," Bob replied.

"What? Where is it?" Mr. Elliot asked.

"I sent it to a Mexican lawyer and asked him to annul the marriage. Señor Canessi gave me the name of a reputable lawyer and told me what I needed to do," Bob explained.

"You're kidding. You already sent it?" Mr. Elliot asked, his voice rising in volume. Referring to Peter Welsh, the FBI agent, he asked, "Does Pete have a copy?"

"I don't know. I showed it to Pete, but I had no way of making a copy," Bob responded.

Pete was stunned when Mr. Elliot approached him. Yes, he had looked it over, but he hadn't realized that Bob would send it off before the trial. The marriage certificate was a key piece of evidence against B.

B had been moved from the Mexican jail to a federal facility in Nogales, Arizona, three days after we returned home. He remained there until he was transported to the Pocatello County Jail two days before Christmas. On Christmas Eve, Gail posted bail, allowing B to return to his family.

Pete warned us to keep our distance from the Berchtold family. "I know you'll see them at church and school, but keeping Berchtold out of prison is their first priority, and we're working to put him back in. Gail is a nice lady, but she is still married to him."

Bob said, "I hope I never have to see or talk to him again."

"You'll have to see him at the hearing, but you don't have to talk to him," Pete said.

"I hate the thought of a trial," I said.

"I know, but you're going to have to face it," Pete explained. "The judge will decide after the hearing if there's enough evidence for a trial. Just remember what he did to you—and to this entire community. I feel sorry for his wife and children, but this guy needs to pay for what he did."

Greeting Christmas Day with enthusiasm and gratitude was marvelous. Returning home after visiting Grandma Broberg's house, something seemed off as soon as we walked through the door. The air was nippy and we thought the furnace had gone out. I followed the girls into the hallway and peered at the thermostat. The temperature inside the house was below sixty degrees, and cold air was gusting in from the end of the hall.

Bob proceeded down the hall to the den. He hollered, "I think we've had a thief in the house. There's a window wide open in here." The girls dashed into the den as Bob shut the window. He warned, "Don't go downstairs until we explore the house."

Bob and I went from room to room, checking to see if anything was missing. Everything appeared to be in place except for two drawers askew in Bob's dresser. Searching the drawers, Bob found money still concealed. The only missing item was a cherished ring that had belonged to his father. A search of the house revealed no intruder, but because the doors were still locked, the open window perplexed us. It was twelve feet from the ground. Newly fallen snow from the previous day covered the backyard, and there were no footprints. Our suspicions weren't discussed until our daughters were downstairs. Bob's eyes were inflamed, and his voice was snappish. "I know it was B. He probably wants that incriminating marriage certificate. Wait until he hears that I sent it back to Mexico."

Shaking my head in disbelief, I said, "He must have a key to our house. Tomorrow, we better get new locks on the doors."

Jan's Diary, December 25, 1974:

We got home from Grandma's and somebody was in the house. Dad said it was B, but looking out the window, there were no footprints, just snow. It's them. They are watching me, and I'm scared.

It's Just Kid Stuff

A few days after Christmas, Gail called and asked to visit with Bob alone. Although reluctant, Bob gave in to her pleading.

Gail was sullen when she arrived. Bob and Gail conversed privately for an hour. After the meeting ended, Gail walked to the front door, wiping her eyes with a tissue. She left without speaking a word.

Bob was subdued and said, "Her husband sent her over to do his dirty work. She asked us not to testify against him. If we do, he's going to do everything he can to prove us as unfit parents."

"What's he talking about?"

"Oh, don't you know?" Bob cried out, his anger rising. "He claims we contributed to his mental problems because we knew he was under treatment for depression, yet we encouraged him to spend time with us. Instead of protecting him from Jan, we literally threw her at him as if he were her caretaker and we were neglecting her," Bob growled. "Unfit parents? He's the unfit parent! Bottom line, MaryAnn, Gail is pressuring us to save her family no matter the cost to ours, and she does not want us to press charges."

Vacillating back and forth, we thought about the grueling future, but how could we stop it? Did we have a choice? Bewildered, I blurted out, "I hate the thought of seeing their family torn apart! I really do."

Staring blankly at me, Bob rubbed his brow nervously, "As much as we hate what happened, he broke the law, MaryAnn. It was wrong."

I whispered, "Why did he marry her?" Tears welled up in my eyes and began trickling down my cheek. "Did Gail talk about that?"

"I didn't bring it up. I want to believe Jan, that it was a lie, but the evidence is clear. We did the right thing by bringing the law into this. He has to pay for his crimes."

"And Jan?" I asked. "People all over this town will be talking, asking questions, like Mrs. Johnson did at the grocery store. This will be terrible when the public hears about it."

Bob's voice began to quiver. "MaryAnn, there is something else Gail talked about, and you need to hear it. I've felt so ashamed and angry about this and suffered intensely while trying to work up the courage to tell you. I can't believe I was so stupid." Bob's voice broke into a stifled sob before he continued. As he gained his composure, he blurted out, "B has accused me of being homosexual and is telling everyone, who will listen, that he is a victim of my advances towards him. He claims he was protecting Jan when he took her away from me." All the color drained from his face.

Stunned at his words, I looked at him and asked, "What makes him say that? I'm shocked—and who better knows that you are perfectly innocent of his ridiculous accusation? I've lived with you for more than thirteen years and have the proof! Why would he say that?"

I waited for Bob to respond. Choking on his emotions, he recovered his voice and told me about B coming to pick him from the store a few months ago. While they were driving, B had complained about his wife and their lack of sexual intimacy. Bob continued, "He divulged that he couldn't stand his marriage. He said that it had been months, in fact almost a year, since he'd had any kind of sexual release. Then without skipping a beat, he announced that he had an erection and needed some relief. I smirked and said he should turn the car around and go home to deal with his problem. After a few more minutes of cajoling me, he said, 'Oh, Broberg, just reach over here and help me out.' I said, 'You're not serious, are you?' But he kept begging. With a flip of his head, he challenged me by saying, 'Broberg, just do it—it's just kid stuff. Nothing worse than what we did with our brothers and cousins on the farm. Come on—give me some relief.' We were laughing and joking, and he kept asking, and then, MaryAnn, like an idiot teenager, I . . . I . . ." Bob's voice choked as he sobbed. "I did it. He is trying to destroy me. I knew it was wrong when I did it—of course, I did. I know it's going to be a terrible issue at the trial. I'm so so sorry. The remorse I felt has plagued my every waking minute. I've struggled to figure out how I would ever tell you. I hope you know that I love only you and have no feelings for him—only regret. He is accusing me of being something I am not. Please try to forgive me, MaryAnn, and know how sorry I am. Can you stick with me while I do everything to make my life right again? It's going to be extremely hard."

Bob's piercing blue eyes brimmed over with tears. I felt numb.

Forced Affidavits

A late afternoon phone call on December 30th from Berchtold's lawyer took us by surprise. She asked if we would be interested in meeting with her and discussing a proposal that might save us from an unwanted trial. If so, she would be at her office with details. After a few hours of deliberating, we decided to find out what she had in mind.

Patty, the lawyer, had been a customer at the flower shop. She was friendly to Bob, but was not someone I was well acquainted with. We entered her office hoping she would help us. We were never warned by her or anyone else that we should not speak to her without an attorney. No one from the FBI had told us who we should or should not speak with. We hoped this would bring Jan back to us quickly. We later learned that she had a legal obligation to let us know that we had the right to bring our own attorney to the meeting, but she never said anything to us about that. Sadly, our trusting nature was still our enemy in these uninformed choices.

We didn't even know if we would benefit from having our own attorney because we weren't the ones on trial. No one prepared us for this—not the law enforcement nor the FBI. When we got to her office, B's attorney presented affidavits for us to sign. Among other things, they stated that we believed Jan had been unharmed while in the company of Berchtold and that he had been given our permission to take her. She then stated, "If you do not sign these affidavits, you should expect a long, drawn-out trial. Furthermore, we are prepared to make a case that you and Bob have been unfit parents, that you have endangered your children, and that Bob is a homosexual."

My heart sank. I felt physically sick. Bob and I are unfit parents? How could she possibly prove that? My poor husband was already embarrassed and would be subjected to further false accusations. We wanted to go back to a normal life and did not want Jan dragged through the unnecessary trauma of a trial, where she would most likely have to testify. I could not live with any of it. Patty left us alone to make the decision. We sat in shock and disbelief.

Bob and I read and reread the affidavits while struggling with our own sense of justice and fretting about the impact the trial would have on so many people. Feeling desperate and backed into a corner, we signed the papers. We went home subdued, but hopeful that the whole thing would now be put behind us. It was a long and dismal New Year's Day.

The day after New Year's, Berchtold's attorney contacted the State prosecutors and announced that we had willingly signed the affidavits.

Within a matter of hours, the Federal Attorney called us from Boise and was explosive. "What have you done? How could you make such a statement and let this criminal skate? This is a disgrace to the law profession. Why did you go see her? Why didn't you call me? Don't you know not to make a deal with the criminal's attorney? That's my job. I do the negotiating." His voice shook with rage.

Bob listened. Then he said, "Firstly, no one told us. We've never had a legal problem. We've never had an attorney. Secondly, we are sick and tired of this entire mess and want to put it behind us. We can't take anymore. We want to get on with our lives."

"That will not happen until we get through the trial." Working to control his anger, Mr. Elliot's voice softened. "And whether you like it or not, there is going to be a hearing. I will not let this jerk off the hook. Meanwhile, stay away from his attorney and any other person associated with the Berchtold family."

When Agent Pete Welsh came by, he was bewildered. Instead of hitting us with another lecture regarding our stupidity, he sympathized with our arduous ordeal. "I understand why you signed the affidavits. Berchtold has a tough attorney. It's her job to get her client off and if anyone could win, it would be her. You can be assured she will tear the prosecution apart."

Bob and I looked at each other with dismay. It was deeply embarrassing to realize how naive we were about the legal system.

Pete waved his hand back and forth, "What's done is done. The newspaper has your affidavits and it will be broadcast to the public. For your sake, you need to call the prosecutor's office and let them help you write a statement for the news media." Leaning back on the sofa, Pete rubbed his neck. He looked first at me and then at Bob, gently nodding his head, "You know, this is everyday business for us." Pete paused and pursed his lips. With a hint of a smile lighting his face, he said, "Can I ask you a question?"

We both nodded, still dazed from our ignorant decision.

"Have either of you ever been in court before?"

Bob shook his head, while I confessed to being in traffic court once for a speeding ticket.

Pete grinned, "That doesn't count. It's our fault for not preparing you to face the legal aspects of a heavy-duty trial. We should have walked you through it before they got to you. You need to toughen up and prepare for the worst. You are good people. Don't let anyone tell you different."

The reaction to the news article infuriated some people in the community. We received several anonymous phone calls. We were called "chicken," "stupid," and "disgraceful liars" for not wanting to prosecute. How could we let a kidnapper off and make the community unsafe for children? It was our obligation to put him away for the sake of society.

Two days after the affidavit was published, our statement appeared in the newspaper:

Broberg's Explain Feelings—Berchtold Bound Over for Trial

Robert E. Berchtold, 38, was bound over Wednesday afternoon to Sixth District Court for trial, following Magistrate Dell W. Smith's denial of a defense motion for dismissal of the case on the grounds of insufficient grounds for prosecution.

Berchtold has been charged by the state with kidnapping in connection with the Oct. 17 disappearance of 12-year-old Jan Broberg, reportedly later found unharmed with Berchtold in Mexico.

In an attempt to provide an explanation for affidavits filed in the Federal and Sixth District Courts, the Broberg family released the following statement late Wednesday afternoon through Deputy Bannock County Prosecutor Howard L. Armstrong, Jr.:

Statement from Robert and MaryAnn Broberg:

Due to the statements that have been made, and due to the possible misinterpretations and misunderstandings that might have been placed upon our affidavits, we wish to make the following comment:

Because of our anxiety and the traumatic experience that we and our daughter, Jan, have gone through during the past few months, we feel that this is a period in our lives that we would like to forget and certainly wish had never happened.

With this in mind and being grateful for all of the help that we have received, and for the fact that our daughter has been restored to us unharmed and just as pure as when she left, we felt that the easiest way for us to pick up the threads of our lives was to have all connections with the last few months severed as soon as possible.

We now realize this was foolish and there is nothing we can do or say that will alter the things that have happened since October 17, 1974. We are now prepared to go forward with whatever testimony we have and tell the truth and will sincerely trust in the law enforcement officials, the courts, and all concerned to see that justice is done.

Chapter 10
THE HEARING

January 3, 1975

The morning of the hearing was cold and snowy. The county's prosecuting attorney, Garth Pincock, would handle the hearing. He was a neatly dressed middle-aged man. He asked us to come an hour early, he could brief us on the proceedings of the hearing. When we visited earlier, Mr. Pincock was reassuring; however, today he was less pleasant and was more focused on preparing us for the defense since our last confrontation had been so devastating. He stressed that we only needed to answer the questions truthfully, "Don't be alarmed. You're good people who have been victimized by Berchtold. I'm not going to let his attorney tear you apart."

Jan was the first to give a testimony. It quickly became clear that Jan was emotionally unprepared. Walking into the courtroom and seeing B for the first time, since her abduction, caused her to turn so pale that I thought she might pass out. The judge decided to close the hearing to the public and have each of us face B and his attorney independently.

After Jan was escorted out of the courtroom, Bob asked, "Well, how was it?"

Jan replied, "It went good."

The Federal Attorney surprised us when he said, "Her denial of being kidnapped wasn't the best news of the day." As I took the witness stand,

I tried not to look at B because his sad, pleading eyes could be very persuasive. I felt as though I was betraying him as I answered the questions directed at me.

His attorney was intimidating. She seemed to want me to be seen as an unfit mother who hadn't protected Jan from B. I knew I had always been a loving mother who cared deeply for my children. The attorney changed direction and asked about B's depression and my knowledge of it. I couldn't give her very clear answers because B had always been so upbeat and gregarious.

She asked, "Why would you allow your daughter to go with him alone when you knew he was emotionally unstable?"

I quietly answered, "I never viewed him as being unstable." I was embarrassed to have my judgment questioned like that. A sense of doubt about my own competence as a mother rose inside me. I hoped my explanation of our family friendship would show why I felt confident B was a trustworthy friend—one who would do anything for our family. Nothing surprised us more than for B to take off with our daughter.

The line of questioning frustrated me. The attorney seemed to misconstrue all my answers. I dug my fingernails into the palm of my hands as I explained:

"Yes, I knew there were marital problems between him and his wife."
"No, I didn't know he suffered from ongoing depression until long after he left with Jan."
"Yes, I felt it was a tragedy that our child was taken by Berchtold."
"No, I never gave him permission to take my daughter."
"No, I do not believe Jan was sexually molested by Robert Berchtold."

The questions drained me. With the hearing over, the prosecutors and Pete were confident there was just cause to sentence B in trial. They needed Jan and I to take a harder stance against him. If we didn't, they said it would be hard to convince a jury. Pete stressed that we needed to leave our friendship with B behind and stand firm with the law.

B's Crocodile Tears

B was standing by the classroom door waiting when Jan came out of her Sunday class. He told her that she was perfect in court, and that he wanted to tell her more about Zethra, but there were too many people around. As he passed, he whispered, "You'll be hearing from them soon."

Since Jan's departure from Mexico, the voices hadn't bothered her. B clearly hadn't had a chance to play his terrible recordings near her since then, but none of us knew about those recordings then. Everyone at the hearing wanted Jan to say that B had kidnapped her, but she couldn't lie. Jan really believed that the people from that planet had done this, but she could never admit this publicly. Her fear of ceasing to exist and retribution to her family was extreme.

Maintaining Our Distance, or Not

I was relieved when the hearing was over, but my anxiety rose when we learned there would have to be a trial. Thankfully, B's lawyers hadn't won their case based on our affidavits or on Jan's insistence that she had not been kidnapped.

In the meantime, B and his family continued to cross our path. It was so awkward seeing him at church and around town. It was impossible to ignore every member of the Berchtold family. The kids were still friends and classmates. None of them thought those adult legal problems should interfere with their friendships—and I didn't try to stop this. For some reason, I felt obligated to support it. When Jerry got sick with a mysterious illness and was hospitalized, we naturally included him in our daily prayers. Jan pulled together a "basket of love" that was filled with notes and surprises to give him for when he came home from the hospital. We took it to him at the hospital.

Bob was against our support of Jerry, and he demanded that we maintain our distance. We needed to follow the prosecutor's advice. Bob was resolute. That night after dinner, he sat down at the kitchen table and said to me, "It's not okay–others can help Jerry and the family, but not us."

"How do we cut off our feelings for them when we rub shoulders everywhere we go?" I countered. "Maybe the girls need to go to a different school or stop going to church," I suggested, almost sarcastically.

"Don't be foolish," Bob remarked, as he drummed his fingers on the table. "MaryAnn, we can't continue to be friends with the Berchtold's. I know that sounds terrible, but we have no other option."

"I don't expect us to be best friends ever again," I said, before continuing, "but showing Jerry some compassion is our Christian duty."

"Don't—" Bob interrupted. "Have you forgotten what B did or was it some kind of nightmare that only I remember? Honey, we have to face the fact that B has a problem that is much bigger than us. I hold no malice toward Gail or the kids, but the door has to close between our families—forever."

"Why should the rest of the Berchtold family be punished for what B did?" I stubbornly asked. Arguing emotionally but genuinely, I added, "They've been in our girls' lives for nearly three years. On one hand, we're told to be understanding and forgiving, and on the other hand, we're expected to spit in their faces and nail B to the wall! I'm fed up with it."

Bob was fed up with my stubborn attitude. He left the kitchen and retreated to his easy chair. The frustration between us was growing more intense every time we talked about the Berchtold's. I found comfort in what I thought was my Christian sense of mercy and forgiveness and was convinced there must be some way to work through all the muck.

Gail and I stayed in touch as we worked on a quilt project at church. As we busily hand-stitched an elegant floral pattern, the conversation around the quilting frame, with the group of women, was lighthearted. I felt good about being friendly with Gail like this. After the quilting session, Gail and I talked privately in the parking lot. We knew things couldn't be the same, but we hoped that it would ease the hurt if we could remain friends.

Within hours, B called, gushing over the possibility that the past could be mended. My cheeks flushed as I listened to him, but I displayed a strong front and said, "I still don't think we will ever get back to being friends like we were. We have a trial to go through and Bob's feelings run deep for what you did."

"Oh, this will all be resolved. You and Bob are both so stressed," B said. "Relax and stop your worrying."

"There are too many scars, B," I said. "You will never come through our door again."

B continued his persuasion. He asked, "Didn't Jan come back just fine? Has she said I did anything awful to her?"

"I can't talk about this with you," I said. B sighed and spoke more apologetically, "MaryAnn, I'm so sorry for hurting you. I didn't mean to. Please believe me."

I was quiet, unable to respond. B continued, "I was desperate, and I just cracked. It wasn't intentional. I'd been off my medication and I don't know what happened. You and Bob don't know how much I've depended on you. I can't count the times I thought life wasn't worth living, and you gave me a reason." This tugged at my heartstrings. I swallowed hard, trying not to give in.

B's voice trembled, "As I sat in that horrid Mexican jail and saw you and Jan through a crack in the door, I wanted to die. You looked so worn out. You are usually so beautiful, but you were clearly stressed."

"You'll never know how hard it was," I said, shuddering at the memories.

"Since I've been home, I've wanted to tell you and Bob how awful I feel," B said with his voice full of emotion. He began to cry. "Can you ever forgive me?"

"No," I said. "Day after day, I cried. Susan, Karen, and Bob cried. Bob nearly had a nervous breakdown. If you really want to know, that experience of not knowing where our daughter was felt like a knife piercing my heart!"

B continued, with emotion lacing his voice, "MaryAnn, can I ever make this up to you and Bob? Tell him I'm deeply sorry. He was so upset at the hearing. It kills me to know how much he hates me. Bob knows Jan is like a daughter to me. I would have died before I let anything happen to her."

B's tactic was working on me. He was getting to me. I wasn't sure how it was possible, but my feelings began to shift, even if ever so slightly. Then B gently slipped in the words, "Remember when I told you I wanted to go on a trip? It was you I really wanted to be with, not Jan. But you are so damn devoted that you ignored me, and I made a ridiculous choice by taking Jan instead. If you had said yes and had gone with me, this mess wouldn't have happened."

There it was—his attempt to convince me that he had wanted me all along. "Did you honestly think I would or ever could do that to Bob or Gail?" I responded wildly, but I could feel my heart pounding quickly in my chest. He could sense I had a crush on him, and he was using it to his advantage.

"I've been in love with you since the day I met you, and you know it. I was crazy to take a twelve-year-old on a trip when she wanted to go home, but by then I couldn't bring her back to you because you had called the FBI and said I kidnapped her," B said, trying to convince me that I, rather than he, had done something wrong.

I was so confused, but I finally stammered, "I have to go." Hanging up the receiver, I burst into tears. Throughout the rest of the day, I was preoccupied with that call. I thought of the great times we had had together. I also remembered the months of torment, the jail, the marriage, those disgusting affidavits, the hearing, and all the waiting for the trial. Of course, one of our biggest worries had been whether B had molested Jan. Yet, it was clear I was still such a naive woman; I wanted to believe he hadn't hurt Jan, but there still had to be a better explanation about why he got that marriage license.

When B's hearing date finally arrived, the court granted him permission to move to Utah. He got a job at the car dealership where his brother worked. He visited his family on weekends and still came to our church with his family. Using his charm, he was starting to win back goodwill from the members of the congregations. He seemed to operate like this everywhere he went to get people to believe his supposed good intentions. He would shake hands, smile, and joke. He would often glance at our family and give us a friendly nod and smile. This behavior irritated Bob beyond words. At this point, he was not fooled by B's easy demeanor. B still called me while Bob was at work. I often resisted answering the phone, out of fear that it was him, but when I did pick up, and it was B, I would try to cut the call short. One day he said he was finally ready to reveal the details about "the marriage." I had to know the truth.

I gave Bob an excuse that I was going to spend some time with my mother in Utah, but I packed a few things in our station wagon and drove to meet B instead. When I arrived, he was sitting outside his motorhome with a very serious look on his face. His quiet disposition was an unexpected change from his usual chipper self. He told me how grateful he was that I had come to see him, and he told me how fantastic I looked in my new seersucker pantsuit. He opened the door to the motorhome so we could go in and talk without others hearing our conversation.

I stepped into the same motorhome he and Jan had lived in for all those weeks in Mexico, and I took a brief survey of the cozy living space. The radio was playing country music, and I felt a twinge of nostalgia for better days. B knew I loved country music. I sat on a small sofa just inside the door. I was so nervous and said, "I can only stay a few minutes because my mother is expecting me in time for dinner."

"B," I started, "help me understand why you married Jan."

"Oh, MaryAnn, you have to forget about that marriage," he said as he moved closer to me. "The only way I could see clear for Jan and me to get back home was if we were married. Otherwise, I'd spend the next ten years in a Mexican jail trying to get back to the United States, and Jan needed protection. They would have tried to separate her from me, and I knew I had to get her home safe." Gaining momentum, B explained, "It's not like we had a real ceremony. I paid some guy to get me a marriage certificate so Jan would be safe."

"Oh, I guess that makes sense," I said, feeling more confused, but somehow calmed. "Was that part of your mental breakdown? Your depression?" I probed.

"MaryAnn, you've got to understand. All I ever wanted was for you and me to be together. Sure, I was depressed, but every time I saw Jan, I thought of you. Every time I saw her cooking, I imagined you cooking. Everything she did reminded me of how much I wanted you. Our time in Mexico made that so clear to me. Everything I felt was all for you, MaryAnn. Wouldn't it be a perfect life if you and the girls could move down here to Utah and we could become our own family?" he asked, directing the conversation away from Jan and anything to do with why he married her in the first place.

Oh, he was good. This flattery was convincing me that he wasn't lying. I could feel my defenses starting to crumble. "B, you always seem to know the right things to say to make me feel like it will all work out," I responded.

He flashed his winning smile and moved closer, "I promise you it is going to work out," he said, "I can see our life together full of vacations, sunshine, love, and laughter. That is how we're all going to live forever."

It sounded so simple and it relieved some of the stress I felt from the pain we were all living through. I had become infatuated with him and feeling this way. He came close enough to whisper softly in my ear, "You know, Bob does not appreciate the miracle he has with you."

My heart raced. After fourteen years of marriage, the rush I once felt from feeling desired, that was rare in my relationship, and I began yearning for again. It had been so long since Bob and I hadn't had the weight of the world on our shoulders and could share this kind of exchange. I was surprised how loved it made me feel. B's flattery exhilarated me in a way I hadn't felt in such a long time. We reminisced for hours about those early days. We talked about the getaways, the fun times and laughter, and even our seemingly innocent flirtations from the beginning of our friendship. I felt giddy, and wondered if he could hear how loudly my heart was beating in my chest.

The minutes I intended to spend with B turned into hours. B went so far as to shed tears of regret, begging for my understanding and forgiveness. I was caught off guard by my feelings. I wanted to forgive him, and

I could feel the attraction, which I had always tried to push away, start to grow.

The night wore on and I was surprised to realize I wanted to stay. B leaned in to kiss me, and I didn't stop him. Spending the night with him was a mixture of forbidden excitement and horrifying reality all at once.

Leaving the motorhome the next morning, I convinced myself that B was right. The marriage to Jan was only his strategy to make it possible for him and Jan to get back into the country. I fooled myself into believing that his feelings for Jan were not because he was in love with her, but they were actually intended for me. In that moment, I wanted this to be true, but as the hours-long drive wore on, my momentary escape turned to worry. I was carried away by the idea of getting away from the heaviness and worry that had been my life. It was so nice to feel a man's desire for me.

What had I done? I knew it was wrong, but being with him felt so natural. What if B was my real soulmate? I sobbed through my confusing thoughts. What would this mean for my future? What about Gail and their children? How could I tell Bob? How would I face the church? This was so much against my long-held moral beliefs, and I would be condemned. What would the girls and I do? Would we move away? Could I start a new life with B? Did I want to? The conflict played out in my head as I tried to make sense of what I had done and what I intended to do about it.

Summer 1975: Could We Close the Door?

With B living in Utah, and my feelings for him warming, I thought it might be okay for Karen and Jan to spend small amounts of time with Gail and the boys. We would meet to visit at the park or at one of our homes. Bob held firm and insisted that we stop contact, but I kept allowing it.

The trial that had been set for the summer was delayed again. This was good for B, although Bob and I became increasingly agitated with each other. He questioned my feelings for B and tried to make me see how untrustworthy he was. Bob said, "I believe in forgiveness, but to forget? Never! I can't trust him. It's too bad things ended up like this. If he would just take care of his own family and leave ours alone, we could at least be neighborly again. However, I will never allow him to be close with our family again."

My judgment was clouded by B's constant efforts to charm me. I tried to soften Bob's hardline stance against B and his family. "Maybe there won't even be a trial," I said. "B didn't abuse Jan and he is making great strides. Our church friends are urging us to forgive and forget. After all, are any of us perfect?" I could see that my own indiscretions weighed on my mind when I asked that question.

B made a feeble attempt to make amends by calling Bob. The conversation ended quickly when B tried to explain how upsetting it was for Bob to have involved the FBI over such a huge misunderstanding. He said that this is what ruined his chances of bringing Jan back in a timely way. Bob immediately saw through B's words and hung up on him.

Forever B; Red Roses Too

The summertime was helpful for the kids to get on with life. Jan was cast as the lead role in *Oliver!* —the community's summer musical. Susan also got a part. On the opening night, Karen came and sat next to Bob and I after checking in with her sisters backstage. She mentioned everyone talking about a dozen red roses that had been delivered to the green room for Jan. Scribbled on the card were these words: "Love you. Forever, B."

Bob was furious. He said, "So, you don't think B has designs on Jan? Explain this, MaryAnn."

I didn't feel the same. I could hear B's explanations in my ears, believing he cared about Jan's best interests.

It seemed that B was busy with his mental offensives in multiple ways. Shortly after the musical ended, something frightening happened at the flower shop. Bob got an urgent phone call from a stranger who needed funeral flowers for her father, who had passed away in Logan,

Utah. The family had forgotten to order them, and the viewing was the following day.

The stranger asked if she could pick up the flowers in the morning. During the phone call, Bob could hear live music blaring in the background, which he found strange.

The next morning at seven o'clock, the phone rang. It was Bob at the shop, and he sounded shaken. "I just had a weird experience, and I'm nervous," he said. "When I pulled into the back of the store, a man and a woman were sitting in a car all cuddled up. It was odd, but I hustled into the shop and kept my eye on them through the window. I stepped away to pull some flowers out of the icebox, and when I looked again, they were gone, so I let it go. I was busy trying to get the casket piece ready in time, but I had a strange feeling to double-check whether or not I had locked the shop door. I checked and made sure that the door was locked. A few minutes later, I was sure I heard someone trying to get in the door. After getting my bearings, I called the police and asked them to come over."

"Maybe it was the lady wanting her flowers," I suggested.

"No one was there, so I gave the police a description of the car and one of the officers left to look for it. I called the mortuary in Logan and gave them the deceased's name, but there were no services scheduled for that name. The police and I suspect it was a hoax to get me in the shop alone. But why?"

A chill raced through my body. Immediately B came to mind. Why would I think he had anything to do with this? I tried to dismiss the thought, but couldn't.

Bob sounded calm, "I think it might have been someone trying to rob the store. When that lady called last night, it sounded like she was drowning her sorrow at a bar."

"Just come home—now!" I said emphatically. After that, we both weren't sure whether or not to suspect B. Would he go that far? Bob became more cautious, doubling down on his demands that we stop all association with the Berchtolds. He was very clear with the girls, "Stay away from places where the Berchtold's go, including the park. I'm sorry, but it has to be this way."

The girls didn't get it. They felt as if they were being punished. B was furious when he heard about it, and he blitzed us with a series of phone calls. "What's wrong with Bob?" he would ask me. "Why isn't he letting our kids see each other? Doesn't he know what he's doing to them? If he is upset with me, tell him not to take it out on the kids." The kids were one of B's main ways of keeping a line of information and connection open with Jan.

Not long after, Gail decided to move closer to B's work in Utah. She needed help with the kids and hoped that the move would improve their fragile marriage. Bob was elated to have them gone; the rest of us cried.

Gail and I exchanged letters and phone calls, which kept us all connected. They often invited the kids to visit. Gail finally talked me into bringing the girls for an overnight visit. Bob was very angry with me. He outright demanded that I put an end to our friendship. He would not tolerate it any longer. We got into a heated argument, and I accused him of forcing me to give up a friendship I cherished.

Even with Bob against it, I secretly planned to visit Gail and the kids. I was torn between a sense of doing good, keeping a friendship alive, and my own guilt for having an affair with B. We set off for Ogden and when we got there, it seemed like old times. Karen and Susan got the tour of Gail's new house with Jimmy and Joey. B was there, and Jan and I slipped away with him to go and check out his new side business at a flea market where he was selling items he'd gotten in Mexico. He gave Jan a pretty gold necklace and gave me a handmade black leather cape.

Then, B took us to his brother Joe's house, which was not far away. Joe offered us RC Cola on ice and cheese curds out of his thinly stocked fridge. After taking a few sips of my Cola, I sat down on an overstuffed chair, feeling strangely tired. My eyelids were too heavy to keep open, so I laid my head back and dozed off. I don't know how long I'd been asleep when something startled me back awake. I woke up long enough to see B walking across the living room partially naked, but I could only keep my eyes open for a few seconds. My head was spinning.

Approximately an hour later, B woke me and said, "Hey, sleepyhead, button up your shirt. Jan's finished watching, *I Dream of Jeannie*, and we need to get back." I quickly buttoned my blouse and we piled into his Lincoln for the trip back. Still groggy and dizzy, I couldn't make sense of what had just happened.

As we stood in Gail's kitchen, B pulled out two packages for Karen and Susan. The girls were delighted. My head was now pounding, and I felt unsteady. Karen noticed and became concerned. She asked why I was swaying back and forth, as if I were dancing to music no one could hear but me. I didn't know why, but I had to give an excuse, so I told her my thyroid was acting up and that the medicine I had taken had probably reacted with my body.

I felt strange the rest of the night, but we still enjoyed a night of dinner, games, and conversation together. We had missed this so much. That night, the kids slept on the trampoline under the big oak. I went to bed hoping nothing inappropriate had happened between B and me that day. I wanted to feel good about my decision to come, but my suspicion triggered intense feelings of guilt and shame.

I still felt a little guilty when Bob and I talked about it at home the next day. He was sullen and didn't ask a single question about our trip to Ogden, but instead handed down an ultimatum: "Until this trial is past, you cannot be a part of the Berchtolds' lives. I will not have my girls in harm's way any longer. Our children have always been your first priority. What is going on with you? You need to stop indulging the Berchtold's feelings, and you need to get over yours too," he demanded.

I'm not sure if it was my guilt or my sense of mercy that spoke up, "Where is your heart, Bob? Gail needs a friend, and I intend to be one."

"This is not about Gail," he said. "You are mesmerized by B. You need to decide who is most important here, me or B?"

I was shocked that Bob could tell I had feelings for B. I denied it, but a big part of me knew Bob was right. My confusing feelings for B were now a major problem, and I had to figure things out because my marriage was in jeopardy. What had happened to our "ideal" family?

As the summer went on, the trial was postponed for a third time when B fired another attorney and hired a new one. B was often spotted around town, apparently in preparation for the trial. When a fourth trial was announced, we heard little from the prosecutor's office. We heard that B's. new attorney, the fifth one now, had been working to settle the case out of court. Bob and I hoped there would be a way to avoid the extreme stress and emotional toll a trial would mean for us, especially for Jan.

Jan was constantly anxious. She knew she had to hide the truth of her mission. She never knew when or if the voices would come. That entire summer, weeks would pass before she would hear the high-pitched voice once again. Very late one night, she was asleep in her downstairs bedroom. Her eyes snapped open when she heard the voices quietly calling her, "Female companion." Panic swept over her when she saw the ivory-colored box on her dresser. With her heart pounding, she again listened to the now-familiar message. "Complete the mission with your companion," the voice said, "or very bad things will happen."

In fear, Jan nodded her head. She would do whatever it took to keep her family alive. Ordered by the voice to close her eyes and go back to sleep, Jan obeyed. She pretended to sleep, but was unable to do so. She dared not move, hoping the unseen visitor would assume she was sleeping and would leave. After what seemed to be a long time, Jan subtly peeped toward the dresser. The box was gone! Afraid to get up, she tossed restlessly and waited until dawn before she creeped out of bed. Jan looked for the box on the floor, under her bed, and in the dresser drawers. She rummaged through clothes, shoes, and mementos, but the box was nowhere to be found. Certainly, she concluded, the power of her visitors was not of this world.

End of Summer

With summer in full swing, Jan had much more freedom. She took advantage of the time for bike rides, being with Caroline, and having secret meetings with B. The voice told her to call him every week to discuss a time and place to meet. B said that he had heard from Zethra that there were other people assigned to help them with the mission. If Jan received notes or phone calls from strangers, she must not panic. She was just to do what she was told and immediately destroy the notes. One note arrived giving her a number to call later that day, along with pocket change so she could use the nearby pay phone. When Jan called, she immediately recognized the voice on the other end as Zethra's. The warning Zethra gave was frightening and traumatizing. Zethra said that if B went to jail, Jan would be assigned a new male companion, one she didn't know or love. Jan was terrified to think that an unknown adult man could replace B as her companion.

She finished the phone call and then called B, telling him she was scared. He reminded her that everything would be fine if she did exactly what she was told, which reassured her. B also warned her to stay away from all males of any age. Jan didn't like that. She said, "My friends think I'm weird. They all like guys, but I can't." It was impossible to have any kind of normality with all of this hanging over her head. The pressure was taking its toll on Jan.

Chapter 11
MASTER OF DECEPTION

March 1976

We spent the past year wondering whether or not there would be a trial. This took an emotional toll on all of us. Bob and I were exhausted trying to keep our marriage together and trying to provide a sense of safety and normalcy for the girls.

I answered the phone one afternoon, while Bob was at work, and I heard B's anxious voice on the other end of the line. He and his attorney had been discussing a plea bargain with Federal prosecutors, which could eliminate the need for a trial. This was B's ultimate hope of not getting any jail time. I tried to stay calm. I said, "Oh, this is quite a surprise. It certainly has to be a big deal for you. What will it take to settle?" I was hoping to find a way to relieve the ongoing burden of my own guilt while tearing myself away from any more communication with B.

"Is this another situation like the affidavits?" I asked, suspicious of his motives and thinking that he might be trying to trick us into something again.

B struck out vindictively, "For hell's sake! It's nothing like that. I already told you, MaryAnn, that I won't agree to their conditions without knowing what Jan thinks. This is for her."

"And how will this concern her?" I asked.

"Do you want to go to trial?" B snapped, his frustration with me now obvious. "Or would you like it if I mentioned a certain 'something' to a certain someone? I thought this is what we all wanted. Either you bring Jan or there will be no plea agreement," he said before slamming down the receiver.

I agonized over what to do. I was getting more and more confused about my feelings for B. I was starting to sense that he may never have had any real feelings for me in the first place. Bob's patience had worn thin, and our marriage had truly suffered. Bob said he would do anything to see B behind bars. "I don't want any of my girls around that man. I will do whatever is necessary to protect them. If you can't agree with that, I'll have you removed from this house."

Plea Bargaining

Bob's threats echoed in my ears, but I decided I had to meet B with Jan. I picked the girls up from school. Driving home, I explained that Jan and I had to run an errand and I dropped her sisters off at home. As I drove toward our meeting with B, I told Jan what we were doing and why. She had a worried look on her face. "Mom, you know what Dad said," she reminded me. "We're not supposed to talk to B."

I nodded, but also explained, "Jan, if B will work this out and we don't have to undergo the trial, life will be better for all of us." This managed to calm her down a bit.

B was parked and waiting on the side of the road. The minute he saw us, he jumped out and came over to our car, oddly scooting into the front seat next to Jan. "You're late. I thought you weren't coming," he said, flashing a forced smile. "This is very important. I don't want to decide until I tell you about the deal."

But instead of talking about those details, he leaned toward Jan and started asking questions about school. I squirmed with anxiety. I couldn't take it any longer and interrupted, "Look B, what's the plan? We've got to get home."

"Oh, relax. You need to lighten up," he said rudely.

Noticing that Jan was biting her fingernails, B stopped and stared intently at her. She looked timidly back into his eyes. After a few moments, he glared directly at me. "This has been a very hard day. The feds aren't going to let me go free. Either I plead guilty and receive a reduced sentence, or I go to trial and we all get dragged through the mud."

Jan's eyes widened as she looked at B and then at me, expecting some kind of reaction. I made certain my eyes didn't show how I felt, but inside I thought I would burst. I thought to myself, *could we be so lucky? Would he plead guilty and get this over with by going to prison?*

"My lawyer thinks I could get off completely if I went to trial, but that would cost us plenty," B slowly exhaled, his shoulders dropping and his face downcast. He did not move or speak for several moments. B's head jerked slightly as his mouth tightened. "Jan, I'm only thinking of you. If there is a trial, you are the one who will suffer the most."

I thought, *Oh, isn't he so clever! Playing the "good guy" for Jan. What a manipulator!* In my mind, I was shouting, *You took her! You are the guilty one!*

I wanted to convince B that it was a good idea to take the plea bargain, but I also wanted to stay in his good graces. I thanked him graciously for thinking of Jan. I told him, "We don't want Jan involved in a trial either, and it seems like you hold the key to stopping it. I know it's a lot to ask, but for her sake, there doesn't seem to be an alternative."

B's eyes narrowed. His jaw was firmly set. Turning to Jan, he asked purposefully, "What do you think I should do, Dolly?"

Jan shrugged her shoulders, "Uh, I don't want you to go to jail."

"Well, it's either that or drag you through a whole lot of crap." B's eyes were pleading with Jan by this point, and he asked, "Think you could love a jailbird?"

I was shocked by his off-color remark, and I said, "We've got to go!"

"So do I," he said. "I have to go back and let my attorney know. The feds want my answer today."

I stared at him emotionless, sensing how deeply I had wanted something B would never give me, knowing that what I had with Bob might be forever ruined. More importantly, I painfully realized just how inappropriate he was being with Jan.

B finally blurted out, "Well, you two are no comfort at all. What I'm doing is for you, Jan."

What did he expect us to do? Cry? Beg him to change his mind? The news was such a relief, but I only dared to hope inwardly.

He went on, "If I knew you wouldn't be hurt, Jan, I'd fight like hell. But you know the truth, and in time everyone will know." He stared at Jan with great intensity for an unusual length of time. His fixation on her made me extremely uneasy.

He curled his mouth into a smirk and winked at Jan. "Don't you worry, Dolly. It's working out just fine. You're doing everything just right. Trust me."

I noticed that Jan's eyes were as large as plates. I glanced at B and then looked back at Jan. The color had drained from her face and tiny beads of perspiration dotted her forehead. She crossed her arms over her stomach and began swallowing hard. I knew something was very wrong with her. "Honey, are you sick?" I asked.

I put my hand on her head and she slumped down in the seat, waving me off. B grimaced, opened the car door, and got out.

A minute later, Jan forced a slight smile and said to B, "I'm kind of sick. I think it was my lunch." I began to grasp that there was something unspoken going on between them. What didn't I know? How could I get Jan to trust me enough to tell me? She obviously isn't okay. Now I was on high alert.

"I've got to go see my attorney now," B explained. Hurriedly, he kissed Jan's forehead, smiled, and said, "I'll let you know what happens." He reached into the car and patted Jan's arm. Cocking his head to the side, he said, "Remember, you're my special Angel, Dolly. Don't worry, I promise everything will work out the way it's supposed to."

I had had enough of this. I tried to talk to Jan during the drive back home, but she was completely shut down. Laying her head back on the seat, she closed her eyes, obviously disturbed. I knew his words had upset her, but there was something else in the unspoken exchange between them that was eerie. *What is really going on here?* I thought.

Later in the day, B called to report that a plea bargain had been worked out. He had agreed to serve some jail time, with details to come after a federal judge considered the agreement.

Confessing the Truth

Bob didn't say a word when he came into the house after work; however, the feelings on his face were plain. "I guess you know B was in town today."

"Yes," I said.

"He called the store, but luckily I wasn't there," Bob said coldly.

"He is pleading guilty. They've worked out a plea deal and we won't have to have a trial," I said, hoping this would satisfy Bob.

He quickly answered, in a sarcastic tone, "Oh, is that what you decided was best?"

Trying to soothe his emotions, I responded, "Don't you think it is a good plan? It's what we wanted to happen. He is guilty."

"What I think obviously doesn't matter anymore," Bob said in disgust. "Why did you take Jan? I don't want him near her or any of my girls! I thought I made that perfectly clear."

I was devastated that Bob knew I had gone to meet B. "Did you have someone watching me? It doesn't matter what I do—it's never right," I said defensively.

"And it never will be as long as he is in the picture," Bob responded. "I'm sorry, MaryAnn. I can't take any more."

"Well then," I said, angry that he was being so flippant with me. "It's time for me to clear the air and tell you the worst part."

Bob looked at me with equal rage and asked, "What else don't I know?"

I had to tell him. "I've been unfaithful to you, and B has been holding me hostage for months with his threats to expose it," I blurted out, "Before he tells you, I want it to come from me."

Bob was stunned. His face fell, and he burst into tears. I had expected an explosion but saw only pain instead. The explosion wouldn't happen until later. The pain in his eyes broke me. I started sobbing and left the room. I felt guilty and devastated. I was finally grasping the damage I had done. *How could I have let B convince me to have any kind of sexual encounter with him after the pain he had brought into my life by taking Jan? Professing his love for me was such a farce. How had I not recognized his intentions? I was afraid. From day one, he used me, and all of us, to get to Jan. What about Karen and Susan? Had anything happened with them? Was there any way to salvage my kids and marriage through all of this?*

The atmosphere in the house was ice cold after my confession. Bob and I didn't speak to each other the rest of the evening. Lying in bed, I stared restlessly in the dark. Bob had reached his limit. I sadly knew he was right. That night, my thoughts ran wild. B really frightened me. What he said about needing Jan's approval, and the look he gave her, bothered me intensely. Something finally struck me to my very core. I had allowed myself to be flattered by a master of deception. Why hadn't I seen it clearly before now? I had allowed B's devious ways to come between me and the most important people in my life—my husband and our children.

The next day, after the girls left for school, Bob and I had a bitter argument. Refusing to listen to anything I had to say, he reiterated how I had jeopardized the safety of our girls, and said that he would not allow it any longer. Bob said he would get a restraining order to keep me out of the house unless I left voluntarily. I was devastated.

Later that day, Bob had me served with divorce papers. The shock hit me like a ton of bricks. In despair, I banged my head on the wall before throwing a few clothes in the car and driving to my mother's home in Garland, Utah. As I drove, my mind raced between feelings of disbelief and despair. Trying to compose myself, I began thinking sensibly. Analyzing my predicament, I became aware of how much I had been avoiding. I had been such a fool. More importantly, Jan needed our protection from B. Something was very wrong with her. I couldn't put my finger on it, but I just had a feeling.

After I got to my mom's place and began explaining the situation, my mom instantly knew it wasn't Bob who was to blame. My mother adored my husband, as did my eight siblings and their families. Bob had a gift for seeing peoples' best qualities and focusing on them. With genuine love, interest, and a great sense of humor, Bob had endeared himself to my entire family. My mother couldn't imagine how I had created so much chaos. Her straightforward advice was to "get home and fix this."

Getting little sympathy from my mom, I went to stay with my sister Eileen. "How could I have been so brainless?" I said to her tearfully. "I've let so much die between Bob and I. Everything's a mess." She listened carefully and gave me this wise advice, "Since Jan's kidnapping, your lives have been anything but calm. None of this is like you, and most certainly it is not like Bob. The stress has pushed him over the edge."

I nodded and said, "It's been such a tough year for us all."

"Just get in your car and go home," Eileen said, "I will call Bob and let him know you are on your way."

I had been away from Bob for a week and I hoped that, by now, he would have cooled down. My mind and heart were now clear, and I knew I had to head home no matter the outcome. The journey back to my life with Bob was full of unknowns, and I knew—even if he would consider letting me come back home—things would be extremely difficult. As I drove all those miles, I cried and worried, as I now understood that I had been used and manipulated by B. I was filled with rage. He had led me down a path in which a handful of half-hearted sexual encounters could destroy my relationship with everyone who really mattered to me—Bob and my girls. They were all I wanted. I would do anything to keep them. I felt as if death would be better than living, but I pressed on.

Walking into the kitchen, I could see that Bob's face was quite subdued and less angry. I had prepared several speeches while driving home, but standing in front of him, I forgot them all. We looked at each other for a few desperate moments, hoping the other would be the first to speak. "I'm so sorry. Will you let me come back?" Sobbing, I fell into Bob's open arms as he lovingly patted my back.

He whispered in my ear, "Welcome home." Relief and gratitude swept over me.

I next greeted the girls and apologized for leaving without saying good-bye. They each tenderly said how happy they were that I was finally home.

Bob and I both regretted what we had done to create a difficult home environment. We knew we would have to work hard to repair our family relationships. We dug in with renewed commitment. We spoke with our children and expressed our unconditional love for them, promising to work through any contention in our home.

As our discussions continued, talk of the Berchtold family entered the conversation. Each daughter expressed her desire to remain close friends with the Berchtold children, hoping to see them whenever possible. Karen again reiterated, "It was wrong that B took Jan, but she came back okay, so what's the big deal?"

"Besides, B is going to jail, so we kids could still do things together, and he wouldn't be around," Susan added.

As Jan listened, she became agitated and threw the book she was reading across the room. She stormed out, yelling, "I wish everybody would stop blaming him. It's not his fault. Maybe someday you'll all understand."

We were shocked at her outburst. Her reaction reinforced my gut feeling that something much deeper was still going on. Getting to the bottom of it had to be my top priority now—while also repairing our broken marriage.

For a year, we had gone through so much anger, distrust, and betrayal, so many secrets, and such deep trauma. Removing the wedge between us would take all of our effort, but Bob and I recognized that at some point we needed to stop blaming each other for what had happened in the past and needed to find ways to renew our commitment to each other and revitalize our relationship.

And little by little, we did. We openly discussed all the factors that had led to the poor condition of our marriage. I was finally able to see the wisdom in eliminating the Berchtolds from our lives. I could see how B had cleverly discovered our Achilles' heels and had taken advantage of all of us. He had subtly infiltrated our lives to win our trust, and succeeded in gaining access to Jan. That was all he ever truly wanted.

Our children's close friendships gave B more leverage, so we had to cut them all off. Sadly, continued connection to Jan had come through me and B obviously resented Bob's resistance. In hindsight, I realized that B's motive was to break our marriage apart and turn us against each other. This would remove Bob from his position as protector and father. We recognized that we had both been blinded by B's cunning. Our eyes were now wide open to the importance of building a strong and secure relationship—not just for ourselves, but for the protection of our children.

Chapter 12
B NEVER LETS UP

Spring 1976

The next invasion of Jan's privacy occurred during one Spring night. Zada's voice shattered her sleep. The box was in her room again.

Jan held her breath. In the same shrill, high-pitched voice, the repetitious messages came as in the past, but this time adding that the male companion had been found pleasing before the councils of the universe. He was worthy to continue the mission with her and the time was near for her to be with him once again. It was important for her to follow the male companion. Jan was so shaken at hearing the unexpected piercing voice that her body tightened as if she were paralyzed. Moments later, she bolted from her bed and rushed into Karen's room. She was extremely distraught. In a shaky voice, she whispered, "Karen?"

Karen only grunted as Jan trembled in fear and crowded herself next to her sister's sleeping body. Karen mumbled, "What are you doing?" as she moved to the side of her tiny twin bed. Placing her hand in Jan's, she fell back to sleep. Intently, Jan listened to every sound in the dark night. Holding Karen's hand brought her some measure of comfort, and sleep eventually came.

The next morning, Karen asked what had been going on, but Jan dared not expose the reason she had invaded her sister's bed. She made up a story about getting spooked because she heard a scratching sound outside the window.

After that experience, Jan found it difficult to sleep in her room. She often slipped into the family room at night or talked Karen into sleeping in her bed while she rolled herself up in a blanket and slept on the blue hanging chair B had built into her room.

Following this intrusion, Jan began receiving specific instructions from strangers. The first was delivered to her at school. She had never seen the guy before, but he walked up to her, called her by name, smiled and nodded knowingly, and then handed her a note. His grungy appearance startled her. He looked to be about twenty years old and wore a grease-smudged t-shirt and dirty Levi's that were torn on the upper thigh, exposing flesh. His unkempt hair was long and straggly. She watched him casually walk across the beaten-down grassy trail toward Terry Street. He never looked back. Her heart pounded as she read the brief note that was written on a torn piece of lined paper: "It's time. A way has been opened. Don't put it off. Remember your mission. Call this phone number. Do as instructed."

After getting home from school, she slipped downstairs. Using the push-button phone in the family room, she dialed the number. A male voice answered the phone and told her to ride her bike to the Anderson Trailer Park on Saturday morning. When there, someone would talk to her. He then told Jan to destroy the note after hanging up. Jan walked across the room, lit a match from the box by the fireplace, and threw the burning paper into the fireplace.

It was raining on Saturday morning and Jan knew her mom wouldn't want her to ride her bike in the rain. Jan was busy dusting the family room, trying to find an excuse to leave the house, when her mom called to her downstairs and said she was going grocery shopping. Relieved, Jan jumped on her bicycle after her mom left and pedaled furiously to the park, as instructed, about five miles from home.

The small trailer court was junky looking. All the trailers were old and in need of repair. There was no grass, but only weeds and gravel. As

Jan got off her bike, the door to a trailer opened and a man with a short brown beard hollered, "Over here." Fearing for her safety, Jan stood in the pouring rain and looked at him. Another figure looked over the man's shoulder, and with relief, Jan recognized B.

She hurried up the wooden steps and into the trailer. The place was dirty and smelled bad. Another man was sitting at the kitchen table holding a cigarette. The male door greeter took a seat at the table and poured coffee into mugs. Jan knew she was in a strange place with the wrong people.

B smiled and gave Jan a hug. "You made it. I was beginning to worry. Sorry it had to rain, but you are amazing. Take off that wet jacket and let it dry." Jan followed him to a couch. They sat down and B continued to explain. "I didn't dare come anywhere near your house because I'm being followed. We have to be extra careful with everything from now on. Now that the mission is so close to being worked out, my life is in danger."

Jan nodded as she watched the two strangers out of the corner of her eye. They appeared uninterested in what was taking place.

"Did you get the message from Zada?" he asked in a quiet voice.

Jan nodded.

"I did too, so I've been working on a plan. I'm going to open up a game center in Jackson Hole this Summer, and you have to come. I'll be getting a divorce, and I'll work out a way for us to get married. It's going to be hard, but what else can I do? Your parents will be the hardest to convince, so we better start thinking about how to get you to Jackson."

B looked anxiously at his watch. Seeing Jan shiver, he motioned with his finger and said, "Come with me." She followed him, and they left the trailer. He walked her around to the back of the lot, where he had parked his car. Starting his car, he adjusted the heater, letting warm air blow on Jan's trembling body. "I hope you don't get sick again," he said. "I'm not around every day to make sure you take your vitamins. You don't have much time before you have to get home, but I need a little time alone with you before you take off. So, tell me what you think about this Summer?" he asked.

"It would be fun, but my parents won't let me," Jan replied.

"Let me worry about that," B said, pulling her close and throwing his jacket over her. "It has to work out. Even if your parents refuse to let you come, I'll figure out a way."

Other messages followed. With each delivery, Jan's anxiety increased. Instructions to meet unknown men in unfamiliar places frightened her, but she dared not ignore the messages. She knew they were watching. Fearful for her very existence, she obeyed without question. Occasionally, a brief message was given over the phone, but most disturbing were the whispering voices in the middle of the night, reminding her that B was her chosen male companion and that she must complete her mission. The box would appear out of nowhere, and it would be gone just as mysteriously.

Disheartened, Jan thought, *I'm supposed to have this special child before I'm sixteen. If B is in jail or gets killed, then what? I don't want another male companion. What do they mean exactly that I'll cease to exist? How would they kill me and my soul? Things are getting bad. I want to forget about everything that's happened. But, I can't.* Despondently, Jan closed her eyes and wept.

***

Life would seem normal to me, at times, but each time the phone rang, I hesitated to answer, afraid it would be B. When he called, I responded politely, but briefly.

Bob was more direct, "B, we are doing fine and don't need any interference. Your stewardship is your family. Don't call here again. Good-bye."

A few days before Memorial Day, I picked up the receiver and heard B's jubilant voice. "Hi! Where have you been? Or have you just been ignoring my phone calls?"

"I've been busy working at the store," I replied anxiously.

"How are things going between you two?" B was clearly inquiring about the status of my marriage.

"Wonderful!" Bracing myself, I took a deep breath and then exhaled. "B, don't call me again."

B sighed, "Be assured, I'm out of your lives. I think it's great you're working things out." His voice had a pleasant, cheerful ring.

"Good," I replied with relief, "I have to go. Bob's expecting me at the shop."

"Okay, sure. I'm just passing through, but thought you'd like to know that Jerry and I are on our way to Jackson Hole to open up a game center."

Surprised, I said, "Wow! That's a change from the car business. Hope you do well."

"Oh, it's going to be fun. You guys will have to come up," he said.

I thought, *Doesn't he get it? This is unbelievable. No matter what he's told, he won't give up.* "I have to go. Good luck," I said.

"Has Jan told you that she wants to come and work for me this summer?"

I was stunned. My mouth dropped open in utter disbelief. "What did you say?" My voice had raised a decibel or two. "What are you thinking?"

"It's not my idea; it's Jan's."

Unable to control my fury, I pounced on him. "I don't know how you are talking to Jan. Get out of her life and stop meddling in our family."

I slammed the receiver down. Who did he think he was? The audacity of him thinking we would let her go! He's finally supposed to be serving jail time. How is it even possible that he is opening a game center in Jackson Hole?

School closed for summer vacation, on a good note, when Jan was chosen to be the drill team leader for the next school year. It seemed to be a great opportunity to celebrate and take a summer vacation to relax in California. Excitement mounted as we put our plans in motion. However, Jan's anxiety began to surface as the week progressed. Finding enough courage to approach me, she set the stage carefully, not wanting to be misunderstood. In a nonchalant manner, she said, "I need a job, but I don't want to babysit."

I nodded my head and smiled. "Well, guess what? Dad thinks it's time for you to work at the flower shop."

Jan frowned and ignored the proposal, "Did you know B is opening a family fun center in Jackson Hole?"

My stomach dropped. Taking a deep breath, I said, "Yes, I heard about it. How did you find out?"

"From Jerry. He's already up there working." With a sizable amount of enthusiasm, Jan related what she knew. "It's really going to be neat. They've got all these fun machines and games, and it's for kids only. Adults aren't allowed. I could buy my own school clothes and drill team stuff with the money I earn and—well, you know—all the other things I need. What do you think Dad will say?"

"I can tell you right now, the answer is no! Period. Parents don't let their thirteen-year-old kids go away to work for the summer."

"I'm almost fourteen, Mom. I'm not a kid anymore! Now Dad hates B for no reason!"

"Your father doesn't hate him, but he doesn't want you around him," I said. "He still hasn't served time for his kidnapping charge. B doesn't use good sense, Jan."

Jan's eyes narrowed and her nostrils flared, "How many times do I have to say it? He didn't kidnap me! We couldn't come home because you guys called the law. Now you're going to ruin this too."

Stunned at her outburst, I defended my position. "Well, you are not going! Just get it out of your head."

With her hands on her hips and wagging her head back and forth, Jan said, "I want to get out of this town. Do you know how people look at me? I can't stand to stay here because you blew a little thing all out of proportion. Everybody treats me funny. I'm not a normal kid anymore because of what you did."

With tears running down her face, she turned around and ran out of the room.

I opened my mouth to speak, but didn't. What could I say that would make a difference? I didn't know why she felt like this. I wondered how long B had been plotting this. Jan was dealing with a lot of emotions, but I was sure that if we left it alone, it would all blow over in a few days.

Her father's arrival from work brought the issue to the surface. Jan passionately explained that she had a place to live with some good people. Jerry would be there, and she would make four dollars an hour.

Bob gave his answer without mincing words. "No, Jan. You're not going. Don't even think about it. B can't be trusted. Furthermore, I don't want you talking to him on the phone at all."

Jan's eyes welled up with tears and a wave of disappointment swept over her face, but not a sound came out of her pursed lips.

We moved our vacation plans up. We invited Jan's best friend, Caroline Hansen, to go with us, hoping this gesture would appease Jan.

Berchtold was in town on June 8, 1976, to receive his sentencing, which amounted to five years in prison in total, but with forty-five days suspended. The days he had spent in jail before being released on bond would be counted toward his served time. It was shocking to realize that he would only serve a total of fifteen days and the rest would be suspended in the Bannock County Jail.

With B in town, I watched Jan's every move. I didn't want her to leave the house in case he had a plan that included her. Knowing that his influence was powerful and that anything was possible, our trust level was at zero.

Jan nervously announced, "I think I'll ride my bike over to Caroline's."

My response was immediate, "I'll drive you." Instead, she practiced the piano.

Our two-week California vacation took place immediately after school was out, and Caroline, whom we loved like daughter number four, came along. It was delightful to be together and away from the constant chaos. It was also comforting to be far away from Berchtold and his constant phone calls. It was a great time to give our girls undivided attention and to recapture some unity and fun as a family.

Realizing the hold Berchtold had on Jan, Bob, and I seriously discussed selling our business and moving. One of Bob's employees was interested in buying our shop, and we discussed the possibilities. As they began looking for financing, Bob and I were exploring other business opportunities in Utah.

After a weekend trip, we returned home hopelessly discouraged–neither of us felt it was what we wanted to do. Within a couple of weeks, the financial picture soured for the buyers and the plans never came to fruition.

Instead of selling, Bob decided to remodel and expand the shop. He threw himself into an extensive remodeling plan, secured a bank loan, and laid out his ideas with a building contractor.

Calls from Berchtold came all the time. He claimed that Jan would not listen to him, and he was determined for Jan to come to Jackson Hole. I hung up every time I heard his voice—after telling him to quit calling. Ignoring his phone calls was impossible. He was relentless, and back in those days, the phone would ring forever if no one answered it. I screamed at him several times and told him to quit calling us. We knew from the phone bill that no one at home was making calls to B because it cost money for every long-distance call, and Jan wasn't allowed to call him. If she was calling him, she was calling collect on his dime. Knowing it was impossible for us to stop receiving his calls, we would pick up the phone, and simply hang up once we knew it was him.

B would often get a few words out before we could slam the receiver down.

One call came after another—first angry, then worried, then threatening, "She keeps saying she will run away if you don't let her come."

Exasperated, I raised my voice, "Forget it! Leave her alone and quit calling."

The next call, B's anger escalated. "Believe me, MaryAnn, I will not give up what I've fought so hard to get, no matter what I have to do! I've paid too high a price to let go." His voice was determined and threatening.

In a fit of rage, I struck back. "Fought so hard to get? You're a sick son of a bitch! Don't ever call here again!"

B screamed back with equal fervor, "You'll be sorry! If I have to, I'll take her to the jungles of Africa or South America, and you will never see her again!"

Trembling, I slammed the receiver down. I had no doubt that he meant every word. Shaken and distressed, I drove to the store to talk with Bob. He offered comfort and calmed me down. "When I get home, I'll talk to Jan," he said.

Jan's restlessness was disconcerting. Explaining our fears didn't make a difference. She didn't respond. She avoided looking at us while wiping away tears. We asked her to explain B's accusations about her running away, but Jan, who was previously always a willing communicator, now refused to talk. Her demeanor deeply troubled us.

I pleaded, "Jan, what's going on? Talk to us. Can't you see what he's doing to you?"

Jan shook her head, "Just let me go to Jackson Hole and everything will be all right."

"I can't let you do that, honey. I love you too much," Bob said.

Looking at her father, she begged, "If you loved me, you would let me go. It's not B's fault."

"No, honey. It is his fault because he is trying to persuade you against our wishes. Even if this doesn't make sense to you, it has to be this way."

Jan didn't respond. She sat quietly and stared into space. Bob and I were sick about the change in her behavior during the past few weeks. She had become moody and easily agitated.

Over the next few days, Jan steadily voiced her plan. She was going to Jackson, and no one could keep her from going. It was alarming to see her so insistent and stubborn—something we had never before witnessed in her. Her sisters had no insight either. Karen invited Caroline over, hoping Jan would confide in her best friend. Alas, that didn't happen.

Jan Flees to Jackson Hole
July 27, 1976

Returning home from running an errand the next day, I found Susan crying and holding her arm.

She had fallen from her bike. Jan had been very thoughtful and had tied a dish towel around Susan's neck to support her battered arm.

"Where is Jan?" I asked, as Susan continued to cry.

Karen answered hesitantly, "Well, she went on a bike ride earlier."

I replied, "Her bike is in the garage."

Karen looked sick. "I heard her on the phone giving someone our address, then a car honked, and she left."

I rushed over to the phone book and found it opened to the number of a taxi company. I rushed the girls to the car in a panic. Trying to comfort Susan, I reassured her that we would get her to the doctor—as I wildly sped onto the highway and headed to the airport.

With my heart pounding furiously, I grasped the steering wheel so tightly that my knuckles turned white. Listening to Susan's mournful cry, I quickly processed my thoughts. *Jan didn't have money for a plane ticket. This is ridiculous. I've got to talk to her. She can't go see that sick pervert.*

Assuring the girls that it would only take a few minutes, I parked at the curb of the terminal and rushed in. Jan had already gone through security and was near the front of the boarding line. From across the airport, I yelled, "Jan, you can't go! You are not getting on that plane!"

She held up a wad of cash and said, "It's too late! You can't stop me!" Then security opened the doors to let people board, and Jan walked outside, across the tarmac, and up the stairs onto the plane.

With tears running down my face, I ran to the car. Through my sobs, I choked out, "I didn't know what to do." Karen tried to comfort me. She said that Jan was determined to go, and there was nothing we could have done to make her stay home. By the time we arrived home, Susan was asleep. I woke her and took her to the living room, where she rested on the couch. I promised I would take her to the hospital soon.

Meanwhile, we found an envelope on the kitchen table that Jan had left for her father. When Bob got home, I handed him the letter, and sat unresponsive as he opened the envelope and read:

> *Dear Dad,*
>
> *I'm sorry that things didn't work out the way you wanted. But I know down deep that this is what I truly want. This is a very unique situation, and I hope that you can understand. I know I haven't been the best daughter in the world, but I hope that someday we can have the kind of relationship a father and daughter should have. I love all of you, and I'm sorry if I've hurt any of you. But life goes on and we have to live our lives the way that we see fit. Maybe I'm selfish and blind, but I'm trying. I care about all of you. Thanks for understanding. I guess I'm pretty lucky.*
>
> *Love, Jan*

Unable to provide any sensible details about how I had let Jan board a plane and disappear, I just placed my head down and cried, "She wouldn't come with me, and I couldn't create a screaming match in the airport. I'm tired of dealing with her hostility. Susan needed me, and that unreasonable brat was acting like she was twenty-one. Damn her, damn him. I just don't care!"

Bob shook his head and looked bewildered. Karen cried, overwhelmed with the emotions of the day, as well as never having heard me swear before. After watching me rant and rave, Bob's anger turned to Berchtold, "I have never wanted to kill anyone in my life, but I want to kill him. He's a menace to society! That animal!"

I felt defeated, and I judged myself an inept failure as a mother—even more so when we took Susan to the emergency room, where X-rays showed a fracture. While the doctor was putting a cast on her arm, I thought, *You idiot! Susan deserves your time and attention right now. Karen's constantly trying to comfort the rest of us, and she's barely twelve years old! Pull it together, MaryAnn. You're the parent—act like one! Think about Jan later.*

After Susan was given a pill for pain, she settled into bed. Bob went to the medicine cabinet and brought me a sleeping pill. I had never used them before, even when Jan was missing, but I was exhausted and traumatized, so I didn't protest. Jan's entire personality had changed. Her demeanor was serious, solemn, and almost rigid. Bob pulled the covers back on the bed, opened the windows, closed the blinds, and demanded that I sleep while he took charge.

A new day brought me to my senses. What should we do to get Jan back? Jan needed to be deprogrammed from Berchtold's hold. He had somehow managed to brainwash her. It was beyond belief, but deep in my gut, I just knew.

In her mind, Jan tried justifying the way she had left home. It had not been her intention to hurt her parents, but until the "special baby" came, she couldn't explain anything to us. In time, we would understand. B had told her it was up to her to either get on with her mission or fail. Was she ready to endure the consequences? She cared about her family too much to let us get hurt.

B met Jan at the airport and expressed his delight, "You're going to love it up here," he remarked. "There's lots of planning we have to do in a short amount of time. I've got you scheduled for a doctor's appointment tomorrow, but tonight we're going to the Pink Garter to see a play. This will be a good place for us to live when everything settles down." Giving birth sounded scary and painful to Jan. Her slender, underdeveloped body weighed in at roughly eighty pounds now. She had grown a couple inches taller since she was twelve, but there were still no signs of puberty. She hoped an alien birth wouldn't hurt as much as she imagined a human birth would.

Asking why she had to see a doctor, B explained, "You are sick too often, and I think it's allergies. In all these years since your mom had you tested, she never bought you medication. I want to make sure you are healthy and in good physical condition when you become a mother yourself."

Jackson Hole was buzzing with tourists, and Jan found the fun center a busy place. Lots of kids were in and out all day. She thought parents weren't allowed, but that wasn't true. Some of the adults had more fun than their kids. Jerry and Jan worked together providing customers with tickets and change and keeping the center clean. Cast members from the playhouse came over to chat and told Jan they would show her around the theater. Jan was ecstatic. Her ambition in life was to be an actress. Different shopkeepers in the plaza would ask B if Jan were his daughter, and he would laugh, roll his eyes at Jan, and say, "Well, something like that."

The Sewing Machine and Loads of Gifts

Before she had time to make any money, B told her about a phone call from his attorney. It was not good news. Jan had to return home because her parents were ruining everything. If she didn't go back, they were going to have him sent to jail. Frustrated, B said he would talk to other people who were part of the plan. She needed to do whatever it took to make the plan work. Her parents wouldn't like it, but they were backed into a corner, and they would have to fight to get out of it alive. Promising B she would follow the plan, Jan gathered her belongings while B loaded his car with gifts he had bought for her fourteenth birthday.

***

Our family's plan of action was to hire a lawyer and proceed with a civil lawsuit against Berchtold. I called Berchtold's attorney and informed him of what had taken place, "Berchtold's enticement is more than we can handle. We are filing a lawsuit against him. We want our daughter home and out of his clutches. We want him out of our lives forever."

B's attorney asked us not to proceed until he had an opportunity to talk with his client. Berchtold was given an ultimatum: "Get that girl back to Pocatello, or you'll be charged with child endangerment."

Saturday afternoon, the phone rang, and Bob answered it. "Dad, I'm at the Mini-Dome and I need you to come and get me," Jan said. "You need to bring the car." She offered no further explanation and hung up.

As Bob drove into the parking lot, he saw Berchtold's car. He also saw Jan standing nearby surrounded by shopping bags.

Seeing Bob approach, B hurriedly climbed into his car. He shouted, "Thanks for everything," and blew Jan a kiss before speeding off.

Bob was furious with Berchtold. Jan angrily loaded her things into the car.

When they arrived home, Jan threw open the door and stormed into the house, her arms filled with bags of gifts. She ran down the stairs to her room, unloaded the merchandise, and went out to the car again. Bob removed several items from the back seat and set them on the garage floor. Neither Bob nor Jan uttered a word. I was silent also, allowing the situation to play itself out. It was obvious that Berchtold was trying to buy her affection now.

Bob finished the unwelcome chore and slammed the car door shut. With eyes flashing with rage, he walked in the back door carrying a portable sewing machine. "This is only one of the gifts Jan received for her birthday," he told me. "B bought her a camera, piles of new clothes, all kinds of trinkets, and who knows what else. I told Jan it is all going back. She is very upset, and so am I." He stormed out of the house toward the patio.

I spoke to him through the screen, "Did you ask Jan why she flew up there and where the money came from?"

"No! I'm too angry right now to be reasonable. Berchtold is . . ." He paused, never finishing his thought, but clenched his fists and shook with rage.

Jan kept silent as she flitted up and down the stairs, carrying her new possessions to her room. I turned to her and said, "I'm so thankful you are back. Can we talk?"

Avoiding eye contact, her answer was curt, "Not right now!"

Later that evening, I overheard Karen quizzing her. Jan enthusiastically talked about her excursion. "Working at the fun center was okay, but I don't like to play those pinball machines. I helped take money, make change, and stuff like that. The most fun was going to the Pink Garter Theatre. When I'm old enough, I'm going to be in plays there. The people were really nice to me. Jerry and I did some shopping, but I didn't get to stay long enough to do much."

To our bewilderment, teenage rebellion had raised its ugly head in the middle of our family chaos. Perhaps a professional could identify her defiance and understand why she was determined to follow B's demands. Our immediate concern was finding a good counselor.

Orders were given that no one was to speak with Berchtold when he called, and we were to leave the phone off the hook after each of his calls.

"But he'll really be mad if you don't take me back to the doctor," Jan said.

"What doctor?" I asked, aggravated. "He took you to a doctor?"

"Yeah, to an allergy clinic. B said he had to see what was wrong with me."

Annoyed, I snapped at her, "Oh, good grief! You had allergy tests when you were five years old. B knows that."

"But he said I need some good medicine that will help me, especially when he takes me riding. I want to be a good rider. He said there are lots of places to go in Jackson Hole. I want to go back!"

I was furious and spouted off, "What's he trying to prove? He's not your father. You didn't need those tests again."

Jan shrugged her shoulders and replied, "Well, I told him I didn't want to, but he said he couldn't get medicine for me unless I did."

I explained, "You know that we're upset about what you did. You are not allowed to talk with him, with Jerry, or with any of the Berchtold's."

Jan turned her colorless face upward and looked at me. Her eyes were wide and questioning. "But why?" she whispered.

"You belong with us, not him. Even though you might think our decisions are not the best, it's our job as parents to look out for you. He's trying to take away our responsibility over you as parents, and we're not going to let it happen. He told me he would take you far away and we would never see you again. I couldn't stand that."

Leave Her Alone

Jan said no more. She sat on the kitchen chair with teardrops falling down her cheeks. Her arms slid across the table, and she dropped her head on them. Gentle sobs emerged as she wept. I chose not to console her. It was more important that she knew we were not giving in. If we were going to keep B away, we had to be tough.

After Bob arrived home from work, we sat on the patio while I questioned B's motives. "Why would he make her go through allergy tests again? He's up to something."

Bob retorted, "That's the pattern of his life, but there might be something else Jan's not telling us."

Looking anxiously at Bob, I knew the high probability that Berchtold had violated Jan, "What do you think he's done?"

Bob put his face in his hands and heaved a heavy sigh, "I can't even think about it. I get too sick. Do you think Jan would ever tell you?"

Thinking about the challenge, I moaned, "I don't know, but I'll try."

That night, I attempted to have a more explicit mother-daughter talk with Jan. I felt awkward, and I stumbled around trying to find the right way to bring up sensitive issues. After a few feeble efforts, I decided she needed to know that the FBI thought B was a man who preyed on children sexually. She listened intently, but never commented. Her eyes were sympathetic as she watched me struggling. I hoped she could feel safe and tell me if there had been any inappropriate behavior from B, but she said nothing. Exasperated, I blurted out, "Has B done anything bad to you? Has he touched you or been sexual with you? If he has, you need to tell me."

144

Jan emphatically shook her head to assure me. "No! That's sick! He would never do that, Mom. Don't be gross!" I wanted to believe Jan since she had always been an honest child. It had been unthinkable earlier for me to believe that B could violate her. He had children of his own, and as far as we knew, he was a loving father. But something deep in my gut told me otherwise—that Jan was protecting him for some unexplained reason.

Bob went to an attorney to seek legal advice. He said, "What rights do we have to protect ourselves from Berchtold? He continues to harass us with phone calls and has threatened to take Jan again."

The attorney scowled, and his bushy eyebrows formed a straight dark line across his brow. "Basically, none," he replied. "He isn't breaking the law unless he attempts to hurt one of you. Legally speaking, your personal rights aren't in jeopardy, unless he commits a criminal act."

"What if he's molested our daughter?" Bob asked.

"Without her admission or any evidence, he's free and clear. But I'd take her to a counselor pronto." The attorney paused, scratched his head, and leaned back in his chair. "Why don't you file a civil suit against him? Whether it would do any good, I don't know, but he might leave you alone, and it would bring attention to the authorities."

"Once he hears that, he'll be even more volatile," Bob answered.

"He'd be a fool to try anything," the attorney said.

The following afternoon, the phone rang. I answered it, only to receive a tongue-lashing from B. He had heard from Jan that the FBI had said he was a child molester. The hair on the back of my neck bristled as I blurted out, "You rotten snake. I know you've molested Jan and we'll get the truth. I hope they throw the key away when you're sent to prison."

B screamed back, "Did you tell her I had little-girl problems and didn't have the capacity to enjoy adult women? How could you be so low to say that to her? I will have Jan, so help me God. I have made promises to her I intend to keep!"

Later in the day, Jan ignored her father's warning and rode her bike to Caroline's. Determined to make his point, Bob drove over and brought her home. Explaining to her why we were being so protective didn't seem to make an impact. "Just let me go back up to Jackson," she demanded.

"No, Jan! I can't let you. Your mother and I don't want Berchtold near you. You don't understand how dangerous he is. He might take you again. We are trying to protect you!"

"Dad, I want to marry B!"

The words reverberated thunderously in Bob's ears. He was flabbergasted and didn't know how to respond. He blurted out, "Jan? Do you know what you're saying? You're too young to even think about marriage."

Refusing to look at her father, Jan stared ahead as he drove down the street. "Because something has happened that is maybe bad. I don't want to live in sin for the rest of my life. If I married him, I wouldn't have to."

Bob flinched at the news, swallowed hard, and for a time could not breathe. His face drained as he fought back tears. He asked, "Can you tell me what happened?"

Jan shook her head.

Bob felt his throat tighten as he begged her for more information.

"Whatever has happened, you don't have to marry Berchtold. It would be the worst mistake of your life."

Jan hung her head. She became silent and unresponsive. Tears fell from her downturned eyes.

"Don't give Berchtold another second of your life. He is telling you lies and making you feel guilty. He's a wicked man. Please listen to me. None of this is your fault. You haven't sinned. You are young and innocent, sweetheart. I will not let him do anything to hurt you. Let me help you."

When they arrived back home, Bob was an emotional wreck. Jan was subdued and remained silent. The following day was Sunday. Jan ignored Bob and I. I felt as if I had been punched in the stomach. *How could we not have seen the monster? How did we all fall prey to him? How would we protect and help our daughter through her unimaginable pain?* I was angry, sad, and disgusted with myself, and with Berchtold at the same time. Bob had been right all along. Our only consolation was seeing our three girls relating with one another normally.

On Monday morning, August 9, 1976, I went to pick up a few items at the grocery store. Upon my return, Jan was gone. I panicked and called Bob. She returned shortly after, but she sat outside in the garage looking extremely distraught. I was relieved to see Bob drive up.

Jan watched him get out of the van and walk into the house, and then she began screaming, "Now you've done it! You finally got to him. B said he never wants to see or talk to me again. I hope you're happy!" She ran downstairs to her room, slammed the door, and stayed there most of the day. We looked at each other and knew that she had once again found a way to talk to Berchtold.

Bob invited her to join us for family time together, but she refused.

We all noted her nervousness. She went in and out of her bedroom several times, and would come into the family room, but would not stay there while anyone was there. I later asked if she would watch TV with me while I ironed clothes, but she refused and returned to her room. It was after midnight when I concluded that she wasn't going to talk to me, and I went to bed.

Chapter 13
GONE AGAIN

August 10, 1976

Jan stood trembling in the cool night, nervously watching for a blue sedan to appear. Her shivering could not be attributed solely to the night air. It was 1:30 a.m., an odd time for a girl who was barely fourteen to be standing in the shadows of her home waiting for a ride. Her fear caused doubts about the entire situation. Her thoughts were scattered. *I can't believe this is happening. I don't want to go, but I have to.* Jan's heart ached as she anticipated her family's shock when they discovered she was gone again.

Twice tonight, B had tapped on Jan's window to let her know he was there. The first time, Jan had silently mouthed the words, "Mom is still up," and motioned toward the family room. After I had turned off all the lights and had gone to bed, Jan sat nervously in her dark bedroom anticipating B's next signal. She nearly jumped out of her skin when she heard three soft taps on the windowpane.

Distinctly remembering Zada's horrible intrusion in her life, Jan was not sorry to leave her downstairs bedroom behind. She had been constantly afraid of hearing that awful voice again.

Now it was time to do what she had been dreading. Jan stood on the blue padded chair B had hung for her three years earlier, and she crawled through the small basement window in her room.

Jan thought, *My parents can't understand. I've tried to find an explanation for them without getting anyone hurt or killed, but nothing worked. If they would just let me be with him, things would be different. Dad doesn't want me to see him again. Someday I won't have to hide all these dark secrets. I wonder if someday they can all know about the mission.*

Jan shivered as she contemplated her assignment. Inside her chest, a knot of anxiety pushed hard against her ribs. She tried to reassure herself. *It's going to be okay.*

Jan surveyed the neighbor's unlit homes before slinking behind a pine tree at the corner of the street. She glimpsed a car slowly creeping down the darkened street with its headlights off and her heart thumped wildly. B had told her he was going to park around the corner by the Mini-Dome and would be in a blue Ford Sedan. *That's it!* she thought, stepping out momentarily so B could catch a glimpse of her before she darted behind the tree again. A flicker of the car's headlights gave Jan assurance that B had seen her.

Jan remembered the sharp words that had been exchanged with her father earlier. *If they only knew this was for all of us. Zada said that once B and I get married, everything will be okay. B keeps reminding me that my parents have to believe in me.*

Jan quickly glanced at the neighbor's bedroom window, knowing that the widow lady could see her if she happened to be up and looking. *Hurry, B,* Jan anxiously thought as the car moved cautiously along the quiet street.

Again, trying to justify her actions, she reminded herself, *Dad and Mom both think B is bad, but he's been so good to me. What would happen to me if B weren't around to protect me? He's scared too. They threatened to give me a new male companion if something happens to him. A stranger would be terrible.*

The car stopped. B reached over and opened the door. Jan dashed from her hiding place and sat in the front seat of this unfamiliar car. She pulled the door shut. Even the clicking of the door sounded unusually loud.

"Hi, Angel," B said, smiling affectionately. "I see you got the other backpack."

Distressed, Jan responded breathlessly, "Yeah, I kept it hidden in my closet, but I didn't bring any clothes."

"Good girl!" he exclaimed in a shrill, approving voice. "That's what I told you. This is the beginning of a whole new life. I'll take over from here and will buy you all new clothes and everything you need."

With that remark, he put his arm around Jan and pulled her closer. She looked from the corner of her eye toward her home and thought about her unsuspecting family. B left the lights off until he reached the end of the block. Turning onto Center Street, he guided the car toward the interstate. A hard, sickening lump lodged in Jan's throat as she read the words overhead that indicated the direction they were headed: "Salt Lake City."

B saw Jan struggling with her emotions as she dabbed at her eyes. "Quit your worrying. Everything is going to be okay. Bob and MaryAnn will understand soon enough. Did you do everything I told you?"

"Yes, I think so." Jan's voice quivered.

"Did you have any trouble getting out through the basement window?"

"No," she answered. "It was open."

"Yeah, I know." B snickered slyly. "And did you leave the note for them?"

"Yes," she replied in a shaky voice. Jan knew she was going to cry, but was trying not to. After all, she wanted to prove that she was strong enough to go through with the plan. Crying might make her look like a baby.

"Did you write it like I said?" he inquired.

Upset, she responded, "Uh-huh!" She swallowed hard, feeling pressure from B's interrogation.

B giggled, "That's great, honey! Once they realize you're not their little girl anymore, we'll be able to have a good relationship with them."

"I don't want to talk about it right now," Jan said.

"Okay," he replied. "I'd rather talk about our future, anyway." With a smug look on his face, he stated, "Can't wait 'til we go to Hawaii—snorkeling and cruising from one island to the next—you in a grass skirt doing the hula. Woo-Woo!" Jan didn't respond. "How about a Jungle Safari? Africa would be a fabulous place to go. Most people think of it as a big adventure, but it's a very romantic place." Looking longingly at Jan, he pulled her closer and said, "We'll need a couple of rifles. I can teach you to shoot. I'm a pretty good marksman." Speaking with delight and giving Jan a squeeze, he proclaimed, "Our lives are just beginning." Determined to change Jan's sullen attitude, B asked enthusiastically, "Where would you like to go?"

Jan stared straight ahead, into the dark night, shrugged her shoulders, and remained silent.

"Hey, cheer up. It's not the end of the world, you know." When Jan did not respond, B asked, "Is my Dolly tired?"

Jan pursed her lips together and nodded.

"It has been a hard day for me too," B said. Then he continued to probe. "What happened after you called me today? What did Bob and MaryAnn say when you told them the big, fat lie that I never wanted to see you again?" he asked with gusto.

"Nothing. I didn't want to talk to them, so I just went to my bedroom and stayed there all day." Jan swallowed hard. "Zada tried to tell me that Mom and Dad aren't actually my parents. I don't really believe them."

"Oh, Dolly, be careful what you say. You know they hear everything. This is hard for you to understand because Bob and MaryAnn are wonderful people and have had an important purpose in your life. But honey, you're a special angel, a chosen spirit. I knew that the moment I laid eyes on you. Try to be patient. Everything will fit in time. Remember when Zada—"

Jan's anxiety level rose at the mention of Zada's name, and she cut B off. "I don't want to talk about it! I get scared every time I think about them." Agitated, she began to squirm. She put her hand over her mouth and shouted, "I feel sick!"

B gently rubbed her leg, in an attempt to comfort her. He couldn't see her face well enough in the dark of the night to tell if she was really sick, but he supposed it was nerves. He said with a firm voice, "You'll be okay."

A few moments later, Jan announced, "I'm going to throw up!"

B slowed the car, "Hold on till I stop." He pulled quickly onto the side of the road, reached across Jan, and opened the passenger door. Jan immediately leaned over and hung her head out the door. Holding her stomach, she swallowed hard, and waited. Nothing happened.

B asked, "Are you okay, Dolly? What can I do?" Jan moaned and waved her hand, wanting B to stop talking to her. The cool night breeze brought her some relief, and she soon announced that she was feeling a little better.

B looked closely at Jan's pale, perspiring face. Then he hit the steering wheel with a vengeful blow and snapped, "Hell, this is hard! Why can't Bob let go? You don't deserve this." B rummaged around in his pocket and pulled out a pill. "Here, this will help. It's a relaxer. I think you've got a case of the jitters."

Jan swallowed the pill with a bottle of Squirt that B had pulled from a cooler on the floor. She then slid down on the seat and curled into a ball. "I think I'm okay now," she responded weakly.

B tenderly patted her small form as he pulled back onto the highway. "Just remember everything you've been told. The Black Family is very nice. I wish you could have met them when they came to Jackson Hole this summer. You'll love being in California. They have a cute little room waiting for you, and there is nothing for you to worry about. Everything has been planned out perfectly."

Without a Trace

The following morning, Bob went down to Jan's bedroom before work, hoping to redeem himself. Instead of finding Jan, he found a note on her pillow:

Dear Bob and Maryanne,

You won't let me do whets [sic] right, so I will do whets wrong. I am leaving without B, and do not plan on coming back until you accept me as me. I cannot accept your religion or your screwed-up morals. I just want to be me and have B. Please, before all of us are destroyed, let me go.

Jan

Referring to us as "Bob and Maryanne" was disturbing enough, not to mention misspelling my name and the word "what." Jan was a straight A student, so we knew that she knew better. *Had she been instructed to do this? Was making those obvious mistakes her way of signaling to us that she was being coerced? Her last sentence was alarming. What had B done to her?*

Bob called Pete Welsh, the FBI agent, and gave him a brief explanation. Pete immediately came to our home.

"She seemed to be doing so well, until this summer," I said, and then I came clean. "B used me as his open door to Jan. I wised up, but too late. He got her, anyway."

Pete shook his head, "Berchtold is a master at deceit and has a convincing tongue. Her note indicates that she left on her own, which most likely will preclude the FBI from involvement. He knows this. Do you want me to report this to the police?"

Not wanting media coverage, we were hesitant. Pete explained his reasoning. "If she is reported as a runaway, it will protect you from the press because runaways aren't released to the public. Unfortunately, the downside is the fact that runaways are not actively sought by law enforcement like a missing person would be."

We preferred keeping her disappearance quiet. Our emotions were so fragile that we thought that dealing with anyone except family might push us over the edge again.

"I still have the tape recorder," Pete announced. "It hasn't been used since you last had it. I'll bring it by." He quickly returned and advised, "Record every call that comes in. Be calm and talk to people as you normally do. Things worked out the last time—maybe not perfectly, but we did get your daughter back." Pete paused as he looked at our shocked faces. "Are you guys going to be all right?"

"I can't believe this is happening again," Bob replied with tears welling up in his eyes.

I remained stoic. Slient, but upset, I was steadfast to find this wolf in sheep's clothing. We would bring our beloved daughter home—no matter what it took!

Later in the day, a large, burly detective named George Shail stood at our door with a friendly smile and a warm handshake. Ready to assist us, he needed details so he could begin an investigation.

I hadn't expected to hear from B. There was no doubt in any of our minds that B was behind Jan's disappearance. Consequently, I was beyond surprised when I picked up the phone that evening and heard B's voice. He sounded frantic. I recorded his call for the police. "What in the hell has happened there? I just had a phone call from Jan saying she ran away from home. Do you know how she left? What she took?"

"Stay out of this, B!" I warned. "We'll take care of getting Jan home."

"Oh," he whimpered, "it's all my fault. I shouldn't have told her I never wanted to see her again."

His false emotions were unbearable, and I snapped back, "That's the smartest thing you've ever done. Be sure you mean it."

"It's obvious you're not concerned about Jan," he snarled. "That little girl could be anywhere and you couldn't care less."

For once, B hung up on me this time.

B called again the next day. I was not home, but Bob answered. As soon as he heard B's voice, he hung up. B called back, begging Bob to hear him out. He declared that he was drunk and had been for three days. He cried, telling Bob that he could have everything he owned—his car, money, kids, anything Bob wanted—if he would give him permission to marry Jan.

"Over my dead body!" Bob declared emphatically, slamming the receiver down.

Two days later, B called again. "Have you heard from Jan?" he asked.

"No," I replied.

"Neither have I. I tried drinking myself to death and just spent twenty-four hours in the Jackson Hospital." I'm so worried about Jan." His voice was whiny. "Jimmy's here with me, but I'm taking him back to Ogden today. I'll come back here in case Jan calls me." Again, he asked, "Have you heard from her?"

"I said no!" was my curt reply.

"What in the hell got into her?" B asked. "I tried so hard to convince her that things could be worked out, but she wouldn't listen. I did tell you she was going to run away, MaryAnn." There was a brief pause as I waited for him to say more, and I wasn't disappointed. "There's something else I need to tell you, MaryAnn. I don't want to add any more worries, but I think Jan is a lesbian."

"You damn liar! You have to be twisted. You're a pervert!" I yelled before slamming down the receiver.

An hour later, he called again. Breathlessly, he said, "MaryAnn, I just hung up from talking to Jan, but she wouldn't tell me where she is. You'll never believe what she did the night she left." I monitored every word he uttered with skepticism, hoping I could find a hint of Jan's whereabouts. Berchtold's singsong voice was full of drama. "I can't believe she did this, but she walked up to the interstate and flagged down a truck driver. She told him she was a runaway and wanted to go home. Can you believe that?"

His explanation did not ring true. Firmly, I said, "Jan's afraid of the dark and would never have the nerve to do such a thing."

Miffed by my response, he fired back, "Well, that's what she told me. Obviously, you don't care. I'm just relieved to have heard from her."

I was silently seething from his disgusting lies, but I bit my tongue and let him continue.

"She told me not to worry because she has money and is getting a nice sun tan," he laughed. "Isn't that good news? She actually sounded pretty good—like she was free. Now, I can take Jimmy home. If I hear anything else, I'll call you."

I was repulsed.

As the police began their investigation, they learned that Berchtold had opened a checking account under the name of Jan Broberg at the Jackson State Bank. At the allergy clinic, she was listed as Jan Berchtold. She had been given a prescription for allergy medication. All of that seemed irrelevant to the question pounding in my head every second: *Where was she?*

***

When Jan arrived at the Blacks' home, she was confused and anxious. What had her family done when they found out she was gone? Where was B? He had given her that pill to help her relax, but what had happened after that? She barely remembered being dropped off.

B hadn't told her much about the Black's except that they were nice and would take good care of her. She didn't need to be afraid, and he was certain they wouldn't pry into her life. She wondered, *Are the Black's some of them? Are they aliens in disguise?* They didn't ask her any questions about why she was there, and within a few days, Jan's fears about them decreased. The family made no demands, treated her well, and allowed her to be a recluse.

B kept telling her she had to be brave because everything would be over soon, and she could go back home. Jan wondered how that would happen. The unknown caused her sleepless nights, and soon black circles appeared under her piercing blue-green eyes.

B's daily phone calls were the only thing that kept Jan sane. She begged him to get her soon. He ranted about the FBI throwing him in jail again, but more than that, he feared the demands Zada was making.

"We have to do what they say, or they will take Susan. It doesn't matter what they do to me, it's you I'm worried about. Be brave, Dolly, for just a little longer. Your folks have to give in. I wish they knew what we're going through because of them."

The unknown kept Jan on the edge. She was experiencing nightmares, reliving the vivid experience she had encountered two years prior. *Why me?* she often asked. Every night when she tried to sleep, the memory of the fateful day when she had first been held captive by the aliens invaded Jan's mind. With all her might, she tried to erase the thoughts, the voices, and the mission—but none of it would go away.

***

It had been two weeks since Jan had disappeared. The local police still had no clues as to her whereabouts.

On Wednesday afternoon, Bob was at work. He answered the phone and heard a shaky voice say, "Dad, its Jan." There was a tremor in her voice, and she was trying very hard not to cry.

Stunned, Bob slumped onto a stool and cried out, "Oh, honey, where are you? What's going on? We miss you and want you to come home. Tell me where you are, and I'll come get you."

She sounded frightened, and the strain in her voice alarmed Bob. "I can't tell you where I am, but I want to come home and go to school. Have you signed the papers?"

"What papers? For what? I haven't seen any papers."

"Giving me permission to get married," she blurted out. "You should have gotten some."

"From whom?"

"I don't know," the trembling in her voice continued.

Bob stood firm, "Jan, I have told you before, and I still mean it, I will never give you permission to marry that devil. I love you too much to do that." Bob waited for a response. All he heard was a soft guttural moan. He pleaded, "Please, Jani, come home."

Jan sniffled quietly, "I can't, Dad. Not until you sign the papers."

"Honey, I can't do that, but I love you, and we all miss you. Please know that I would do anything in this world for you—except let you marry Berchtold."

Jan's voice was weepy, "If you love me, you will sign the papers."

Realizing she was not going to abandon the issue, Bob said, "Jan, call your mother. She misses you terribly. Please, will you do that?"

She cleared her throat in an attempt to control her emotions. "I don't know. I might."

An operator came on the line asking for a deposit of more coins to extend the call.

Anxiously, she exclaimed, "Dad, I've got to go! Just sign the papers, and everything will be all right. I want to come home!"

Bob sat stunned with the receiver in his hand. Choked up, he began to weep.

By chance, I stopped at the shop just minutes after her call. I found Bob extremely distraught. Faulting himself for not getting through to Jan, he was experiencing bitter despair. "She wouldn't listen. She just kept saying over and over that I had to sign some papers. I don't even know what she's talking about. I feel so helpless. What else could I do?"

Having no answer, I leaned against his shoulder and cried with him.

Two days after Jan's call to her father, I heard from Berchtold. He asked if I had tried calling him. He was afraid he had missed my call.

"What reason would I have to call you?" I asked.

"I thought Jan might have called you or Bob," he said.

Thinking about Jan's phone call to her dad, I said nothing. Had he been with her when she made the call? I hoped he would explain about "the papers" for the recording machine to capture.

Berchtold continued, "I've been in Phoenix for the last four days."

"In Phoenix? Why there?"

"I have people who are helping me search, and one of them thought he had found her, but it turned out to be a false lead."

"That's too bad," I replied blandly.

"Jan told me she was getting lots of sun, so I figured Phoenix was a good lead."

I responded with a grunt.

He stammered, "Uh, by the way, it's the end of Summer, so I'm closing up the fun center."

I said nothing.

After a few moments, he said, "Did you know Gail and I were divorced? It was finalized a couple of weeks ago here in Jackson."

Surprised, I replied, "Oh, I didn't know."

His nonchalant attitude was expected. "Oh, we haven't been compatible for years. Gail knows this is best for both of us. I'll still take care of her and the kids, but I've got to get on with my life and find happiness."

I could have vomited. Everything was now conveniently prepared for him to marry Jan. Where was he hiding her?

Chapter 14
SACRED HEART ACADEMY

August 18, 1976

It was a hot, sticky day in southern California when B made the call he had been planning long in advance. "Hello, is this the Sacred Heart Academy?"

"Yes, that's correct," a voice replied. "May I help you?"

"With whom am I speaking?" he asked firmly.

"I am Sister Maria Terese."

"Please, I need to talk with Sister Charlotte."

"I'm sorry, sir, but Sister Charlotte isn't available. Would you like to leave a message?"

"Are you in charge?" he asked.

"Of what, sir?" she asked.

"Enrollment."

"Well, if you're making inquiries about criteria for placement, I can help you."

"All right, then," he said, sounding agitated. "I'm in desperate need of help."

"Please, sir, what can I do for you?"

"I'm in an extremely tricky situation, and I need our conversation to be kept confidential," B said. "I'm an Agent for the CIA, on assignment for President Ford. I've been stationed in Laos for some time. I'm sure you've heard what's happening there right now. The Communists are overtaking the country, and all Americans are being evacuated so they will not be killed. I barely escaped with my daughter. It's been a horrible ordeal."

He choked up. Sister Maria was moved and said, "I will pray for you and your daughter and—what about your wife?"

"My wife died of cancer a few weeks ago," he said. "It's been very hard on my daughter. My job doesn't permit me to spend as much time with her as I would like, especially right now. I'm going to talk with Gerry— oh, pardon me, I mean President Ford—and see if he can give me a new assignment."

"Sir, how old is your daughter, and what is her name, and yours?"

"I apologize. I am forgetting my manners," he replied.

"You should know that anything you reveal to me will not be divulged to anyone outside these sacred walls. But Sister Charlotte, our administrator, will want to know certain details."

"I need a private school for my daughter to attend. Her name is Janis Tobler, but please, you must promise to keep her identity hidden from anyone who comes to inquire."

"Of course. I understand," Sister Maria responded. "I promise you that we will look after her."

"And you can call me Frank Tobler," B added.

"Well, Mr. Tobler" she said, "just to let you know, our students are of all ages and come here from all over the world."

B cut her off. "The Secret Police have investigated your school," he said, and then he took control of the conversation. "Let me tell you about Janis. She is barely fourteen years old and is quite small for her age, but you will find her rather mature. She's heartbroken that I can't stay here in California with her. I'm all she has left, but my assignment is so demanding. Janis is a bright, intelligent, religious girl who needs the care and safety of your school. Her mother, who was a devout Catholic, would be so happy to know she is attending a Catholic school."

"Mr. Tobler, I'm sure it is very hard for you, as well, to have suffered such a terrible loss," Sister Maria said, beginning to feel sorry for the loss of this emotional father.

B interrupted Sister Maria: "Janis is in hiding right now. I have an important meeting with President Ford and the Chief of Staff in Washington, DC, over these next few days, but I will be coming to Los Angeles this weekend. Can I bring her then?"

"Mr. Tobler, our boarding school doesn't open for two weeks. You would need to speak to Sister Charlotte about getting her placed sooner," Sister Maria said.

B again brushed over her hesitancy. "She is quite homesick right now, and she is also frightened. Please don't ask her a lot of questions. I can answer anything you need to know. She has a few personal things because we escaped Laos with only the clothes on our backs. Some of our friends didn't make it," he went on. "Janis is traumatized. She is worried about her Laotian friends who were left behind during the bombings." There was a long pause as "Mr. Tobler" sniffled and cleared his throat.

"Mr. Tobler, you needn't worry about Janis. We will take excellent care of her," Sister Maria said. "We look forward to meeting her."

"How soon can you take her?" B asked.

"I'll have to discuss this with Sister Charlotte."

"If only you could find a place for her at your school now. My biggest concern is making sure she is protected from outsiders. She's been through so much."

"I will speak with Sister Charlotte and see what we can do. Where can I reach you?"

"I will call you in the morning. Time is critical. Please tell that to Sister Charlotte."

"Well, we do have another early arrival. Perhaps we can make an exception for such extreme circumstances."

"Oh, it will mean so much to know she is with you wonderful sisters," he effused.

"Certainly. Please call tomorrow, and may God be with you."

Jan's Diary, August 20, 1976:

B called yesterday and said he was coming today. I can't wait to see him. Hope he has some good news about me going home. The Blacks are really nice. They have two daughters older than me. They think B is my dad. I think B met them in Jackson Hole when they visited. They are very Catholic. Every time they bless the food, they cross themselves. Maybe they want me to as well. Makes me feel funny. I wonder how Susan and Karen are doing. Fine, I hope. I sure love them! I wonder if I have alien powers; then I would be able to transport myself into Karen's closet and read the Boxcar Children to them again. That was fun, fun, fun.

Three Weeks In

It had been three weeks since Jan had disappeared, and it was hard for me to keep things together. Jan's school registration was two days away. I needed to tell her drill team adviser too. I was desperate for the right thing to say to people, so I called Gail for more information.

"B is back from Jackson Hole and tells me Jan wants to marry him," Gail said. "According to B, she sounds very persistent. I know this sounds awful, but if she were my child, I would give my permission. I mean, how can you stand it, MaryAnn? I'd rather have her married and know where she is than to go through this uncertainty."

"Gail, have you lost your senses?" I asked, utterly shocked. "What if it were your own Jill, fourteen years old, demanding to marry a forty-year-old man?" I was so angry at her obvious lack of concern for how terrible this had been for us. "Jan hasn't even started puberty," I added. "We are

desperate to have her home, but we will never allow her to marry B."
Then, against hope, I asked, "Have you heard from her?"

Her reply surprised me. "I haven't spoken with Jan, but B is here. Do
you want to talk to him?" I didn't, but I needed some answers, and I hoped
he would slip up and give me tips as to her whereabouts.

B got on the phone. "I talked to Jan a couple of days ago," he said,
"and she told me she called Bob last week to get his permission to marry
me. She's pretty desperate, but she said she won't come home until you let
her marry me." I was incredulous, but I held my tongue. "Just to get her
home, can't you say yes? I have a Salt Lake attorney who would put some
papers together. Would you like me to talk to him about it?"

I kept him talking just in case he let any details slip that could be used
against him. We had been recording our calls and sharing them with the
police. I knew his calls were important in helping the investigators build
any kind of case against him.

"What happened to your Pocatello attorney?" I asked, calmly.

"I fired him," B said. "I wouldn't have served any jail time if he'd done
things right." I was almost beside myself. Where was he hiding Jan, I
wondered, and was Gail in on it, or was she just scared and manipulated
by him like I had been?

"I want you and Bob to come down and meet with my new attorney—to discuss this with him."

At this point, I wanted to scream, but I managed to keep my voice
even. "Do you think we're crazy? Whatever is going on, we won't be a part
of it."

"You want her back, don't you?" he threatened. "You wouldn't listen
when I tried telling you what Jan wanted. I told you she needed some help
because she was so mixed up. Now look at what's happened." He was so
cunning, obviously trying to put the blame on me and Bob.

Doing everything I could to hold my temper, I said, "B, just get Jan
back home. That's all we want."

"She's pretty determined about this marriage thing," he said again, sighing deeply "I have a solution, but it will freak you and Bob out." I braced myself for what he would say next.

"We could go to a justice of the peace in a small Utah town, and with your consent, we could do it very quietly. No one would even need to know. It might be the only way to get her to agree to come home. I know you're going through pure hell not knowing where she is."

I was very disturbed by his suggestion, and I slammed down the receiver. I couldn't handle his crazed determination to marry Jan. I hoped that anything he said could be used as evidence of a blackmail plot and that the law could charge him. I told Detective Shail about the call so he would know to listen to the recording.

Pete stopped by to listen to the recording. "He's clever. Until Berchtold actually shows some kind of written document, there's no legal proof he's intending to marry Jan," he said, discouraged. "He's smart enough to know how the law works. In order to avoid any legal responsibility, he's putting all the blame on Jan, hoping she will go along with the runaway story."

Detective Shail agreed. "At this point, it would be hard to prove in court that he is coercing her into marriage. He obviously has a plan, but we still don't know where Jan is, and we don't want to jeopardize her safety."

Bob agreed. "He wants us to get so desperate to get Jan back that we would give our permission to let them marry. I won't ever do that, no matter what the outcome."

B was our only link to Jan's whereabouts, and it was still a good advantage for law enforcement to have him on the loose, at least for now. If B felt less threatened, they believed he might take some liberties and talk more freely, hopefully giving something away. If we gave him enough rope, he just might hang himself, they said.

Pete couldn't officially be involved in the case due to our decision to list her as a runaway, but he was still very sympathetic to our dilemma. "Waiting is tough," he said. "He will make a mistake. Keep yourselves busy. That will help."

Thankfully, Detective Shail offered a small shred of hope for Jan's location. "Berchtold closed Jan's checking account at the Jackson State Bank on August 27 and presented the teller a card that bore her signature. Not only that, but a few days earlier he picked up a prescription under the name of Jan Berchtold at the allergy clinic. It seems like he might be getting ready to make a move."

Unable to fathom how devious B could be, I asked, "What are you saying? Is she now nowhere near Jackson Hole? That would be hard to believe. Where could he possibly leave her while he is there?"

Catholic School
August 20, 1976

Jan looked anxiously out the attic window and watched cars pass down the street. B said he would be in a rental car because he had flown in. She peered at each passing vehicle with anticipation. *We're going to some fancy hotel when he gets here,* she thought. At last, a car stopped in front of the house. As she strained to see who it was, she recognized B climbing out of the driver's seat. Her eyes filled with tears, and she grabbed her small bag and bounded down two flights of stairs to the main floor.

He greeted the Black family and turned just in time to catch Jan as she flew into his arms. "Hi, Dolly," he said. She was so grateful to see a familiar face. The stress of all this was getting to her. He bent down and hugged her. "How's my girl doing?" he asked, looking into her eyes.

"I think she's happy you're here," Mrs. Black said. "She's been rather quiet and lonely."

B thanked them for their help in protecting his daughter and taking care of her. Jan trembled as she thanked each of them for their kindness. B and Jan quickly departed. Jan was so happy to be safe with B. She kept telling him how relieved she was that he was there now.

"It's so good to see you too," B said. "You don't know what a hard week it has been. It's been a worry having you stay with people you didn't know. What a trooper you are!"

"When am I going home, B?" Jan asked anxiously. B shook his head and confessed, "Not for a while. Things haven't worked out yet with your parents. We need to talk. I've been working on some things, and you're going to have to stay in California for now."

Jan became emotional, "I don't want to be gone from home any longer."

"Let's go get a bite to eat, and we'll talk about it," B said in a comforting voice. Then he added, "It will only be a while longer. I want you home too. I hate having you here when I'm so far away, and I'm not going back until I know you're safe."

Homesick

In the hotel room the next morning, B woke up early and was startled to see that Jan was not in the bed. He had told her the plan about going to Sacred Heart Academy, and he was worried how she would take it. Panicked, he scanned the room and saw her curled up in a chair near the window.

"What's the matter?" he asked.

"I couldn't sleep," she said. "I've just been thinking."

He went and knelt beside her. "About what?" he asked.

"About school and pretending to be Catholic."

"Oh, I see," he said.

"I can't be Catholic. All that stuff—the rosary, catechism, confirmation, confession. I don't know what they're talking about. I don't want to go!"

B had told her his scheme, but had avoided discussing the details of how Jan would disguise herself in her new environment. It was evident that she was nervous and upset about having to pretend. She was very unsure how she could talk about Catholic things as if she actually knew about them.

"Oh, Jan. It wasn't supposed to be like this. I would take it all away if I could, but Zada insists that you must do this until Bob gives in. You have to do what they say. Please, honey, you've got to go through with this."

"I want to go home." She started crying. "I don't want to go to a Catholic school. This is stupid. I'd rather be dead than have to do this."

"Don't talk like that!" B said. He tried to gather her into his arms, but she struggled to free herself.

"I'm not a little kid," she protested.

"It's going to be okay, Jan. Believe me. It'll just take time, and I know it won't be that long. If Bob and MaryAnn knew why you wanted to marry me, they wouldn't hesitate for a minute."

"Then tell them!" Jan blurted out.

"You know what would happen if I told them. Nobody can know—at least not yet. Could you really stand to see those terrible things happen to your sisters? I know how much you love them both. Can you imagine Karen being blinded or Susan being taken, and going through all of this or even worse?"

Jan closed her eyes as her body trembled. "No," she whispered.

"Please be patient! It will all work out for the best. We must believe in the plan and do everything we've been told." B drummed his fingers nervously on the arm of the chair while he watched Jan's disappointed reaction.

To help Jan calm down and feel safe, he said, "I've got something else to tell you."

"You're not supposed to know, but one of the Catholic Sisters is in on the plan with us and will be looking out for you. She is the reason you are going there."

Startled, Jan questioned, "What? One of them? Who?"

"I don't know which one," he said. "Dolly, don't be frightened. Whoever it is, she will be on our side. These nuns are women who have devoted their lives to God."

"Is she like Zada?" Jan asked.

"Oh, I really don't know," B said. "This sister has a different job than Zada. Just remember, when anybody asks, tell them that your mother died and that I am your father. You will be safe at the school until it's over. I promise. I've never lied to you, have I?"

Jan turned away from him. She wanted to ask questions about having the special baby. Would they be able to raise the child? Would the baby be taken away from them? However, she was too exhausted and distraught to talk.

B knew Jan needed cheering up. He thought for a moment, and then he jumped up from the chair and said cheerfully, "Hey, we should go to the beach today and get some more of that golden sunshine. You've got the beginning of a beautiful tan, and it looks ravishing on you. We won't have to think about anything else except having a good time." He crossed the room to where she was standing, pulled her face up to his, and kissed her.

Jan grunted and rolled her eyes upward.

"Stop worrying. It's going to be fine," he said. "Come on—let's go!"

The beach was crowded and hot. Jan was buried up to her neck in sparkling sand, with sunglasses covering her eyes. It was clear she was trying to block out all of her fears.

B leaned in and said, "I hate to see our day end, honey, but I have to drive all the way back to Utah tomorrow and then go back up to Jackson Hole. It's time to close up the fun center."

Jan remained motionless. B studied her exposed face, examining every feature. "Hell, you're beautiful. I love all those cute little freckles across your tiny nose." He rubbed his finger softly across her nose and cheeks. "And those high cheekbones are just like your mother's. Why did God make you so perfect?"

Jan closed her eyes and remained immobile. B carefully pulled the sunglasses away from her eyes and blew the sand off her face. "Look at those eyelashes—so long, dark, and simply wonderful. If our children look like you, they will be awesome."

Why did he say that? she thought angrily. Jan shook off the sand and stood up. "I'm ready to go, now!" Picking up her beach bag, she marched quickly towards the dressing room.

Realizing that his impulsive words had set her off, B backpedaled. "Jan! I shouldn't have placed that burden of thinking about our children on you. I wasn't thinking. You've got enough to worry about. I'm sorry. Wait, I'm coming!"

Ignoring his apologies, Jan entered the dressing room and changed out of her swimsuit and into a pair of pink shorts and a top B had bought her on their shopping spree.

At the car, he again begged for her forgiveness.

They were both quiet as they began the ride to Flintridge. Jan peered out the window while they traveled the mountainous road toward the school.

The beautifully landscaped Flintridge campus, sprawling across fifty-two acres of canyons and semi-developed terrain, crowned a peak of the San Rafael Hills. The Spanish-style buildings that housed the sisters and students had once been the Flintridge Biltmore Hotel. On top of the hill was a library and an auditorium. The campus, surrounded by small cottages, contained a swimming pool, tennis courts, and a music department. The entire grounds were enclosed and protected by security guards and fences.

A large green canopy sheltered the marble steps in front of the building. Jan climbed the steps, wondering what she would experience beyond the doors. As they walked into the foyer, a sister scurried to greet them. She identified herself as Sister Ignacious. Jan's only exposure to the Catholic Sisters had been when she played Gretel in *The Sound of Music*—and those nuns weren't real. It was a relief not to feel threatened by this warm greeting. B bantered with the nuns as if they were old friends. He joked about the wolf someone had said roamed the hillside. "I almost changed my mind about bringing my daughter to this untamed territory," he teased.

After the introductions, Sister Charlotte took them on a tour of the grounds. "Students come here from around the world. We have students from fifteen foreign countries who live on campus—and others are day students from the immediate neighborhoods, such as Pasadena and Glendale. Sister

Charlotte explained that "the girls build strong and enduring personal friendships with both faculty and students. Some of our students are motherless, so the sisters are accustomed to being mother, friend, and tutor, as well as teacher." Sister Charlotte paused as she realized her words might have been a bit upsetting for "Janis" due to the recent loss of her own mother.

Seeing no signs of distress from the young girl, she continued: "At Flintridge, there is a special emphasis on fine arts. The drama teacher is an actress who has done tours and even had some starring roles. The music department is outstanding as well, attracting especially gifted students."

Excitement welled up within Jan. *Someday, I'm going to be an actress,* she thought. *B said being here would require the finest performance of my life. He's going to help me get in a movie. Wow! I might like it here after all.*

"Janis, you will be staying in one of the cottages with me and a sweet girl from China, Jacinta Lobo, just until school starts. Then you both will move into the dorms. Jacinta is a fine musician, and I hear you are too."

B graciously thanked Sister Charlotte, telling her he would bring Janis on Tuesday afternoon before he left for Washington, DC. Having the chance to look over the campus and learn about the opportunities that awaited made Jan an excited chatterbox for the remainder of the day.

"Isn't Flintridge everything I told you?" B said, enthusiastically. "You're going to love it. Now let's celebrate. I'm taking you to the Hollywood Wax Museum, then to the Chinese Theatre, and then we'll have a special romantic dinner."

"But B," Jan said, "I don't know anything about Catholics. You've got to help me."

"I will, but not today," he said. "Today, we're going to have the time of our lives."

The First Day at the New School
August 24, 1976

As B pulled the car up to the entrance of the school, Jan was feeling anxious about her first day. The thought of facing a totally new and foreign environment was so frightening to her that she could hardly breathe.

Downplaying her fears, B flattered her, "Do you know how incredible you are? Relax. I know you can do this—for us—and for them. The only thing you need to remember is that you are Janis Tobler. The sisters won't be hard on you because I told them you're having a tough time coping with the death of your mother. Okay? I can't tell you enough how much I love you. This is going to kill me—leaving you like this."

"I know," Jan said quietly after taking a deep breath. "Don't worry. Do what you have to do."

"What a girl," B said, taking her hand and kissing it. "I love you," he whispered passionately. After a few searching looks for her approval, he opened the car door and jumped out, motioning Jan to slide across the seat to exit through his door. He removed two small bags of new clothes from the trunk. Because the students wore uniforms to class, Jan didn't need much other than underwear, socks, shoes, and pajamas.

With Jan standing beside Sister Charlotte, B repeated how sorry he was to leave. "Take good care of my daughter," he said. Then, after planting a friendly parental kiss on Jan, he strode confidently to his car. The clanging of the security gates closing as he drove away jolted Jan into a somber mood.

Thankfully, Jacinta Lobo was an energetic, bright, and friendly roommate. Her petite form and dark features fit the image Jan had envisioned. What she didn't expect was how caring Jacinta was. Both girls had unusual circumstances that brought them to Flintridge early. They had two weeks to build their friendship before other students arrived.

Rosary Beads

Jan studied up on Catholicism, and Jacinta practiced the piano. Jan was a good piano player, but Jacinta was much more advanced. *She must either practice hours every day to be so good, or she's a prodigy,* Jan thought.

Each morning, the girls attended worship services. Before long, Jan was proficient at reciting the rosary and other prayers. The ritual of crossing herself became a habit, although it never felt natural. After they finished their studies and chores, the girls played tennis, swam, and relaxed in the outdoor gardens as they talked about girl stuff.

Jan avoided talking about herself, and Jacinta never probed, even though Sister Ramona had told Jacinta about Janis's mother's recent death and her terrifying escape from Laos. Jacinta's impeccable manners would never allow her to press for more information. Jacinta's English wasn't perfect, which gave Jan the opportunity to help her. Jan's focus on her new friend took away some burden from her own pain, although she missed Caroline and her sisters so much.

Jan's Diary, August 26, 1976:

I miss my wonderful parents. I wish I could tell them how very thankful I am for them. My mom, for doing so much for me, for having patience with me, for loving me, for teaching me how to be a good person. For our wonderful talks. I really love her. I'm thankful for my dad because of all he did for me, for providing for me, loving me, teaching me Christ's gospel, and helping me make decisions. And for the time he spends with me. Even when I act mad at him, he says his funny sayings: "I'n it great?" "Every day's a bonus!" "Life is good." If I didn't have my parents, I couldn't live. They've got to understand and let me come back.

Weight of the World

Nights were most difficult for Jan. They had a strict curfew, and Jan was a night owl. Jan had a hard time turning off her thoughts about home and her future. It was usually then that her tears began flowing. The first time Jacinta heard Jan sobbing; she was taken by surprise. She got out of bed, knelt by Jan's bedside, and gently patted her back. After the crying subsided, Jan asked Jacinta, "Do you ever get so lonely for your family that you can't stand it?"

Jacinta replied, "When I feel bad, I blow my troubles to the wind. That makes me feel better."

"Sometimes I feel as if I want to die," Jan said. "I don't think I can handle feeling like this." She wept as her new friend placed her soft hand on her face and comforted her.

"Tomorrow we will go to the top of the hill and throw all our troubles away. You will feel better. Okay, little Janis?"

"Okay, Jacinta," Jan whispered. "Thank you for being such a good friend. I need you." Jan threw her arms around Jacinta and hugged her. "I'm feeling better already."

Guilt was overwhelming Jan for many reasons. She didn't feel right about the sexual interactions she had been having with B. She had also been taught all her life that her body was sacred and that it was a sin for anyone to touch her private parts. B had taught her a few things in Mexico, but even with her breasts undeveloped, B still caressed and kissed them. It felt good sometimes, but mostly she felt bad because it was wrong and made her uncomfortable. B kept telling her that this was the plan and that someday it would be time to make the baby. All of her friends were having their periods, but she hadn't started yet. *Maybe that was because she was half alien*, she thought.

She wasn't ready to be a mother, but the aliens had told her that the rules on their planet were different from those on Earth.

Chapter 15
OVERWHELMING GRIEF

August 23, 1976

Since school was to begin soon, I called the principal and told him Jan would not be coming. I couldn't discuss the situation with him, but I asked him to pass the news on to the drill team adviser. Principal Soderquist wished Jan well and said, "She will be missed. Jan is a good student, and she is well-liked by both teachers and her classmates. I am so sorry for your troubles." Later, I wondered if he thought it was odd that we never requested Jan's transcripts or school records.

Keeping the matter of Jan's disappearance secret would be challenging since it had been imperative to let family and close friends know. Since this was a high-profile case, if anyone spoke about it, word of her absence could spread like wildfire, which would botch confidentiality and potentially endanger Jan.

Karen faced questioning daily from Jan's peers. Where was she? Why wasn't she in school? Why was she not at the drill team's practices?

Karen remained loyal to our decision and answered, "Jan is staying with my Grandma Buck. She'll be home soon." Among her friends, only Caroline knew the truth, and she admirably kept the confidence well.

On the first day of September, I had a surprise visitor—Gail. She had just delivered her ex-husband to the county jail for his fifteen day sentence. That was hardly justice for kidnapping Jan nearly two years ago.

"Have you heard from Jan?" I asked hopefully.

Gail's demeanor was cool and distant. She emphatically replied, "No, but I've come to pick up the sewing machine B gave Jan for her birthday. It was very expensive, and I could use it."

"Gail, I'm sorry, but I'm not returning anything B has given Jan until she is back home. You tell him that," I said.

I was determined not to give even an inch to B, and I was sorry he continued to manipulate his ex-wife.

Fifteen Days Gone

After B was released from the Pocatello Bannock County Jail on September 16, I desperately wanted to follow him. I felt certain he would visit Jan. It was an irrational thought with our private investigator watching him, but I needed to do something. I persuaded Bob to go with me to Salt Lake City. Spying on B might be the only way to find Jan.

B was employed as a salesman for an arcade-and-pinball-machine investor. He worked in a building that was in a rundown and rather sketchy area—a sharp contrast to the beautiful Visitors Center and Tabernacle located in the heart of Salt Lake City's Temple Square. Parking on the street near the building, I hoped to find activity at the business, but it was Saturday. The business was closed.

Our next stop was at the Salt Lake City International Airport. As Bob drove around the parking lot, I noticed Gail's green Station Wagon. Pulling into a vacant space, Bob cautioned me to be careful. I went over to the car, tried the door, and found it unlocked. Waving to Bob, I got in. On the seat was an entry ticket into the parking lot, dated to September 19, 1976. My heart raced with anticipation. *He's gone to see Jan,* I thought.

I looked around in the car a little more and then went back to report to Bob, "According to the parking ticket, he came in here yesterday at 11:18 a.m. I also found a receipt from Mountain West Distribution showing the purchase of a JVC TV/radio yesterday."

"Undoubtedly, another gift," Bob said. "Let's go in and check airline schedules."

"If he left yesterday, I doubt he'll come back today," Bob stated. After collecting airline schedules, we returned to the motel.

I stayed up late studying each schedule, anxious to figure out a destination. I worked through a dozen different scenarios. Would Jan be harmed if B felt threatened? We spent Sunday at the airport watching passengers get off various flights. Bob was at one end of the airport, and I positioned myself at the other. Becoming weary of watching arrivals, we decided to talk with ticket agents. "We're trying to find out if a relative is on this next flight. Would you mind checking your passenger list for Robert Berchtold? What about Frank Farr? Hank Hutchinson? Bobby Tobler? Jan Broberg?" Several of the congenial agents let us scan their lists. To our disappointment, neither person was listed by any name we knew on any incoming flights.

"We can't watch every flight, dear. And what can we do if we do find B, unless Jan is with him? There is little chance of that," Bob explained.

I knew we needed to pick up our girls at my mother's house and then go home. Reluctantly, we returned to our car. The green station wagon was still in the parking lot. With heavy hearts, we left the airport knowing B would return and that we would not be there to catch him.

Jan's Diary, September 12, 1976:

B brought me this tiny TV radio, but I'm not allowed to watch TV in my dorm. I sneak it under the covers so I can watch Charlie's Angels and Love Boat. I love Farrah Fawcett; she reminds me of Karen— she'd be her. I'd be the one with long brown hair, and Susie would be the angel with short hair. I wonder what Sister Ilene would think if she saw the antenna? An alien invasion? Jacinta thinks it's cool and laughs at me. Hah! Hah!

179

On the day Jan had been reported as a runaway, a private eye had seen her name on the police log and called us. The police were already investigating, so we hadn't felt his services were necessary. But as time passed on with no clues, desperation had changed our minds, and we hired him.

After he had been on the job for ten days, we asked for an accounting of his work. His information coincided with what the police had reported. He believed Jan was hiding out in Ogden, Utah, disguised with heavy makeup. Really? That was it? That tipped me off that he was inexperienced. We terminated our agreement. He tried to overcharge us, but after some negotiation, he accepted a check for what we all agreed was an okay amount. Bob and I were getting stronger at standing up for ourselves and for each other.

From that moment on, every day became a search for Jan. Knowing Jan's nature, I concentrated on key details of her personality. She had to be busy either in school, theater, or arts and crafts projects.

During the first kidnapping, B had been chagrined because Jan's boredom had centered around her desire to return to school. *Okay,* I thought, *what kind of school and where?* She had to be close but invisible to law enforcement scrutiny. For the next several days, I pored over volumes of telephone directories at the local library, searching for private schools in surrounding states. I mailed many copies of this letter:

> *I am writing to you with an unusual request by asking for your help in locating our missing daughter. We have reason to believe she has been placed in a private school by an individual who claims to be her father. A description of our daughter:*
>
> *Name: Jan Broberg (could be under the alias of Berchtold); Birth date: July 31, 1962; Age: 14; Weight: 85 lbs.; Height: 4'10"; Hair: light brown; School year: 9th grade.*
>
> *She has a sprinkling of freckles across her nose, high cheekbones, a dimple in her chin, and a distinctive bump on the first knuckle of her left-hand ring finger. She is very petite and very active, has a charming personality, loves to act, plays the piano, sings, is bright and*

intelligent, and loves outdoor activities such as swimming, horseback riding, and gymnastics. A picture is enclosed.

As concerned parents, we are most anxious to locate her and would appreciate a collect call from your school should she be enrolled or has inquired about enrollment.

The individual responsible for her disappearance has several aliases. His given name is Robert Ersol Berchtold, alias Frank Farr, Bobby Tobler, and Hank Hutchinson. He has blond, wavy hair and is 5'8" tall, 145 lbs., and 40 years old.

If you have any questions regarding the validity of this request, you may contact the Pocatello Police Department and ask for Detective George Shail.
Thank you for your time.

I mailed several dozen letters, but received only one reply—from the Judson School in Scottsdale, Arizona:

Dear Mr. and Mrs. Broberg,

We received your letter and are in deepest sympathy with your dilemma. I am sorry to inform you that we have had no contact with your daughter. However, we are keeping your address and letter in our files, and if she does come here, we will contact you immediately.

We wish you good luck. Enclosed is the picture of your daughter you sent us.

Sincerely,

Henry G. Wick, Director

B's phone calls became more sporadic, but he always said, "Jan won't come back until you give her permission to marry me."

Our response was consistent: "Sorry but tell Jan that will never happen."

"How can I tell her? I don't know where she is," B said.

"You seem to have more contact with her than we do," I said. "When or if she calls, tell her we miss her desperately, and ask her to please call home."

"I guess it's up to me to find her since you don't seem to give a damn," he declared angrily.

Hope

Bob's excited voice rang through the telephone line on the morning of October 4, 1976, "MaryAnn, guess who Bishop Meyers saw yesterday on his way home from Salt Lake? Berchtold!"

"Okay, so . . ." I said, waiting for more.

"Yeah, well there was a girl sitting on Berchtold's lap." My heart leaped. Bob continued: "Tom was out near the Lagoon Amusement Park with the boys from the church on a youth outing, when B passed their car. A bunch of the kids in Tom's car laughed when they saw a young girl driving, and they made snide remarks about "Old Berchtold" cuddling some young chick.

"So, do they think it was Jan?" I asked.

"No," Bob replied. "Tom said she was small and blond, but she looked younger than Jan, more like age eight or nine. The boys had a better look and made those remarks, and then dropped it. He didn't say anything to the boys since he knows we are keeping everything quiet!"

My rush of adrenaline dissipated with this disappointing news. I groaned and began to cry. "Oh, that sick, perverted idiot. I want to tear his heart out like he's doing to mine. Where is she? What has that creep done with her?" I asked.

"I'm calling Detective Shail," Bob said. "MaryAnn, things are going to be okay—I know it. Just hang on."

Bob, who had been sick in bed with despair, was now beginning to sound positive. Having been hardly able to go to work, he now suddenly became fully engaged in our quest to locate Jan.

My imagination ran wild. Now another young girl is being victimized, and where is my daughter? Thinking the worst, I continued to cry, going from room to room pounding on door casings and verbally beating myself up. Furious, I shouted aloud, "How stupid, blind, and ignorant can one person be! Look at what you've done! You're disgusting. How can you stand yourself? It's your fault, and who's paying for your stupidity? Your innocent daughter!"

Stating my feelings verbally was therapeutic to my soul. Hearing the condemnation aloud reminded me that I was human and was more ready than ever to crush Berchtold and his hold on Jan.

The anguish of having been conned by B weighed so heavily on my mind that I felt I was being suffocated. I was driven to my knees and voiced the most mournful and sorrowful plea I had ever uttered. Full of hostility and resentment, I asked, "Why should Jan be the one suffering? This isn't her fault. How could this happen to her? Why is Jan paying for my awful mistakes? I deserve the punishment, not her! Let me suffer, not her!"

But I wasn't done. I then turned all my hate toward B. I bellowed aloud, "I hate this depraved, deceptive, corrupted liar! He has twisted and distorted everything that was good in my life! He's a devil—a sick monster!" Sobbing uncontrollably, I felt as if my entire lower extremities were being severed. I experienced indescribable physical, emotional, and spiritual agony. If this were justice for a battered soul, would mercy finally follow?

Eventually, my petition changed to submission and humility, and I prayed:

O dear Father in Heaven, what more can I do? Choking with emotion, I pleaded, *Let Jan be safe. Let her come home. Give me another chance to be her mom. Let me continue to teach her and give her the help she needs and the love she deserves. Let her heal and be whole.*

In return, I promised God that I would be more faithful, repentant, devoted, and indebted to Him. At that moment, I remembered Christ's death on the cross and intensely experienced my contribution to His great suffering. Overcome with grief, I sprawled limply on the floor. Lying there, my body heaved sporadically as the sobbing began to subside. My head was pounding so hard that I thought it would explode. It felt huge and out of proportion to my body. I slowly revived. My quivering muscles gradually relaxed. I pulled myself to an upright sitting position and cradled my head for a long time.

I had never done anything like this before. My nature was normally quiet, calm, steady, pragmatic, and levelheaded, but I finally exploded with the same emotional pressure of the horrible unknown and desperation I had often tried to carry Bob and my little girls through. It was a release I had never before fully succumbed to.

Bob came home for lunch and observed a puffy, red-eyed, weak, and subdued wife. Uttering no words, he placed his loving arms tightly around me. In his strong embrace, at this lowest point in my life, I completely recognized my deep feelings of sorrow and loss. I fully experienced my true, deep, and endearing love for Bob, my husband. With his forgiveness and understanding, this giant of a man was my greatest strength. I was in love with him more than ever. I knew we would have our life back. The realization flooded over me. We, our family, would make it—together.

After school, the three boys who had seen B were interrogated at the police station. Detective Shail explained why they were being questioned. He told them that Jan was missing again and that Berchtold was a suspect. "Do any of you think it was Jan Broberg? Just speak up. It's okay. I want to know if you are sure that it wasn't her."

After a brief discussion, one boy thoughtfully contemplated Detective Shail's words and said, "Well, I only saw her from a side view, and I'm not sure. It could have been her. Maybe."

Detective Shail jumped to his feet and asked, "Would you be willing to appear in court with that testimony if we need it?"

The boy nodded.

Detective Shail was excited. His search could now proceed outside the boundaries of Idaho because of what was stated in police records:

"Jan Broberg was sighted in the Salt Lake area on October 3, 1976, in the company of Robert Berchtold."

Detective Shail, insisting on my presence in Utah, asked me to meet him at the local airport before dawn. The breeze was chilly in Salt Lake, and we were met by a police officer who transported us to the downtown station. Pictures, current information, and the history of Berchtold and of Jan's kidnapping were discussed.

After we were finished, the accompanying officer took Detective Shail and me to Ogden, where once again we repeated our story. I furnished the officers with information about B's relationship during the past year. He had been with a divorcée named Stacey, who worked for B's attorney. Shortly after I had ended our affair, B told me that he had found a "poor substitute" for me. He said that since he couldn't stand to be alone, and since I was no longer interested in a life with him, he had to do something. Stacey's daughter, Danielle, was a few years younger than Jan. The Ogden police were eager to "nail this guy" since it had become clear that children in their community were also at risk.

We were driven to the elementary school Danielle attended. After a lengthy discussion of how to get information from other students as to whether they knew Jan, a plan was formulated. A school event was in the planning stages that would require a group of students to be representatives for an inner-school project. Danielle and some other students were escorted to the principal's office, where photos were displayed. Jan's photo was among them. The students were asked to point out photos of students they knew and to indicate who they thought would be a good representative. Danielle was specifically asked if any of the students were friends. Studying the pictures, she passed by Jan's. She returned to class unaware of the intense search for Jan.

The children were out for recess when Detective Shail came out. He pointed to Danielle and asked, "Do you think she could pass for Jan?" I nodded in the affirmative, thinking it was terrible that Danielle was another one of B's targets.

The police now knew that contact had been made with the young girl, and they planned to talk with Danielle's mother to find out what the association was between them and B. Detective Shail concluded that Jan was not, nor had she been, in the area. My stomach was churning. I thought, *If she isn't here, then where was she? What has he done with her?*

The police had obtained a search warrant for Berchtold's apartment, which was searched that day as well, but they only found a book with weird, disjointed writings and few clothes. "Damn it, George," I said to Detective Shail, "why can't we find anything, any reason to put him behind bars?"

Detective Shail replied, "Sorry, MaryAnn. We're going to get the guy. Believe me."

As the plane headed for home, I crowded into my little spot in the back. The whirring engines drowned out the voices. I was in no mood to hear about the successes or failures from the other detectives anyway. I went over the disappointing activities of the day. What a waste! Jan's photograph had been left with several officers, but it all seemed so hopeless. I quietly cried in the back of the plane.

And Hopeless
September 24, 1976

Immediately after my return with Detective Shail, I began pressing Bob for another trip to Salt Lake. Just maybe, I dreamed, B was hiding Jan in his apartment. Doing nothing brought me exhausting anxiety.

I often stood alone at the dining room window when the rest of the family was in bed, staring into the dark, unfriendly world, wondering about my little girl. Silently, I would pray that she knew how much we loved her—unconditionally—and that we missed her desperately.

Bob was scheduled to attend a wholesaler's holiday open house in Salt Lake City the next week, and I was determined to go too. My jogging partner, Karlene, helped me work out a disguise. I borrowed her blond wig, a loose-fitting blouse, a long skirt, round-rimmed reading glasses, and funky shoes. "Oh, Karlene, am I nuts? Don't answer that—we are doing this!"

Undeterred, we were off. We dropped Bob off at his Open House. He hugged us and told us to be safe and not to do anything stupid. Susan, Karen, and I headed for the apartment complex. Seeing B's Lincoln Continental parked near the entry made my blood turn cold.

Information gleaned from Detective Shail indicated that B lived with an artist named Lydia, whom he had met in Jackson Hole.

Jan had mentioned her once, stating that she was a "large lady and really nice."

I practically jumped out of my skin when I saw him come out of the building. The girls were frightened and ducked down, but I wanted to observe what he was doing. He was moving something from the back seat of his car into the trunk. I had binoculars, but my view was hampered by trees and cars.

He raced out of the lot. Susan volunteered to go in and find apartment 201. I told her that if she wasn't out in three minutes, I would come in after her. Susan ran into the building. Karen looked at me with alarm. I blurted out, "Hurry, Susie, and get out of there!"

Within minutes, she was racing back down the sidewalk. "I found it!" she said breathlessly. "I listened at the door and could hear *Gilligan's Island* on TV."

"Maybe it's Jan! We watch *Gilligan's Island* every day!" said Karen.

"And he's gone to get them a treat," I surmised. "I'm going in."

"Mom, we don't want anything to happen to you," Karen exclaimed. Confidently, I placed the blond wig over my dark hair and positioned the glasses on my nose. "How do I look, girls?"

"Weird," Susan said. Karen agreed.

A man leaving his apartment looked strangely at me. I nodded when I reached the end of the hall. I exclaimed, "Whoops! Wrong floor," and started walking back toward him. He went down the stairs and out the door. I turned around and put my ear to B's apartment door. I thought I heard someone moving around inside. I quickly retreated down the hall. A few minutes later, I crept back and listened, but only heard silence. As I hurried down the walkway toward the car, I ducked to avoid a low branch, but I didn't stoop low enough and I felt the wig leave my head. I looked up and saw it dangling on the tree. I quickly retrieved it and dashed to the car to find my daughters laughing hysterically. I, too, began to chuckle as I thought of my ridiculous charade.

"Well, do you think the FBI will hire me as an undercover agent?" I asked.

"Only for comedy," Karen answered.

"What did you do in there, Mom?" Susan questioned.

"Not much. I don't think Jan is living here. Let's go find your father."

Back home, we tried to make the best of life. Detective Shail encouraged me to keep taking Berchtold's phone calls and have him talk as much and as long as possible.

Pete Welsh checked in most days and reminded us how much time it takes for a criminal to feel comfortable enough to begin taking chances. Pete suggested that we might want to consider hiring a local retired FBI agent who could spend quality time every day checking on Berchtold.

Vern Jensen was a handsome, silver-haired man in his mid-sixties who exhibited a kindly and unassuming demeanor. He made no loud acclamations about his life, service, or accomplishments. His firm handshake and warm smile gave us the assurance that he could do the job. As a family man with grown children, and now as a grandfather, this crime was intolerable to him.

Bob and I were honest about our limited finances, but Mr. Jensen preferred a "gentleman's agreement" that would require no contract, and we could pay at our convenience. He would call us when he had anything of importance. He emphasized patience.

"Berchtold is a man with a criminal mind, and he has taken a great deal of time plotting out this scheme. He's no fool," Mr. Jensen said.

Vern Jensen's approach to investigation was methodical. He warned us not to expect quick results, but he assured us that he would be thorough.

Point of Desperation
October 3, 1976

I received a phone call and heard B's excited voice, "I have some vital information on Jan. One of my connections told me he saw her."

"What did he say?" I asked skeptically.

"I know you have this phone bugged, and I'm not telling you anything except in person. Meet me at the Crossroads Café today."

"I don't think so," I said, unsure.

"Too bad. It's something you should know," B declared.

"Okay, I'll have Bob come with me."

"MaryAnn, you either come alone or not at all. I don't want Bob there."

Without hesitation, I replied, "Fine."

"Crossroads Café. Two o' clock, today—alone."

I called Bob and relayed Berchtold's message. Determined to hear what he had to say, I insisted I was going. Bob tried to talk me out of it. "Call Pete. Let him advise you."

Pete came by to listen to the recording. "Are you afraid for your life?" he asked.

"No, he won't harm me. Something's on his mind, and I want to know what."

"I don't think you should go alone. He's a pathological liar. No one knows his state of mind."

"Pete, I have to go. Even if it's all a lie, I have to hear what he has to say. It's been ten weeks with no word about Jan. What if he really does know where she is and is willing to tell me? I guess I'm hanging on to any little hope."

Pete understood my desperation, "MaryAnn, you're not going un-armed. Do you think you could use a gun to preserve your own life, if necessary?"

I wavered. "I don't know." Then, realizing what was at stake, I confidently replied, "Yes, I could."

Pete then instructed me to go down to his office.

I immediately called Bob and told him what I was doing. He wasn't pleased.

I argued, "B might drop some hint. I'll stop by before I leave. I'm going to call my mom to tell her I'm coming. Randy can be in the parking lot as my hidden protector."

My youngest brother, Randy, lived in Tremonton, just two miles from the Crossroads Café.

"Mom, could you call Randy and see if he can drive over to the Cross-roads parking lot? I would feel a lot safer if I knew someone was watching."

When I went to the FBI office, Pete placed a small handgun in my palm before asking, "Have you ever used a gun before?"

I nodded, explaining that I had shot a rifle at a target range many years before, but not a handgun.

After a quick demonstration of how to use it, Pete told me, "Keep your bag unzipped and your hand near the opening. If Berchtold moves threateningly toward you, use it."

I gulped.

"I never tell people it's okay to shoot another person, but I know this guy could wipe you out. I'll be responsible for legalities afterward. I want you safe."

Feeling determined, I placed the gun in my purse.

He gave a reassuring grin. "Call when you get back home, and I'll come by."

I stopped in at the shop briefly. I hugged Bob reassuringly and reminded him to pick up the girls. Then I hurried out the door.

Tremonton, Utah, on the Idaho-Utah border, is a farming community, and the Crossroads Café was the most popular coffee shop in the area. It attracted not only local farmers, but also long-haul truckers and many road travelers. The café was situated on a dangerous two-lane stretch of highway.

The day was overcast and gloomy, and when sudden fall or winter storms blanketed the area, the Malad Pass was treacherous. I didn't expect my visit with B to be lengthy, and I hoped to be home before dark.

B was waiting in the parking lot when I arrived. I briefly remained in my car as I scanned the lot to find my brother. There were several pickup trucks parked around the café, but I didn't see Randy's car.

I nervously picked up my purse, clutched it tightly, and got out of my car. B approached me and cordially asked, "How are you, MaryAnn?"

"Not so great," I coldly replied. He disgusted me.

"Well, I'm half-crazy worrying about Jan. Let's go in and sit down. I'd like a piece of pie," he said, as he motioned toward the café.

I was relieved because I didn't think anything bad would happen if we were around a group of people. I noticed B nervously looking over the customers. We found a booth near the door. I ordered a soda; he had apple pie.

Our exchange was guarded. He wasn't ready to reveal anything until he had scrutinized the situation. He questioned what we had done about finding Jan, and he asked if the police or FBI were involved. I knew our local authorities hadn't been in touch with him, so he was clueless. I wanted it to stay that way.

"I've told you before that we reported Jan as a runaway and were told it was put over the police wire service. That's all we know. The police said runaways are not actively sought by local law officers. They are generally found when they get in trouble or turn up dead. We have no other leads. I'm hoping you have some news."

"I do, but I won't talk in here," B said in a low tone. "It's Bob's fault that she left. If he'd given his permission for Jan to marry me, we wouldn't be going through this."

"Bob did what was best for Jan," I said.

The contemptuous look he gave me was unnerving. Stubbornly, he persisted. "This is about Jan! She will never come home until Bob gives in. What a stubborn, hardheaded fool! He's always been selfish."

I studied the hateful look in his eyes, but sat quietly, not giving him any ammunition to take shots at my husband.

"I should have finished that bastard off when I had the chance," he remarked through clenched teeth.

My heart skipped a beat as I heard his admission. I stared at him without moving a muscle.

He continued, "I was in that parking garage the morning he went to do his flowers—for his own funeral. Ha! My gun was pointed straight at him. Let's go out to my car. I won't talk in here about Jan. What I heard won't be easy for you." He threw some money on the table and walked out the door.

I felt panic. What does he intend to do when I get in his car? What if he drives off? No matter what, this was the reason I had come. I picked up my purse and thought about Pete's instructions. If I had to, did I have the guts to use the gun? B's confession had left me shaking.

Unlocking his flashy red-and-white Mark IV, B told me to get in. Sitting with my purse on my lap, I nervously fidgeted with the zipper until I realized that might be drawing B's attention. The thought occurred that he could grab my purse and use the gun on me. Turning my attention to him, I listened intently.

He said, "I don't know where she is, but I've been told she is living in a commune with a lot of other people."

"Where?"

"I said I didn't know," he answered, irritated. "He wouldn't tell me."

"Who wouldn't tell you?" I asked anxiously. "Some guy Jan knows. He lives in this place where she's living. She asked him to contact me. He said he doesn't want the law investigating their place. It sounds like illegal activities are going on."

"Like what?" I asked.

B bit his lip. He had a worried look on his face, and then he slowly began to relate what he said he knew. "He told me Jan is . . . shooting herself up." He paused, carefully taking his time.

"What are you saying, B? Jan's a druggie? Jan—who hates needles and can't stand having a shot?"

Trying to be emotional, he whimpered, "I know it sounds crazy, MaryAnn. It's the last thing I ever expected. Somehow, I've got to get her out of there."

"So, what's your plan? You don't even have a clue as to where she is. And how can you believe this guy?"

B began to fidget. My hand moved to the purse opening. I carefully placed my hand near the open zipper. My heart was beating fast. Frantically, I thought, *Don't do anything stupid, B. I don't think I can do this.*

B played with his keys, turning them over and over in his hand. "I haven't worked this out yet, but I have an idea she is in Montana."

"Oh!" I said, startled.

He went on. "I've spent a lot of money trying to find her. Hell, I'm about broke. I found out that there's a commune somewhere in Montana that's run by a group of hippies. I'm going to spend some time looking into it."

I tried to appear gullible to his stratagem, but inwardly, I was enraged, thinking how horrible he was to lie to my face.

"It didn't have to end this way," B said. "It could have been different, but Jan is as stubborn as Bob. My biggest fear is that some creep is taking advantage of her when she's high."

I studied him carefully, thinking he was putting on a very poor performance for a man who I believed had already robbed my little girl of her innocence. His ploy to deceive me was over, but I could not confront him—yet.

"Anything else?" I inquired.

"No. I hope to hell this guy was lying. Do you think he was?"

"I don't know." I relaxed and opened the door.

"Will you call me if you have any news?" I asked.

B smiled, "You can count on it."

I drove two miles to my mother's home, watching carefully for any sign of B. A pickup truck that pulled out of Crossroads when I did was following me at a reasonable distance. After circling the block once, with no truck behind me, I pulled into my mother's carport. A minute later, Randy came to the back door and said, "Mike Westmorland gave me his truck, and I just dropped him off."

I replied, "Oh, that was you following me then!" I related everything to Mom and Randy before calling Bob to let him know I was safe.

"I about had a heart attack when you got into Berchtold's car," Randy said. Then, with a twinkle in his eye, he added, "Mike had a rifle in his truck, and we wondered if we should shoot out his tires. But we decided that we would follow you if he took off. I'm glad you didn't go anywhere."

"I'm relieved this is over," I said.

Chapter 16
GRASPING AT STRAWS

October 20, 1976

"I can't tell you how I got this but look at Berchtold's phone bill for the months of June, July, and August—an enormous amount." Detective Shail pointed out the numerous calls that had been made to our personal number from Jackson. I acknowledged that he had called often, but there had also been calls made to other numbers, many of them pay phones.

"Now look at all the collect calls he received from Pocatello. Most of them were made from pay phones," Detective Shail declared. "How would you like to pay his phone bill every month?"

Nearly every day there had been one call placed and some days there had been two or three. Detective Shail identified the locations of the calls from phone booths on Center Street, the Mini-Dome, a gas station, and a trailer court. It was staggering.

"I wonder how many of these calls Jan was involved in," I said curiously.

"Who knows? But I suspect most of them. None of the calls were long, just often. You can tell when you guys went on vacation, but the day you got back, they started again. What kind of an influence does this guy have on your daughter?"

I shook my head, wondering the same thing. "What are these other calls?" I asked, pointing to numbers with area codes.

"I don't know. Call them and find out," Detective Shail suggested. Handing me the list, he issued a stern warning: "If anyone finds out you have this, it could mean trouble. I'm not about to lose my job or retirement over this little piece of paper. Swear you will not let anyone else know you have it."

I nodded. "I promise."

I immediately began calling the unfamiliar numbers. One number, from Oregon, turned out to be a game machine company with a message giving business hours. I was disappointed.

A few days later, I brought the list out again and called another number. This one was from Arizona. The results were the same—another game business. I thought they were all businesses, so I thought I would try each one to satisfy my curiosity. My third try was a call to California. A lady with a mature, strong Eastern accent answered. "Mary Mount," she said.

Blood rushed wildly to my brain, and I felt faint. "Pardon me—what did you say?" I asked excitedly.

"This is Mary Mount. May I help you?" the voice stated.

"Uh, yes! Are you a school?" I was flustered and felt a warm flush on my face.

"Yes, we are a Junior College."

"May I ask where you are located?"

"Los Angeles," the person replied.

"Oh!" was my startled remark.

"Is there something I can do for you?"

"Well, I'm not sure. I'm looking for someone, but I don't know if this is the right place. Can I call you back?" I didn't know what to say, and I needed to gather my thoughts.

"Certainly. Call back anytime."

"I need your name, please."

"Sister Patricia Irene."

With that reassurance, the conversation ended. The news was exhilarating! Filled with anticipation, I could hardly speak as I dialed Bob to give him this overwhelming piece of good news.

"Call Vern," he shouted excitedly.

When I called, Mrs. Jensen reported that her husband was in Salt Lake City. "Let me call his motel and leave word for him to call you."

My stomach was in my throat all day. After a while, Vern called. As I related my discovery, he cautioned me, "Don't you make one more phone call. Promise me. I'm coming home, and we'll talk tomorrow."

I was elated. It was the renewal I needed to keep my sanity.

I broke my promise to Detective Shail when I revealed the phone numbers to Vern, but I told him I couldn't tell him the source. Vern smiled and assured me it wasn't necessary.

"Be patient. This will take some time to investigate." He did not give us any clues of what he would do or how he would do it, but he simply provided assurances. "Don't get your hopes too high," he cautioned.

Vern kept us informed by simply stating that the investigation was proceeding and his contacts in California were handling the situation very cautiously. Days later, Vern reported personally. His kind eyes expressed disappointment. "Jan wasn't there, but don't be discouraged. Law enforcement in California is working with us, and they are continuing to search. We'll find her."

The Phone Call
October 30, 1976

About a week later, I was doing my Saturday cleaning when the phone rang. I hurried to turn on the recorder before picking up the receiver. A strained, quiet voice on the other end of the line said, "Hi, Mom."

"Jan!" I shrieked. "Honey, where are you? Oh, it's so good to hear from you!" I was crying and laughing at the same time.

"Is Karen there?" Jan asked. "I want to talk to Karen."

"No, she's over at Caroline's," I reported anxiously.

"Caroline's?" There was a touch of excitement in her voice.

"Yeah. You know, just doing whatever—not much," I said, trying to be casual. With a lump in my throat, I gushed, "Oh, Jan, we all miss you. How are you? The girls will be sick that they missed your call. Are you okay?"

"I can't talk to you. I have to talk to Karen or Susan." She sounded strained and anxious.

"Susan is over at Cindy's, but she'll be home soon. Honey, I can't stand not knowing where you are—or how you are. All your friends keep asking about you. When are you coming home?" I was trying to keep levelheaded and wanted to be wise in my choice of words.

"I don't know," she said. "I have to talk to Karen or Susan! When do you think they will be home?" She sounded disappointed.

"Really soon. They'll be so sad to know you called and they weren't here." My heart was pounding so hard that I thought it would explode.

"Well, I've got to go now," she said.

I detected a little tremor in her voice. Panic set in. What else could I say to keep her on the line so that the call could be traced? Everything seemed so trivial.

"Jan, are you well? Are you doing okay?" I asked.

"Well, I've got to go. I really wanted to talk to them. Maybe I can call back, but I don't know," she said hesitatingly.

"Yes, honey, call back," I pleaded. "I will have Karen and Susan come right home. They've missed you so much. You've got to call them, okay?"

"If I can—but I don't know. I'll see. Gotta go. See ya."

The phone clicked, and I heard the dial tone.

Surprisingly, I didn't cry. Several emotions overwhelmed me as I sat clutching the receiver. I was stunned, grateful, confused, and exasperated. I stared into space, thinking of every little thing that was said. *Why wouldn't she talk to me? She sounded okay, but not great. Not scared, but sad. Homesick? Maybe, but what if she wasn't?*

I dialed Bob with the news. He was ecstatic. "I'll be right home," he said. I called the Hansen's and spoke to Caroline's father. He offered to bring Karen home.

"Please, let Caroline come," I begged.

The house was soon buzzing as the girls quizzed me about Jan's call. I rewound the tape and urged them to listen for themselves. Shrieks of emotion pierced the room as they listened to Jan's recorded voice.

Bob said, "Okay, that's enough. We can't tie up the recorder in case she calls back right away, so calm down and don't get overly excited. Let's talk about what you're going to say to her."

After sufficient drilling, we huddled around the kitchen table for snacks as we waited. Karen was appointed the official phone answerer. After two and a half hours had ticked away, my faith began to waiver. Bob decided to run back to the flower shop and lock up. He promised to return immediately. The girls felt positive Jan would call back.

The anticipated call finally came, "Hello, Karen? This is Jan! How are ya?"

"Real good. How are you doing?" Karen said with enthusiasm.

"I'm fine." Then, with a quivering voice, she said, "I wanted to call and tell you I love you so much and I miss you so much." She broke down and began to cry.

Jan's emotions sparked Karen's, and she began crying too. "We miss you, too, and love you!"

"I just wanted to call and hear your voice," Jan blurted out.

"Susan's on the other line," Karen said. "She wants to talk to you."

"Huh?" Jan questioned, not sure she heard. "Yeah, it's me! Hi, Jan. How are you doing?" Susan asked.

Jan enthusiastically responded, "Susie! Hi. Just wanted to hear your voice. How's piano going for you?"

"Good. I've started on my festival pieces, and they are hard."

Karen broke in. "Jan, you've got to come home."

"Oh, I want to! I want to come back and visit you so much! It's all up to Mom and Dad right now. Did they get my letter?"

"I don't know! I can ask Mom—she's right here," Karen responded.

"Tell her I sent her a letter, and it has everything in it. It has all my reasons and explains everything. Oh, I sure love you guys. How are you, Susie Q?"

"I'm doing great, but Karen's having trouble in drill team. She needs help. If you were here, you could help her," Susan said. Her comment evoked a spark of interest.

"She needs help in drill team, huh?"

I stood in the background coaching their conversation, whispering to them to ask certain questions.

"Jan, you've been gone a long time. When are you coming home?" Susan said.

"It seems like forever, doesn't it? Well, I'm not going to say right now. I just had to call and tell you—"

Karen interrupted her by telling her the family poodle wanted to say hello. "Here she is with her ear to the phone. Talk to her."

Excitedly, Jan said, "Hi, Tiffy. How are you? Oh, I love you."

Karen said, "Tiff acts like she knows it's you. She's so cute."

"I just want to talk to you guys a minute." Jan paused.

Karen anxiously said, "Don't hang up, Jan. Caroline is here."

"Caroline's there?" Jan squealed.

At that moment, the operator broke into the conversation and said that Jan only had thirty seconds left. Jan was too emotional to let that detail interrupt her. Caroline's exclamation of "Hi, Jan!" brought a response from both girls.

Their weeping as they connected was deafening. The three sisters and best friend created a vivid symphony of sound. I knew at that moment that Jan wanted to be home. Whatever wicked and unscrupulous plan B had devised, he hadn't destroyed the love and devotion she felt to this circle of girls. They were all united, spirit to spirit.

Jan fired off questions to them as rapidly as they did to her. She continued to express her love for each one of them as she repeated over and over, "I love you guys so much. Oh, I'm just so happy."

Again, the operator interrupted the gabfest and asked Jan if she desired to extend the call. Jan enthusiastically exclaimed, "Yes!"

I picked up an extension and tried to listen, but there was so much crying that I couldn't hear what was being said. It was useless to try to calm any of them as they were electrified with their reunion. Their conversation resumed after Jan deposited the needed coins.

Jan asked, "Are you guys all on the phone?"

"Yes!" they blubbered in chorus.

"So am I, Jani!" I joined in.

"How are you, Mom?" she asked.

"Great, honey. I love you."

"I love you too. Did you get my letter?" she inquired.

"No. What letter?" I asked.

"I sent you a letter. It explains a lot of things." Her voice became shaky.

"Um, when did you mail it?" I asked.

"Oh, I don't know," she paused, trying to determine a date. "It should be there pretty soon."

Jan changed the subject, "I had to call and tell you all . . ." She hesitated. "And hear your voices." She was choosing her words carefully.

Karen proudly announced, "Jan, I'm going to drill team every morning. I marched in the homecoming parade."

"I'm so proud of you," Jan exclaimed.

"It was really hard. I had about ten blisters on my feet," Karen said. They all laughed.

"Do you like it?" Jan asked.

"No!" Karen stated emphatically.

"No?" Jan responded. They all chuckled again.

"Everybody misses you. They want you to be their leader. You're the best!" Karen said.

"Well, that's the breaks," Jan replied.

I jumped back into the conversation. "Jani, are you okay? Have you been well? I've been worrying my head off."

"Yes, I'm well. I just miss you all."

"Are you homesick?" Susan asked. "Do you want to come home?"

"Oh yes," she responded enthusiastically. "Sometimes. I'm getting by okay. I just wanted you all to know I love you." Again, it appeared she was weighing her words. "Well, everything's in my letter."

"I wish it would come," I said.

"Relax. You'll be getting it pretty soon."

"What's in it?" I asked.

"Well, I'm not going to discuss much of anything. It's all in the letter."

Annoyed with my persistence, Jan asked other questions. "How's Tiffy? Has her hair grown back yet? Put Caroline back on."

Determined not to let go, I persisted. "Have you seen B lately?"

"I haven't talked to him for a couple of weeks. He wanted me to contact you before I called him."

"Why?" I boldly asked.

"So . . ." she paused. I thought she was being prompted. "I want you to tell him I called. Call him so he knows."

"Why does he need to know?" I asked.

"I don't know. You call him or something and tell him I've called."

"I don't have his phone number. He's never given it to me. He always does the calling. Do you have it?" I asked.

"Well, no I don't."

Abruptly, she directed her next questions to the girls and asked about school. I allowed them to converse as I tried to plan what I should say next. She had just stated that she was going to call B after her contact with us, and then she claimed that she didn't have his number.

Karen and Susan told Jan that they were both getting straight A's and Jan appeared excited for them.

Jan inquired, "Is Dad there?"

"No, he had to go back to work," Susan said.

"He'll be sad he missed you," Karen added.

"Oh, that's okay."

"He misses you and loves you desperately," I blurted out.

Jan wistfully said, "I'm glad to know I'm still loved."

The connection went fuzzy, and we thought the call was over. When it cleared, Jan was trying to figure out where we had gone. She said again, "I just wanted to hear you guys. You sound so good. Just do whatever my letter says. I want to come home and see you so I can be around you. Put Caroline back on. I'm short for time."

Caroline answered her request. "I'm here, Jan."

"Oh good!" They spent a few moments chatting before the operator came back on the line. Jan began saying her good-byes and said, "I'm out of money."

"Can I send you some?" I offered.

"I'm fine. The letter tells every way I feel. Susan, I love you. Keep up your grades."

Susan and Karen expressed their love for Jan and began weeping again.

"I love you too, Karen, Caroline. I love you all," Jan said, sniffing. "Hug Tiff for me."

"Please come home!" I begged.

"I want to! I'm out of money. Gotta go."

"Oh, Jan, Dad just drove in. Can you wait just a half a second?" I pleaded.

"I don't have any money, Mom."

"Do it anyway. Oh, just say hi to him."

Bob excitedly took the receiver, and they exchanged a few words. "It's Jan? Jan? Jan, how are you?"

"I'm fine."

"Oh, are you coming home?"

"Well, you're going to get my letter."

"We need you. We love you so much, and we want you home."

"I'm out of money now. I just wanted to say I love you."

"Oh, Jan, have you talked to B?"

"Not for a couple of weeks."

"Does he still want you to marry him and all that?"

"Well, I want to marry him, Dad."

"Does he want to marry you?"

"Yes, Dad. Give everyone my love."

The girls shouted into the phone, "Jan, come home! We love you! Hurry home!"

"Know my love, and I'll see you later," Jan shouted back as the call terminated.

It was a disturbing note on which to end our conversation. Jan's words echoed in my ear: "I want to marry him."

The mood following the call was solemn, and we had a time of reflection regarding how Jan had sounded, what she had said, and the uncertainty of her overall attitude. The girls expressed valuable opinions.

We continued our discussion about how Jan had seemed at times to be very excited or homesick, but when talking about the letter, her attitude had been quite bold and unfriendly. Bob and I theorized that perhaps she had to be that way for the sake of whoever might have been with her.

Pete contacted Vern Jensen and Detective Shail. A while later, the group arrived at our place. Pete brought with him John McDonough, the area manager of the Mountain Bell telephone company.

Listening to the recording, Detective Shail complained about the girls and their emotional outburst. "Couldn't you make them stop? Girls, listen to how awful you sound. We can't hear what Jan is saying."

"They were so emotional and happy to hear from their sister," I said, defending them.

"It's okay," Pete stated. "We're glad you all got to talk to her."

We all listened intently to the recording. My heart pounded as I again heard Jan's voice. Mr. McDonough scribbled on a piece of paper. At the conclusion, the men conversed, and parts of the recording were replayed. Mr. McDonough took a black book out of his pocket while he listened closely to the sound of coins being dropped into the toll box. He had it played again.

His awareness about the number of nickels, dimes, and quarters deposited was very precise. Taking a large map from his coat, he unfolded it and placed it on the coffee table. With a pen, he drew a large circle on the map, "Based on the amount of money she put in, she has to be somewhere in this area."

The encircled area included parts of six states surrounding Idaho. The spot that stood out to us was Los Angeles. The men continued to speculate over the entire circled area, discussing all possibilities that existed in any of the cities in the circle. B had previously said he had gone to Phoenix, which was in the circle.

Leaning toward the Los Angeles area, the men decided it would be most advantageous to concentrate efforts there. Law enforcement officers had already been contacted, and if that didn't pan out, other cities would be considered.

Jan's Diary, October 31, 1976:

B left today. It's Halloween, and I had a bunch of stuff to do—things with my friends. I got to call home yesterday and talk to everybody.

Even Caroline was there. Everybody was good. I'm homesick to see them all. B had me write a letter to my mom. Hope she doesn't freak out.

Anxiety mounted as we waited for news. Our thoughts ran rampant. Who has her, and do her captors treat her with any dignity?

A week after Jan's call, her letter arrived. At Pete's request, I didn't open it, but called to inform him. The contents would be inspected for fingerprints and analyzed by the agency. Interestingly, the envelope was covered with a blitz of postal stamps from locations around the United States, but none of the stamps had been canceled with a postal stamp by the Post Office. Shaking his head, Pete said, "He must have a string of criminal friends from every state in the Union. This was not sent through the post office." He concluded that it had been passed from hand to hand until someone had dropped the letter in our mailbox.

Later, after being allowed to read the letter, I tossed it aside in disgust. *When did Jan grow into an adult? Does he think we are that naive? Berchtold dictated every word of this to Jan. It's her handwriting, but not her thoughts. He's a devil.*

Dear Mom:

B said he won't talk to me again until I make contact with you, so I am contacting. He said you couldn't understand why I left home, so I'll tell you a few of the reasons.

I was sick to death of putting on the little girl act just because it's what everyone expected of me. Through the whole mess, there was only one thing I could hang on to, and that was B and his love for me. To this very day, I know he would die for me, but more important than that, he's willing to live and endure everything you and the whole world can throw upon him! He'd go through it all for me. I feel that you just want to own and control me. For what reason I can't imagine, so help me God, I can't.

I begged Dad on the phone to let me just have B and be me, but he acted like I was stupid and that the whole thing was a big joke. I've begged B to come and live with me. I couldn't care less about marriage for marriage's sake, but he won't leave his business and family to risk being with me. I want you to know I blame it all on you and your jealousy and hatred. If you could learn only a little bit of the love you always claim to have, you wouldn't do this to me or B.

I would like nothing more than to start a new relationship with you on a woman-to-woman basis. However, I know we will have these good times with or without you and Dad.

Most of all on this earth, I want to be B's wife, and our love, which I know has existed forever, will go on into eternity no matter what you or Dad or anyone else on this earth does to us. I know this more certainly than any other thing in my life.

Please, Mom, please give me the chance I have fought so hard for and given up so much for. I have found a new life here and can find happiness of a sort, but not like I know belongs to me and B and all of you living as sensible people loving and understanding each other.

I haven't meant to hurt anyone now or in the past. But you have left me no choice if I am going to be able to live with myself.

Please do whatever needs to be done so I can return and marry B. I know life can be good for all of us and nothing has to be lost if we will give the true measure of love Christ gave to us. I pray to God that you will finally understand how I feel.

Love,

Jan

Needle in a Haystack

Anxiety grew as the days passed. Finally, a bombshell exploded when we were informed that B had been arrested and was in a Salt Lake City Jail. Vern Jensen's fine detective work had been passed on to Federal Authorities in the Salt Lake office after Vern discovered that B had not been living at his reported residence, the apartment complex, but had only been using the address as a front. He had actually been living in his motorhome at a hidden location.

The arresting officers had not known what to expect when they approached. They used their vehicle to gently ram his motorhome. B, surprised by the officers' intrusion, opened the door with a puzzled look on his face. He was placed under arrest on a federal warrant for flight to avoid prosecution and for violating parole by not notifying federal authorities of his change of address. A detainer had been filed in the District of Utah for probation violations.

A search of his motorhome revealed a number of wigs and several large photos of Jan in different outfits and disguises. Among the items collected were recorded tapes that an officer described as strange. He said, "The cassettes are basically gibberish, filled with short phrases that make no sense. They are unrelated to the case." He also told us they contained no information concerning Jan or where Berchtold might have taken her. Disappointed, I wondered if B was "writing" another book. He often recorded things to write them down later, or so he had said.

Placed in a Salt Lake City Jail on November 12, 1976, B fought extradition to Pocatello. He denied any knowledge of Jan and proclaimed his innocence.

I couldn't believe he was in Jail. In anguish, I moaned, "Bob, why did they do that? B will never tell anyone where Jan is. What's next?"

"Let's think positive," Bob said. "Pete and George have never stopped in their pursuit of Berchtold, and they won't stop until Jan is found. And I'm certain Vern has done things we will never know—he's so modest. This is great progress."

Bob's confidence in Berchtold's arrest helped me cope.

Chapter 17
JAN'S BEEN FOUND

November 16, 1976

"Jan's been found!" Those words were followed by my shriek—and then tears and exclamations of gratitude. It had been more than three months since her disappearance.

"Can we sit down?" Pete asked. "I don't have a lot of details yet, but Jan was located in a private girls' school in Pasadena, California. She is safe and appears to have been well cared for by a group of Catholic Nuns."

Bob and I looked at each other in silence.

Pete continued, "She was identified by the FBI and is going by the name of Janis Tobler. I guess they discovered her last week, but until Berchtold was behind bars, it's been a confidential matter. Sorry I couldn't tell you anything when they arrested Berchtold, but the situation was still being investigated."

"We've spent a panicked weekend. I'm without words," Bob said as he wiped away his tears, unable to say more.

The excitement in Pete's voice kept my pulse beating fast. "The agents who found her said that she looked healthy. I guess she was scared and tried to deny her real identity, but she cried when one of the agents told her they knew who she was, and that Mr. Berchtold had been arrested. She didn't react much, but just remained subdued. The agent I talked to said she appeared to be rather humiliated, but she wouldn't give details about how she got to the school."

"A Catholic School? Who else but Berchtold would have thought of it?" I said, shaking my head in disbelief.

Claiming to have no further information, Pete said, "I'm not sure when she'll be home, but Detective Shail is making flight arrangements to bring her back. The sister in charge asked that Jan be allowed to stay at the school until authorities from Pocatello arrive to pick her up."

Once more, we rejoiced that Jan was coming home. We fell to our knees as we thanked our heavenly Father for this long-awaited blessing. Complications would certainly line our path, but we would endure. Tears of gratitude and inexpressible joy flowed freely. Jan was coming home!

My thoughts raced with apprehension as we learned more about Jan's circumstances. I couldn't begin to imagine her state of mind. I was so relieved to find out that the nuns who cared for her would continue to do so until she could come back to us. *What was she thinking and feeling?*

Jan's Diary, November 16, 1976:

Sister Charlotte called me into her office in the morning, and there were two men from the FBI waiting. I was scared stiff. They asked what my name was, and I said, "Janis Tobler." One of the men said my name was Jan Broberg. I told him it wasn't, but they had a report and knew exactly who I was. After one man asked me again, I admitted it. They said Mr. Berchtold was in jail and I should just tell them what happened. I refused to tell them anything. Sister Charlotte talked to me and was truly kind. She asked the agents to let me stay with her since she didn't want me going to a juvenile detention center. They agreed and left me in the care of Sister Charlotte.

We learned that later in the day, two deputies from the County Sheriff's Office arrived and told Sister Charlotte they had orders from Jan's hometown police to keep her locked up because she was a runaway. They took her downtown to the Los Angeles Corrections Center and told her that an officer from Pocatello, Idaho, would be coming to get her.

Her night in the detention center cell was horrendous. Jan didn't dare go to sleep. The other girls appeared older and were much bigger than she was. Using awful language, they talked about terrible things and hollered at one another. A couple of the girls with large tattoos repeatedly threatened to "beat the shit" out of some of the other girls that were in the holding tank. The night seemed endless—a waking, living nightmare. Jan had never been so glad for daylight. When Detective Shail showed up the next afternoon, Jan was worn out, confused, and full of mixed feelings. She wanted to go home but hated to leave Flintridge. It seemed like years since she had seen her family. She wondered how everyone at home would treat her.

***

Pete came by the house on Tuesday to remove the recorder. "Are you prepared to face the press again?" he asked. "I'm preparing a news release, and they won't be happy that we kept Jan's disappearance from them." He was right. The reporters were miffed.

Nevertheless, reporter complaints didn't change the circumstances and the fact that this had been the best way to handle an irrational, obsessed man.

The evening news was filled with Jan's second kidnapping and the report that she was found in a Catholic school. The local newspaper previewed the story with the following headline:

"FBI Finds Missing Broberg Girl in L.A."

Since we, ourselves, had been given scant information, we chose to ignore the blitz of phone calls. Needing all the strength we could muster, we decided to focus our energy strictly on our family.

Pete explained the legal procedure Jan would face when she returned. Because she had been reported as a runaway, she would have to spend the night in jail and then appear in juvenile court before a magistrate judge who would decide her fate. Pete felt certain she would be released to us because she was a victim and not a juvenile delinquent.

Anxious for news of Jan, we sat up late awaiting word. Attempting to be calm and patient, each of us had their diversion. Karen and Susan watched TV and worked on a challenging puzzle. Bob nervously read the newspaper. I tried to read, but couldn't concentrate; my thoughts were far from the printed pages I absentmindedly turned. Everyone was more quiet than usual. Occasionally, a brief conversation broke the tense atmosphere.

When the minutes began ticking past midnight, we abandoned our vigil and went to bed. About half an hour later, the sound of a chiming doorbell rang throughout the house. We jumped out of bed, threw on our robes, and invited Pete in.

He apologized for the late hour but knew we would want the latest news. For the first time in our three-year ordeal, Pete's vibrancy and positive attitude appeared deflated. Pete sunk down into the couch. His weary voice related his experiences of the last few hours.

"I was at the airport shortly before eleven o'clock and drove right up to the steps of the plane after it landed in order to save Jan from the news media. Reporters were buzzing around the airport like flies. All other passengers exited before Jan, and Detective Shail appeared at the door of the plane. I got out of my car and waved. I think she was glad to see me from the way she descended those stairs—practically running. She flashed a forced smile and said, 'Hi, Pete.' I asked her how she was, and she just shrugged her shoulders. I whisked her into my car, and she said, 'This isn't the same car you had the last time I was with you.' I said, 'You're right! It's a new one. How is it for you?' and she said, 'Okay!'"

We all chuckled that Jan noticed something as insignificant as a different vehicle. "Sounds like she hasn't changed," Bob mused.

"I explained what was going to happen," Pete continued, "and I drove to the Police Station, where they did a preliminary check-in. She placed a few personal possessions into a basket—not much—a ring and a watch, maybe a little change in a coin purse, but that's about it, and the officer checked it into a locker. She wasn't talkative at all."

Pete's voice cracked as he tried to gain control. After a lengthy pause, he cleared his throat. "She didn't say anything, but just stared at me with a hauntingly wistful look. It was awful." Pete paused for a moment. "Maybe I shouldn't say more. This isn't easy for you."

"No, no! We want to hear," I urged.

"How does she look?" Bob asked.

"Tired, like she hasn't had much sleep. She looks about the same, but her quiet demeanor bothered me. That isn't like your daughter." Pete continued to review the events by constructing the last moments before he had knocked on our door. "I stayed in the cell with Jan for quite a while. I asked her if I could get her anything, if she wanted something to eat, and she shook her head no. I told her I was going by her house to tell you she was back. She nodded her head but didn't say anything. I tried to think of things to say that would make her feel okay, such as, 'Were you treated well?', 'How was the plane ride?', and 'Your folks are fine and really happy that you're home', but nothing seemed to affect her. When I got up to leave, I asked her again if she had thought of anything I could do for her, and she said she was cold and wanted a blanket. After I brought one back, she wrapped herself in it and cowered into a corner of the bed with the blanket pulled up to her neck. She was shivering a little," Pete paused. "I don't know if she was cold or nervous—maybe both. She just sat on the bed looking forlorn and scared to death. I told her I would be back early in the morning to see her." Pete's voice wavered as he stroked his chin. "I hated leaving her alone. It was like leaving my own daughter in that jail. I felt horrible."

"It's okay," I said. "You couldn't do anything else. We're glad you were there and that she could feel some encouragement."

Bob added, "It's hard, but she's home. Who knows what she's gone through? And Berchtold is behind bars. What more could we ask?"

Pete pulled himself up from the couch, "I need to go and let you get some sleep. I'll be at the police station early. Don't worry about Jan. You'll hear from me as soon as I know what's happening."

He tried to be reassuring about Jan, but we were all apprehensive.

The next morning, shortly after eight o' clock, Pete called. "Jan's having breakfast—well, that is, the food is sitting in her cell. I don't think she has much of an appetite, but she's okay. I still don't know about the hearing, but I'm going to take her with me, so she doesn't have to stay here. I'll bring her home when we get through."

Five hours later, Pete pulled into the driveway. I watched through the kitchen window as Jan climbed out of the car. Anxiety spread throughout my chest. Jan looked the same, except she was wearing a ball cap that was covering her hair that was now longer, and her clothes were unfamiliar to us. Most concerning was the look of complete desperation imprinted on her face; her eyes were filled with fear. I swallowed hard and told myself not to become emotional.

Brainwashed by B

As Jan walked through the front door, I scooped her into my open arms. "Oh, Jan," I cried. "I'm so glad you're back."

"Hi, Mom," Jan said quietly. She allowed me to hug her, but her posture was rigid, and she was unresponsive.

I continued to hold Jan close, enjoying cuddling her as I had yearned to do for months. After releasing Jan from the bear hug, I waited for her to reciprocate. She did nothing except stare blankly. I felt awkward and wondered what to do next.

"Well," I said clumsily, "you have some new clothes."

"Yeah, I guess so."

"How are you, honey?" I asked cautiously.

"Fine." Her voice was flat and unfeeling.

A small cut on the bridge of her nose was just healing over. I asked, "What happened to your nose? Looks like you ran into something."

"Oh, I was in a car accident with B. He was letting me drive when a car ran a stop sign and hit us."

I raised my eyebrows at her unexpected answer. "You were driving?"

Realizing that she had just admitted to an illegal act, she looked away and pressed her lips tightly together. Turning to Pete, she asked, "Is it all right if I go downstairs?"

Pete looked at me, and I nodded. "You're home now, and your parents are in charge," he said.

Jan walked downstairs while I frowned. "Vern told us that Berchtold's car had been in an accident. What an idiot! I'm just glad she didn't get hurt."

"Thanks to Jan, we now know what kind of accident," Pete said, shifting from one foot to another. I pointed to a chair, and he sat down. "How's Bob doing today?" Pete questioned.

"He's okay. We had a hard time going to sleep last night, thinking about Jan being in that jail."

"I had a miserable night myself," Pete said. "I woke my wife up when I got home and told her I needed to talk. I was still wide awake at three this morning, worrying about your daughter. Jan was pleased to see me, but she complained that she didn't sleep last night either."

I heaved a heavy sigh, "She looks it. Those are very dark circles under her eyes."

"Considering where she was, I didn't expect she'd get much rest. It's terrible listening to jailbirds hollering most of the night," Pete said, shaking his head. "Oh, by the way, I told Jan she will be seeing Dr. Rush for an exam tomorrow."

"What did she say to that?"

"She wanted to know why. She claims nothing has happened—that she's fine—and she doesn't want to go." Pete shrugged, pursed his lips, and shook his head.

"I wish it were true, but this time she will get counseling immediately."

"Any ideas what counselor she will see?" Pete asked.

"No. We're going to make inquiries through my Doctor," I replied. "We're open to any good suggestions. I only know one child psychiatrist in Pocatello, and I'm not impressed."

"A hearing will be coming up soon, but if she could be seen before the trial begins, it would help a lot."

"How did Jan's court appearance go with the judge this morning?"

"Okay. There were no surprises. He released Jan to your care with a warning for her to listen to you, and he gave a lecture about why she was cited as a runaway. He was stern, but also sympathetic to her predicament."

"Anything else?" I asked.

Pete sat back on the dining room chair and took a deep breath. "Oh, yes. George picked her up in California at the juvenile detention center."

"He said he found Jan hiding in a corner of the holding tank looking like a frightened rabbit. She was quite traumatized."

Stunned, I groaned. "No wonder she looks so pathetic. Pete, I wonder why she stayed at that school so long without telling somebody who she was."

"Brainwashing by one of the most convincing criminals I know," Pete said as he stood and turned toward the door. "I need to run. Call if you have any concerns. I'll check in later. Tell Bob I'll stop by the shop to see him."

I thanked him, and he said, "It's my job. I'm glad she's back, but you do have your hands full. Get her to a child psychiatrist. Oh, and have a Happy Thanksgiving."

Chapter 18
TROUBLES OF RETURNING TO "NORMAL"

November 18, 1976

Jan was not easily persuaded into talking. She appeared apprehensive about anything I said. We concluded that she was probably going through shock from everything that had taken place. I couldn't even imagine how horrendous it had been for her.

Jan's reaction to her father was startling. She stood back several feet and would not get close to him. As he approached her, she recoiled, and a look of panic crossed her face. He glanced at me with a questioning look on his face. Instead of saying anything about it, Bob used his good humor to lighten up the situation, expressing his happiness at having her home. He later commented about how frightened she had been of him, "I need to give her time, but I wonder what's happened."

Bob was extremely patient with Jan. Although she would talk to him, she did so at a safe distance. I remembered a friend of mine, Mona, who as a young adult used me as a shield whenever a male invaded her space. After establishing my trust, she confided in me and told me about her experience of being sexually assaulted. We were certain that some type of sexual abuse had occurred with Jan. Hopefully, she would find the courage to reveal the extent to a confidant or psychiatrist.

The most encouraging aspect of her homecoming was the excitement, laughter, and chatter when her sisters arrived home from school. There were no barriers in the circle of sisters.

Jan's Diary, November 18, 1976:

I got home today. It feels weird. Everybody acts different, and I don't want to talk to anybody except my sisters. I think Dad was going to hug me. I don't want him to touch me. I heard Pete tell Dad that B will probably be transferred from Salt Lake to our jail on Monday. I'm glad he's coming. I miss him a lot, and maybe I can see him. If we could get married, maybe people would stop blaming him for everything. Nobody cares how I feel. They treat me like a criminal and think I don't have feelings. I hate being here except for Thanksgiving. I want to go back to Flintridge. I wonder what the Sisters told my friends at the school about me leaving.

The following day, I suggested to Jan that she call Flintridge and let them know she was home. Her personal belongings were still there, and the staff needed to know what to do with them. Jan shrugged her shoulders, lowered her eyes, and didn't answer.

Receiving no response, I said, "If you don't, I will. I'm not going to ask them any questions, but they need your address. Do you want to talk?" Jan shook her head and retreated to the living room.

Sister Charlotte answered the phone. The moment I opened my mouth, I found myself emotional, "This is Jan Broberg's mother—uh, you know—Janis Tobler?" The sister greeted me warmly and asked how Janis was doing. My voice trembled, and I began to cry, "I don't know how to adequately express our overwhelming joy. We are so indebted to all of you. The Lord heard our pleadings and allowed her to find refuge with you. You are the miracle we prayed for. Please let the others know of our deepest gratitude."

After Sister Charlotte expressed concern for Jan and sympathy to us, she conveyed her feelings and those of her coworkers. "Janis is a fine girl.

She has been exceptional while with us. Not only is she a good student, but she has a great rapport with her peers. She has always been thoughtful and kind to everyone. We will miss her."

"I'm pleased to hear you say that. Jan is a wonderful daughter, and we are so grateful to have her home. Mr. Berchtold has been a major problem to our family for quite some time, but hopefully he is out of our lives and things will be better for all of us."

"I understand this wasn't the first time. My goodness. May God bless all of you, and please give Janis our love."

Little by little, we were informed of B's situation. After learning that Jan had been discovered, he admitted to a parole violation by leaving Utah without permission. He tried to convince a federal judge he had traveled to Phoenix on business and had made two trips to Los Angeles in a desperate effort to convince Jan to return home. They hadn't bought his story. Idaho would be given the first chance on new charges, and then he would have to deal with charges on the federal detainer.

B didn't fight extradition and was moved to Pocatello on a first-degree kidnapping charge, with bond set at $500,000. Even if bail were raised on the kidnapping charge, the federal detainer would not allow the county to release him from jail. He would stay put. A few days later, a headline in the local paper stated, "Berchtold Accused: CIA Impersonation Occurred at School." Berchtold was charged by a US Marshal for impersonation of a CIA Agent. A Federal warrant was filed against him in California. The bond charge was $5,000.

Over the next few weeks, Jan began to reveal events that had occurred at Flintridge. Being exposed to a new life outside her guarded small-town culture had proven to be an education in itself. Theater and drama had been an important part of the curriculum, and Jan had enjoyed these classes the most. After the Christmas holidays, the theater students were traveling to New York for a workshop, and Jan had been planning to go. She expressed disappointment over the change of plans. Among her drama classmates was Melissa Sue Anderson of *Little House on the Prairie* fame.

Berchtold certainly knew what he was doing when he found this hideaway. Jan was enthralled. She was a very fine stage actress already, but had always hoped to be on TV.

We recognized that after the months of exposure to an unaccustomed lifestyle, Jan wasn't emotionally ready to face school or peers. Talking about returning to junior high frightened her. Recovery was necessary, but it would take time. I discussed with her the need for counseling. She begged us to send her back to Flintridge. She insisted that the Sisters at the school hadn't wanted her to leave and that most of them were already counselors. The diversity of classes at Flintridge had been far different than classes at Franklin Junior High, and her schoolwork had been excellent. She asked us, "Why should I have to change now?"

Emotional Warfare

We hadn't entertained the thought of her returning to Flintridge. However, Bob diplomatically stated, "Let us think about it, Jan. I want to do what is best for you and our family."

Jan's Diary, December 15, 1976:

I've been thinking about Flintridge today. I want to go back. I remember when all the freshmen got assigned a senior for a big sister, and I got Charlene. She had blond hair and was really tall. Our big sisters took us places and were supposed to look out for us, but all Charlene wanted to do was party and make out with guys. That college party she took me to was crazy. Some creepy guy kept following me around. He was drunk and was acting weird. I crawled behind a garbage can on the patio and put the lid in front of me so I could hide. I'm still only 5'1" tall, and no one could see me. (Karen and Caroline grew at least a foot while I was gone.) Charlene finally came out of the house but was drunk. I thought we were going to wreck before she got me back to the school. When I told B, he wanted to tell Sister Irene, but I didn't want him to. I didn't want her to get in trouble. I didn't like Charlene that much, but I have a lot of friends that I miss. I don't want to go back to school here. Mom said I need to after the holidays. I feel like a weirdo, and I don't want to explain anything to my friends.

We sought advice from our physician and presented him with Jan's plea. The good doctor stated, "What would it hurt for her to go back there now that Berchtold is out of the picture? There's a lot of information that will be brought out in the trial that could damage her. People are cruel, especially kids."

"We know that," Bob replied, "but Jan is too vital to our family circle. We want her to feel secure and loved no matter the outcome. I can't let her go. What we need is a good psychiatrist. Do you have any recommendations?"

We were given the name of a child psychiatrist in Salt Lake City. I called immediately and scheduled the first appointment for mid-December. We decided Jan could stay home and not return to school until the first of the year. Never content to be idle, she kept busy with projects at home and went to the floral shop with Bob, making small Christmas arrangements under her father's watchful and appreciative eye. It appeared to bolster her self-esteem.

A box arrived via a Greyhound bus with Jan's possessions from Flintridge. She unpacked a school uniform that consisted of a plaid skirt, white blouse, and blue blazer, and then she unpacked a small TV and radio. Seeing the TV, I pointed to it. "Oh, I found the receipt for this in Berchtold's car at the Salt Lake Airport—most likely the weekend he brought it to you."

Jan glared at me and said nothing. Among the few items in the box were some beads. I picked them up and said, "These are pretty. Did you wear them?"

"No," Jan said. "They are rosary beads." She took them from my hands and placed them on her dresser. "They have a special meaning to me. Being a Catholic is not that different from being a Mormon. Both teach you the same stuff—the Ten Commandments, how to forgive and how to pray. They just do memorized prayers sometimes. It was sort of comforting. I don't think you would understand."

I was amazed at just how much she had internalized everything at Flintridge.

Hoping the spirit of Christmas would take its rightful place in our home again, we truly enjoyed the carols and the feeling of peace that was returning to our lives. Jan wanted to do something nice for all the sisters at Flintridge. Over the next few weeks Jan was sewing kitchen aprons and potholders for each sister. She carefully cut characters and flowers from old greeting cards and placed them on bars of soap before dipping the top in wax to preserve the emblems. For each of her close friends, she strung and tied necklaces of colorful wooden beads. After attaching special notes of love, gratitude, and good cheer, Jan carefully wrapped each gift in festive Christmas paper and packaged it for mailing. This seemed more like our Jan.

Our hopes soared.

Preliminary Hearing
December 2, 1976

The preliminary hearing lasted four days, with several witnesses for both the prosecution and the defense. Jan's testimony was the least damaging to Berchtold from the prosecution's list of witnesses. She claimed she had left willingly and that Berchtold had not kidnapped her.

Berchtold's newest attorney filed a motion to dismiss the charge. The judge refused, citing plenty of evidence from the police, the FBI, Catholic sisters, and us for him to face trial on a felony charge of first-degree kidnapping. We were relieved to hear the decision, but Jan was upset.

Emotional Aftershock

Jan's complaints about not sleeping were verified by the dark circles under her eyes. One night I made a good-night visit and found her crying. She said she had bumped her shoulder sharply. "That hurt," she complained, rubbing her bony shoulder. Seeking pity, she continued, "I'm hungry, but nothing sounds good, and I think I'm getting sick. My throat is sore."

"And what else hurts, honey?"

She turned away and said, "Oh, I miss B so much I can hardly stand it."

I gathered her frail body into my arms and cradled her close.

"What am I going to do?" she asked. "I can't eat. I can't get excited about Christmas. I can't sleep. I just worry about him—if I could just talk to him. I can't stand it."

It was hard to comprehend her agonizing plea but remembering myself being manipulated by him helped me understand. I had to temper my anger and listen to her cry for help.

"Could I write to him, or just do something?"

"No, that isn't allowed," I replied.

What is the key to unlocking her mind and removing Berchtold from her life? His control over Jan was frightening.

"Jan, I'm going to get you a tranquilizer. It should help you calm down."

As she gulped down the pill with some water, I studied her swollen red eyes. This was the first time she had shown any emotion during the past three weeks.

Sitting on the bed next to her, I begged, "Honey, whatever is inside you, please get it out. I want to help you, but you have to talk. Cry, scream, holler—anything—but get it out!"

She broke into heartrending sobs as I tenderly embraced her. My own emotions began working their way to the surface. This was the first time she had allowed any affection between us.

"He's such a part of me. I don't think I can stand . . ." She paused for a moment. "I just want to prove to you that I can."

"Can what, honey?"

"Be a good wife and mother," she blurted out.

"Oh!" I said in surprise. It felt as if a knife had pierced my heart. "I know you can be and will be one of the best. No one in this whole world has more to give than you."

"Mom, I don't want to have a trial here. Not for B, me, or any of us." The medication was beginning to calm her down.

She slid from my lap onto her bed and lay face down on the pillow. I looked around the room at her mementos and personal possessions. I thought, *B built this room. Does it remind her of him? Probably. We need to redecorate it soon.*

I began rubbing Jan's bony back, massaging her neck and shoulders. She began to relax.

I raced upstairs, pulled a heavy quilt out of the linen closet, picked up Tiffy, and hurried back down to her room. Jan snuggled the dog as I covered them. Bending down to kiss her, she said, "Thanks, Mom. I love you."

"I love you too, sweetie. Are you going to be okay?" She nodded drowsily. "Sleep tight," I whispered.

Our first trip to see Dr. Smith was a two-hour per person session, two days in a row. Jan refused to talk to him, but he wasn't bothered.

He remarked that he was used to the cold shoulder from young people. We faithfully drove to her weekly appointments in Salt Lake City. Dr. Smith preferred to meet with each of us separately.

Early into the therapy sessions, Dr. Smith asked for our approval to contact Donna Carr, a child psychologist who worked for the Salt Lake School System. She was skilled in testing and evaluating children who suffered from emotional problems. We gave our approval.

The four-hour testing brought encouraging news. Ms. Carr asked, "Mr. and Mrs. Broberg, are you familiar with art therapy?" We said that we were not. "I had Jan do some artwork for me. Disturbed children who have been severely abused draw images in their pictures that show a lot of violence, anger, hurt, and distrust." She showed us a few frightening examples.

"In contrast," she said, "here is one of Jan's pictures. I asked her to draw a picture of her family. Look at what she drew. Do you see anything abnormal?"

Bob and I studied the picture Jan had drawn. We both said, "No."

Ms. Carr explained, "First of all, Jan has put an apron on you, Mrs. Broberg, and you, Mr. Broberg, have a newspaper in your hand. Her sisters are holding some items—a book, a doll—and Jan drew herself carrying pom-poms and dressed in—oh, I suppose her drill team outfit. Everyone has a smile on their face. Take note of the roof she has drawn over all of you standing together inside the house, even your dog. I find that very significant as to the way your daughter feels about her family. She feels you belong together."

The session rejuvenated us. We returned home. Keeping Jan with us had been the right decision. Bob had never doubted.

On Sunday, I awakened the girls so they could get ready for church, but Jan didn't appear. Ten minutes later, I called to her again. "I'm not going to church. I'm Catholic now," she called back.

That wasn't the answer I had expected. I ran down the steps angrily and yelled, "Get out of that bed and get ready for church. Whether you are Catholic or not, you are going to church with us."

The volatility of my response scared me. I felt terrible but didn't apologize.

The following day, I called Dr. Smith and expressed frustration for losing my temper. "She's the victim," I reasoned. "Talking to her about this new religion would have been more civilized. I really blew it."

Dr. Smith asked, "How long was she angry at you?"

"For about an hour after we got home," I answered.

"Is that all? Did she say anything else to you?"

"No. Everything seemed fine after that."

"Good. You probably did the right thing. We'll talk about it when you come in for your session this Thursday."

It was nearly Christmas. Jan and I spent some time at the flower shop helping with the Christmas rush before hurrying to the grocery store, where we picked up a few last-minute items for dinner that evening.

It was late when I crawled into bed. I had barely drifted off to sleep when I became aware of a presence in the room. "Mom, please—help me!" The words were choked with alarming emotion.

I opened my eyes to see Jan standing by my side. Startled, I sat up in bed and exclaimed, "Jan? What's the matter?" She looked terrified.

By this time, Bob had raised his head, "What's the matter? What's going on?"

Tears flooded down Jan's cheeks as she began to sob. "I don't know," she blurted out. "I just feel awful."

I tried pulling her up off her knees and into bed, but she resisted and sternly retaliated, yelling, "No! Leave me alone!"

"Jan, I want to help you. Just crawl in here and talk to me."

Bob quietly said, "I'll go sleep in the den. Jan, you stay here with your mother. Call me, if I'm needed."

Jan crawled into bed next to me. Her small body was trembling and heaving from the tremendous emotional outburst. She accepted my gentle pats on her skinny arm. Eventually, I wrapped my arms around her shaking form.

When she chose to talk, she rehashed her feelings for Berchtold. They hadn't changed from two weeks ago. I periodically brushed back tears—sometimes hers, and sometimes my own. Finally, exhaustion took over. I peered at her small face lying on my pillow, and I watched as she gradually slipped into a restful breathing cycle and fell asleep.

The clock glared 3:15 a.m. I was wide awake. My mind wouldn't turn off. Tears wet my pillow. I felt grossly inadequate to the task of helping my little girl find peace.

Jan and I were both exhausted in the morning. Knowing something had brought her into our room during the night, I prodded. "What frightened you last night, Jan?"

Her eyes were glassy from lack of sleep. Jan said, "I don't know, but I hate my bedroom. I can't sleep there any longer."

"Okay, let's move you upstairs. You can sleep in Susan's trundle bed until we transform the den into your new bedroom. Will that help you sleep?"

A look of relief came over her. Her big blue eyes danced with excitement. "That's great!" She dashed down the steps, loading her arms with belongings and delivering them to Susan's room.

My numb brain flashed, *You idiot! She tried telling you two weeks ago. Open your eyes and mind to every single word she says. You need to listen more carefully!*

Jan never returned to sleep in her bedroom and never visited the room unless someone was in the basement with her. Except for transferring her clothes, the room remained intact.

Jan continued to keep space between herself and her father. It was hard on him. He had always had a close relationship with his daughters, which included warm hugs and good-night kisses, but now he realized she needed time, and he tried to be patient.

Her friends in drill team encouraged her to come back, and they assured her that she was needed.

Flintridge was no longer an option. "Young people have the vibrancy to bounce back and throw off a lot of baggage," Bob reasoned. "Knowing Jan's dynamic spirit, I have no doubt she can do this. We need to keep her focused and positive."

The day after Christmas, Detective Shail called to express disappointment about a basket from Jan that had been delivered to the County Jail for Berchtold. "Please tell her she can't do that."

"What was in the basket?" I asked, trying to hide my dismay.

"Just a bunch of little nonsense items and notes. But wow, doesn't she realize what a jerk he is?"

"I wish she did, George, but Jan still thinks he's wonderful and continues to express love for him. Dr. Smith said this is a complicated matter that will take time, and we're dealing with it the best we can. I thought she understood there was to be no contact with him. We'll talk to her again."

Bob broached the subject with Jan. He said, "He has lied to you, to us, to his family, and to everyone else. You can't believe anything he says or does. Cut him out of your life—now!" With that, he exited the kitchen in frustration.

Jan remained sullen and did not make eye contact with me. After a few moments of searching for the right response to her disobedience, I quietly said, "For your own sake, you need to do as Detective Shail has asked and not have any contact with B."

With a look of dismay, Jan bolted towards the family room.

Chapter 19
JAILHOUSE MISSIVES

January 15, 1977

In the middle of January, Berchtold passed four handwritten letters to a former cellmate and asked him to deliver them, personally, to Jan. Instead of doing as instructed, he gave them to his girlfriend, telling her to see that Jan got them. She told her sister about the letters, who in turn disclosed the secret to their mother. The girl's mother confiscated the letters, reported the incident to the police, and turned the letters over to the police.

Two other letters were already in our possession: one had been sent to Flintridge and one had been dropped in our mailbox without postage, which must have come through his network of—pedophiles? We wondered how many other notes or letters had reached Jan. We didn't know. Pete had told us to safeguard the letters and present them as evidence when we went to trial.

The letters contained passages of undying love and devotion that an appropriately aged sweetheart or lover would have cherished. But the object of the love of this sick, depraved man was a young girl who remained his innocent victim. Three of the six letters are included word for word here (with grammar and spelling as in the original letters):

Hi Darling,

I awoke this morning thinking of you as usual and loving you even more. I remembered you in Oliver and the night you cried when you sang "Where Is Love" especially for me. Honey, remember the song from Oliver, "As Long As He Needs Me," and the meaning it had in the play. Please honey sing it over and over and know I need your love more now than anything on this earth. Remember the movie we saw One Flew Over The Coo-Coo Nest. I have been placed in exactly those same circumstances. Only your love can save me. Evil forces would like nothing more than to destroy us and ruin everything. Please darling don't fail me. Every great event on this earth has been met with evil. Christ himself had to suffer prison and death to accomplish his work. Each apostle was imprisoned then killed by man. Now they would do that to us. I can do no more than love you every minute of my life. This I can do easily. The rest is up to you. I know you love me to with the same love. We have endured so much. I am prepared to endure whatever comes because I look forward to the day all will be made right and beautiful. No matter how dark things look, it all has a purpose. It is you that taught me to believe. Honey, I do! I have so many wonderful memories of good times with you. I live with them daily; it brings you so close to me and gives me so much joy. I always look to the future and how marvelous it will be when the trial is over and there is just you and me, then the special someone who will be added. As soon as I can, I will tell you all the wonderful things I have to tell you. Until then be brave do everything right and don't give up hope. I never will because thru it all there is you.

Forever B

Hi, My Ephnot:

Read then destroy!!! I love You!!!

I remembered today our trip to Monterey as you drove along the coast highway. It was so beautiful as the sun set over the ocean. We would rise above the clouds, the golden sun turning the fluffy floor of clouds all shades of pink and gold. It was a horrible highway but so beautiful to be with you and watch as you guided the car in and out of the cliffs. I love you so very, very much for all you mean to me. Honey I would like to have you answer some questions for me when you write. Did you get all your stuff back from California? The JVC, all your stuffed animals, bowling ball, etc. What did you do from the time you got back until you started school? Are they making you see a shrink? What is your life at home now? Have your parents improved any? Also, I need to remind you of a few things. Remember rule number one. Be careful about any male relationships. Be careful in your contacts with the Church. I have joined the Catholic Church! I hope you still feel as close to the sisters as ever. Is it possible for you to attend the Catholic Church here? We have a time period now to get thru. It can't be more than sixteen months! What happens between now and then I don't know. Just have faith that after this period of testing then all will be made right again. Everything will be so great when we are together again. There is so much I want to do, motorbike riding, boating, hang gliding, snowmobiling, skiing. I want to travel all over the world with you and enjoy every country, people, and adventure it has to offer. I want a beach house in California to go with the cabin in Jackson so we can have the best of summer and winter as we want to. Oh, just being with you will be so wonderful. I dream of evenings by a glowing fire. You are curled up on a rug studying the script of a new movie they want you to do. I am working hard on an-other book. I look up from the typewriter to study the firelight dancing in your beautiful eyes. You smile and wink at me. That's all we need between us to know the world and more belongs to us because we have succeeded where no one else could have stood the test. We know our love was created for such a super special reason and because of this we are blessed above all men. I know we can do it honey. Believe and be brave.

Forever B

Hi Love,

I finally got the book Freckles from the library; your right it is great. I know when I first read it when I was ten, it was you I had in my heart as I lived that beautiful story. Honey read page two hundred and know I know that is the way you feel and always will. I hope I can live to be worthy of that. I read your letters many times each day for strength. You always were the strongest one. When I get discouraged, I always think what Jan would tell me to do. So, I get busy with one of the things on the list you sent in the Christmas package, and I always feel better. What would I do without you? Without your love? I love you so very much. Have you heard from Zada? Did you know she is back at her old job? I got a letter from Sister Charlotte. She said to let you know everything is happening for our good and you are doing everything right. She said to tell you to have faith that by the time you are sixteen everything will be made right if we both do what we know is right!!! I work every day to be more worthy of you and your love. Each night I pray for you and that all your hardships and heartaches will be made easier. Please write me honey. Either to our attorney or like the mailman will tell you. Life would be so much easier if I could again receive word from you. I love you so very, very much and live for the time we are together again. I live just for you.

B

We only had knowledge of one letter Jan had written to Berchtold, which the police had intercepted:

Dearest B,

Hi! I know that you're trying to send letters to me still, but please don't. I'm afraid if you keep trying to send them it will get you into a whole bunch of trouble and I don't want that at all for you! So, since I think it's almost impossible for you to get your letters to me, don't do it. I don't want you to get in any trouble. I hope that you know it doesn't matter. Save your letters and give them to me later. I guess that our brain waves must be on the same frequency because I know how much you love me and how much you appreciate my letters. You don't have to tell me on paper. I take pleasant thoughts of you into my dreams every night and I know that you do too. Our thoughts are on the same path. I know that you love me, and you know that I love you. Everything will work out, but don't get yourself in any more trouble. I know what your letters would say anyway.

I flunked my science test, but I did okay on my Spanish one. I'm helping with the drill team and of "course" it's "improving"!! Thanks for trying. Know that I love you. Keep well for heaven's sake. "Be Good." Keep Smiling.

Love,

Your Dolly

It was a relief to know that her letter had contained no startling news. We didn't know who "Zada" was from Berchtold's letter, but we figured it was one of the sisters at Flintridge. As for Jan's letter, it sounded like Jan. We didn't like what she wrote, but we could live with it. If we could only keep Berchtold away from her, then surely she could be a teenager again and begin to resume her normal life.

Slowly, and with much effort, we were attempting to recapture a normal routine in our home, one day at a time. We were in the midst of a fun family activity, playing a game, when the telephone rang. A male on the other end asked to speak with Mr. Broberg.

Arson, Let It Burn

"I've got to run down to the store," Bob stated. "That was a guy from across the street from our store who said all the window lights are out. He just noticed they're off and thought it looked like smoke in the window."

"Hope everything's okay. Hurry back," I said, grimacing.

Bob grabbed his parka and zipped it up. "I won't be long. We'll finish when I get back. Save me some dessert. I hope it's something nice and hot—it's so cold tonight," he commented, dashing out the back door.

The rest of us continued our Scrabble game. Bob had been gone about fifteen minutes when I heard a siren. A wave of uneasiness swept over me as I thought the worst. It wasn't long before the phone rang. When I picked up the receiver, Bob's frantic voice boomed out, "Our store is on fire!"

His words were inconceivable. I didn't want to believe it. "Bob?" I asked faintly.

"Fire engines are on the way! Don't come down! Stay there with the kids." In the distance, I could hear more sirens wailing.

"Where are you?" I asked.

"Across the street at the loan company. Honey, I have to go. There's a policeman wanting to talk to me. I need to leave right now. Fire engines are on the way!" he repeated.

The girls realized that something was wrong and had come into the kitchen. Stunned, I blurted out, "Our store is on fire!"

Immediately, Jan became hysterical, "Oh no! It's my fault! I knew something would happen! It's my fault!" She jumped around the room in fury.

"Jan! Calm down. How could it be your fault? We don't even know what's going on."

Jan ran into the dining room, and the frenzy in her voice escalated.

Anxious, but uninformed, I began calling family. I couldn't tell them anything except what I had heard from Bob. For twenty minutes, I kept telling the girls to be calm while I paced back and forth listening to one siren after another pierce the night air. Jan's fearful behavior persisted. I couldn't contain the suspense any longer. "Okay," I said. "Get yourselves ready. Wear hats and gloves and grab your warmest coats! Let's go see what's going on."

As I pulled out of our driveway, we could see pillars of smoke billowing into the crisp January night. I parked and saw flames shooting from the building. It was bitter cold as we made our way toward the store. Water hoses, fire trucks, police vehicles, and barriers filled the street. A fireman stopped us from proceeding farther.

Determined to get closer, I grabbed Susan's hand. "Come on, girls. Come this way," I cried out, pointing down an adjoining street.

Jan and Karen followed as we ran down the block to find a different path toward the store. Circling the block, we ran to an alley that would lead us across the street from our store. Fire hoses were all over the place. In the dark, we were able to make it onto the street without interference. We nearly collided with Bob, who was standing back on the far side of the street, helplessly watching our business being consumed by flames. He appeared relieved to see us but was grief-stricken. I grabbed his arm and shook my head, unable to speak.

"Well, MaryAnn, is this the final chapter of this horrible time?" he asked.

I didn't know what to say. We stood gaping at the inferno with our mouths open.

As we huddled together, Bob's eyes glistened with tears. He reached out his arms and pulled us close to him. "Let it burn, let it burn, let it burn! Everything that matters is right here in my arms. Things have been worse, but here we are together! Let it burn!"

It was profound to feel his gratitude at such a bleak moment. Spending these few minutes together as a family grounded us. Jan was crying, wiping away her tears and muttering, "It's my fault." A few onlookers turned to Bob and asked, "Do you know what happened?"

"Two employees at First Security Loan noticed that the window lights were out at about 7:30 tonight. Everyone always loved seeing the Atkin Flower Shop windows. So, after looking at the store for a few minutes, they thought they saw smoke inside, swirling in the front window. That's when they called me. Before I got here, they had already called the police. The two detectives investigating discovered that the back door was open, with the doorknob and deadbolt laying on the ground. The smoke was so heavy that they couldn't get in. They think someone broke into the store and set it on fire."

As we stood there, the freezing cold nipped at our fingers and toes. Bob motioned to the loan office behind us. "They invited me to go in and watch from inside their building. Why don't you and the girls go in there? I'll be there in a few minutes."

We retreated into the office to warm up, but I couldn't stay inside long, not without Bob. I again ventured into the cold night to stand near him while we watched tenants of adjoining businesses removing filing cabinets, desks, and other items from their establishments in a valiant effort to save whatever they could. Many people were in the street now. Curious onlookers stopped to ask questions. Among the observers was a young man whose curiosity was so intense that Bob became suspicious.

Pete Welsh soon arrived at the scene. Aghast at the destruction, he expressed sympathy.

"Berchtold's behind this," I told him. "I don't know how, but I know he's the instigator."

Bob nodded in agreement and told Pete about the young man who asked too many questions for comfort.

Pete didn't acknowledge our accusation. "Go down to the police station in the morning and look at some mug shots. If you see that guy, we'll pull him in for questioning," he told us.

We had been standing in the cold for nearly two hours, and the plummeting temperature was too much for us to endure any longer. I decided to take the girls home. Bob felt compelled to stay.

It was nearly midnight when he returned. His mood was somber. "The fire's still going, but the firemen think it's under control. There are so many hot spots that they expect to remain there all night. The water has frozen around the building, making it hazardous for the firemen to walk anywhere without falling. One of them slipped on the ice and injured his back and he was taken to the hospital. Also, the fire chief broke his hand. Those poor guys. What a night!"

"It's an empty feeling, huh?" I said.

"That's for sure. But honey, there's no comparison between the way I feel about this and the total hopelessness I felt when Jan was gone. And when you left,"—he paused slightly, his voice cracking— "that was total devastation."

I squeezed his hand firmly and kissed his forehead. "Will this ever end? When you called to report the fire," I told him, "Jan went ballistic, blaming herself. Why do you think she did that?"

"I don't know," Bob replied, shaking his head in exasperation. "That reminds me—you better call Dr. Smith tomorrow and cancel our appointment. No business, no money. Who knows when, or if, we can ever start over? I can't believe I didn't increase our fire insurance after the remodeling was finished last month." The look on his face was devastating.

I was overwhelmed at the thought that we would have to find ways to help Jan without professional support, "It's hard to think about anything right now, but we're not giving up. We'll find a way."

As we embraced, Bob's arms fell loosely around me. At the end of the night, I was down on my knees at the edge of our bed praying for greater strength to endure another blow.

Jan's Diary, January 25, 1977:

I've got a sick feeling in my stomach. I'm so glad Dad wasn't in the store when it caught on fire. The store is ruined, and so is the whole building. I feel really awful because Dad can't go to work anymore. I know it's my fault this happened, but I don't know what I did wrong. I've tried to do everything I was told, but maybe there is something I forgot about. Is it because B's in jail and everybody's against him? I wonder if he sent me a message and I didn't get it. I don't know what to do. If B gets out of jail, we need to get married right away. Then things will be better for everyone.

The following day, Bob and I peered through a dozen pages of mug shots at the police station. It didn't take long for Bob to identify the inquisitive young man. Detective Shail urged Bob to keep looking. He had to be certain. I hadn't paid enough attention. My eyes had been focused on the blaze. However, Bob had no doubt this was the man.

Detective Shail and Pete looked at each other knowingly. "This guy was just released from jail a couple of days ago. He was in for burglary. He shared a cell with Berchtold. We'll bring him in for questioning," said Detective Shail.

Lloyd Richard Lockhart was interrogated and confessed to the crime. He implicated an accomplice, Russell Mee, who had also served time in the county jail with Berchtold. He was also brought in for questioning.

The two men disclosed Berchtold's hatred toward the owner of the flower shop, and they unraveled the plot. Berchtold had offered the men a lump sum of money if they torched the shop. Berchtold had explained the layout of the flower shop, indicating that the building was an older structure with creaky wooden steps. A room at the bottom of the stairs was full of boxes, paper, and other flammable materials. Once that room was set on fire, the rest of the place would burn up quickly. He was hopeful that the owner would go into the shop and be killed in the fire.

Berchtold had led the men to believe that he owned a cabin in Jackson Hole. He had told them they could go there and hide out after the crime. He told the men that after he was released from jail, he would hire them to work for him in a new business venture, would pay them $1,000 a month, and would give them an automobile, a mobile home, and an unlimited expense account.

The fire that started in our store had consumed nearly half a block of the downtown area resulting in thirteen businesses having to relocate. The entire contents of our store had been lost.

Bob began searching for a new location for his shop. Ironically, there was space available for rent across the street from where we had stood and watched our store burn.

Bob bought a floral knife and a few other basic supplies. He also purchased a used icebox from the grocery store. With the help of friends and family who rallied to help us paint, construct worktables, and set up a presentable shop, we were ready to open a week later. Fortunately, Bob had stored account information in an old, antiquated fireproof safe, which had fallen through the floor into the basement and was recovered several days later. Our business quickly reopened, and we forged ahead in spite of Berchtold's attempt to destroy our livelihood.

I called Dr. Smith to share the devastating news and to cancel our appointment. "We won't be continuing therapy," I said. "We have no funds to pay you. Please be patient, and we'll get you paid for past services."

"Mrs. Broberg, you can't quit coming," he responded. "You need to see me now more than ever. Don't worry about paying until you're back on your feet. I'm very concerned about Jan."

At his urging, we rescheduled our appointment.

We still owed Vern Jensen money for the detective work he had done. Shortly after relocating, Vern came into the store and put a note in Bob's hand. The note read, "Paid in full!"

"Oh, Vern, you can't do this," Bob stated. "After all, you're the reason Jan is back. We'll get the rest of what's due you eventually."

"You have paid me enough. I insist; I can do this much to help you out."

A week later, charges were filed against Berchtold for second-degree arson and first-degree burglary. That evening, he was found lying on his bed, unable to be awakened. He was transported to the hospital for an examination. Dr. Crandall, who had been treating Berchtold in jail for depression, was summoned. He had prescribed a mild sleeping pill that was routinely given to Berchtold every night by a jailer. Evidently, Berchtold had either been keeping the medication or had received drugs from visitors. He was treated for a minor overdose and returned to the county jail three days later. Until Berchtold had his trial, and until he was convicted and removed from Pocatello, there would be no peace of mind for us.

Jan was shaken over the news. She kept asking if he was going to die.

"No, Jan," her father said. "He's just playing on everyone's sympathy. It's another one of his dramatic displays of being in control."

Spring was in the air. So far, the month of March had brought nothing earth-shattering. Occasionally a caller would hang up when we answered the phone. "I guess Berchtold is checking on us to see if we have changed our phone number—or he's just trying to make us nervous," I said.

"Why don't we get a new phone number, Dad? Then he wouldn't call us anymore," Karen suggested.

"Honey, it wouldn't do any good. He can get anything he wants. I don't know how, but he does," Bob said.

We discussed getting an unlisted number, but because our home phone was also used for business purposes, it didn't make sense. To go underground wasn't our way of living.

He Never Gives Up

It was midmorning, near the end of the month, when the principal called with an urgent message. "Mrs. Broberg, I'm calling to inform you about two girls who were just in our office wanting Jan," Mr. Soderquist said. "They told our secretary that Jan's aunt was in a serious car accident. Supposedly, they had come to pick Jan up and transport her to the hospital. Mrs. LaMonte told the girls that she needed to find out which class Jan was attending at that hour and would have her come to the office. The pair said they would wait outside in the car. Mrs. LaMonte told me what was going on, and I felt I should see if you were home. I know that from all the trouble you've had, this might be another problem."

"Oh no! Where is Jan?" I asked.

"Still in class," he said.

"Good! Thank you for calling. There hasn't been an accident. Do you have any idea who they are?"

"Teenagers. High school age. They don't fit the appearance of your daughter's type of friends," Mr. Soderquist said.

"Keep Jan there. I'm coming."

When I arrived, I didn't see any occupied vehicles in the parking lot. I went to the office and found Jan there with Mr. Soderquist.

"What's wrong, Mom?" Jan asked.

"We didn't tell her anything, Mrs. Broberg. I just asked her to come to the office," said the principal, Mr. Soderquist, narrating the incident once more for Jan's benefit. Ending the account, he said, "I looked out to see where they had gone. They were getting in a car with a guy who had his long hair pulled back in a ponytail. They sat out there for about five minutes and then drove off. I can call the police and describe the car."

"I wish you would," I said. "Jan, Aunt Carolyn has not been in an accident. Do you have any idea who they were or what they wanted?"

Jan appeared shaken. Her wide eyes and trembling lips displayed fear. "No," she said.

"Do you want to come home with me?" I asked. Uncertain, she looked at Mr. Soderquist.

"I don't see any problem if you stay. We'll alert the teachers. You'll be safe."

"It's okay, Mom. Are you going to pick me up after school?"

"I'll be here," I promised.

As soon as I arrived home, I called Bob. "Is Berchtold ever going to give up?" he asked.

"I don't think so. Even though he is locked up, we are not safe from this monster."

Chapter 20
SOCIOPATH OR PSYCHOPATH

May 1977

The defense had filed a motion asking for acquittal of Berchtold due to "mental defect," which would eliminate the need for a trial. An evidentiary hearing would be held to determine if Berchtold was mentally insane and unable to stand trial.

As Bob and I entered the courtroom, we recognized Berchtold's parents seated with a woman near the front. Surprisingly, the courtroom was nearly empty. I wondered if the news media had been barred from attending or had given up.

The Berchtold's turned to watch us enter. I nodded and murmured hello but received no response. B's mother glared at me for a long time until I became very uncomfortable. I looked away and began conversing with Bob, but out of the corner of my eye, I could still see her staring. B was at the defense bench busily turning pages of a manuscript. He avoided looking our way, but he occasionally glanced at his parents, looking quite forlorn.

At 10:20 a.m., court still had not begun. The prosecutor's assistant called us out to the hall and explained that Lockhart was refusing to testify against Berchtold. Him and his accomplice, Russell Mee, had been transported from the Boise penitentiary as witnesses, but Lockhart feared for his life if he ratted on Berchtold. Fellow inmates had told him that others may retaliate against him when he returned due to the buddy system among prisoners who demanded loyalty.

However, Mee was going to testify and reveal everything about the fire and his association with Berchtold. In exchange for his testimony, he would be granted immunity since he was an accessory and wasn't actually there when the fire started.

When the judge returned to the courtroom, the proceeding began. Richard Lockhart was the first witness called.

The attorney asked for the witness to state his name and address.

"I refuse to answer any questions on the Fifth Amendment," Lockhart said, with much anxiety in his voice.

The judge raised his eyebrows and said to the frightened man, "You can tell us your name and address. That will not incriminate you."

The nervous soul turned anxiously to his attorney. "Answer the question. It's okay," the attorney said.

He wiped his hand across his face and blurted out, "Richard Lockhart—Idaho State Prison."

He sank down in his chair and nervously tapped his fingers together, waiting for the next question.

The prosecutor said, "Mr. Lockhart, tell us the reason you are serving at the Idaho State Prison."

Lockhart again stated, "I refuse to answer on the Fifth Amendment."

His attorney stood and addressed the judge. "Your Honor, my client feels that his life is in danger should he answer any further questions. I thereby recommend that Mr. Lockhart be excused from any further questioning in this hearing."

Judge Beebe replied, "Prior to the conditions stated in my chambers, I will comply. Mr. Pincock, do you have any objections?"

"No, Your Honor."

The young man almost jumped from his place on the stand to the floor. His eyes displayed overwhelming relief at being dismissed from his uncomfortable seat.

The second witness was called and stated his name and residence: "Russell Mee, Idaho State Prison."

"Where were you on the night of January 19, 1977?" Mr. Pincock asked.

"I was in the Bannock County Jail," Mee answered.

"Why were you there?" the prosecutor asked.

"I was serving time for burglary."

"Did you know Mr. Berchtold prior to your incarceration in the Bannock County Jail?"

"No, I had never met him until then."

Prosecutor Pincock asked, "Mr. Mee, would you explain for this court your knowledge of what took place prior to the night of January 24, 1977?"

"Well, Berchtold didn't like Broberg. He was very mad at him and said it was his fault that he was in jail."

"You mean Berchtold thought it was Broberg's fault that he was in jail?" Mr. Pincock asked.

"Yeah, Berchtold said Broberg told lots of lies, and he wanted to get even. He talked to us a lot about what he wanted to do to Broberg. He thought if he could run Broberg out of town, Broberg would go to Salt Lake City, and then Berchtold had somebody who would take care of him."

"Take care of Broberg? What does that mean?"

"Beat him up, I guess," Mee replied.

"Why did he think Broberg would go to Salt Lake?" Pincock asked.

"He never said, but he thought if Broberg's business was destroyed, he wouldn't stay in Pocatello. Anyway, he came up with this plan. He said if we burned down Broberg's shop, he would make us partners in his business," Mee said.

"What kind of business?"

"He had a fun center in Jackson Hole, Wyoming. You know, all kinds of game machines and stuff. He said he needed people to go out and set up other fun centers. We'd get a motorhome, $5,000, and an unlimited expense account. He has a place on an island where he wanted to set up the Huckleberry Fun Center, and it sounded like a great idea."

"And did you think he was telling you the truth?"

"Sure, man. He showed us pictures about where it was going to be built and had all the plans laid out. Man, we couldn't turn down that kind of offer, and we told him we would do it when we got out of jail. He drew us a floor plan of the building where Broberg had his flower shop. He said the building was very old, and once a match was lit, it would go like a matchbox."

Mee stopped for a moment. Berchtold never looked at him while Mee provided an account, but rather continued to study the manuscript on the table in front of him.

"He drew us a map and told us how to go in the back door and where the stairs go down to the basement. He said Broberg kept his wrapping paper and boxes in a room down there and the floors were all old boards. He said Broberg kept lots of money in the store. After the fire was over, we were to get some keys to a cabin in Jackson Hole where we could stay until things cooled off. When we both got out of jail, we met and decided to do it on Monday night. We drove downtown by the flower shop, and it was still open, so we decided to go get a beer. Lockhart left and told me he had to go see his wife and would be back to pick me up later. I waited for about half an hour or maybe forty-five minutes before he came back. When he came in, he said, 'I did it! I set the fire!' I asked why he did it without me, and he said he just decided to do it. He told me he had broken the lock on the back and tried to find the money but didn't find nothing. He went downstairs and lit a match to a box of wrapping paper, and all at once almost everything around caught on fire."

Mr. Pincock stopped Mee to ask him, "Then you were not there, Mr. Mee?"

"No, I wasn't, but I would've been if Lockhart had come back to get me," he answered.

"What did you do then?" Pincock asked.

"Lockhart told me to come and watch the fireworks, and we went downtown to watch the building burn."

"Did you see Mr. Berchtold after that?"

"Yes, we went over and told him the next day. We had to get the keys to the cabin from him."

"What did Mr. Berchtold do when you told him?"

Mee paused, trying to think. "He acted like someone would act when they were on the winning team of a ball game. He kind of went crazy. He giggled and danced around his cell, jumping up and down, clapping his hands. He just kept laughing and saying over and over, 'This is just great! I'd like to see Broberg now!'"

An objection was raised from the defending attorney. The judge overruled.

Mee concluded his testimony with a brief, unemotional statement of being sorry for his part in the fire.

The defense attorney attacked Mee's character and credibility as a witness. He made a strong argument about Mee being a thief and a liar. Russell Mee stood his ground and never changed his account of the fire or Berchtold's plan when questioned thoroughly by the defense.

Dr. Crandall was the next witness. He described caring for Berchtold's medical needs while he was at the Bannock County Jail. He was questioned about Berchtold's overdose and suicidal gesture. Dr. Crandall did not feel that Berchtold was suicidal but had been trying to gain sympathy.

A brief recess was called while the court awaited the arrival of Dr. Anderson, a psychiatrist from State Hospital South. He was one of two doctors who had given Berchtold a psychiatric evaluation. Dr. Crandall returned to sit next to Bob and me.

I felt Mrs. Berchtold's cold, icy stare once again. I felt relieved when she got up. Instead of leaving the courtroom, she walked over to me, and in a high, screeching voice said, "MaryAnn, do you remember when you and Gail came to see me, and I told you to keep your daughter away from my son?"

"I remember coming to see you, but you never told me to keep Jan away from him," I said.

She flew into a fit of rage. Her eyes narrowed to small slits and her mouth formed a tight line. "Now don't you lie to me. I did too!" she said viciously.

I refuted her charge, "I'm not lying, Mrs. Berchtold."

She retorted wildly, "Look what you've done to him! It's your and Jan's fault!"

She was trembling with anger. Her fists were tightly clenched. I moved back, trying to get out of her reach in case she decided to let loose. I was grateful that Dr. Crandall was between us.

Bob said softly, "Don't say one word in return. She sounds just like her son."

I turned away, hoping she would leave. She stood there panting heavily. Her daughter came over and ushered her out of the courtroom.

Dr. Anderson's appearance brought the court back into session. His evaluation of Berchtold was an eye-opener.

"Mr. Berchtold is a sociopath. He feels no guilt for anything that has happened, and he blames everyone else for his problems. He takes no responsibility. From the moment he laid eyes on Jan Broberg, he began scheming how he was going to have her. He has a criminal mind and has no remorse for what he has done."

Mr. Pincock asked, "Do you believe Mr. Berchtold is mentally ill?"

"Yes, it is my belief that he is mentally ill."

"Do you believe Mr. Berchtold is a danger to society?" Mr. Pincock asked.

"I do. I feel Mr. Berchtold should be placed in a secure facility that will deal with his psychopathic personality."

"Do you believe Mr. Berchtold remains a threat to the Broberg family?"

"Yes. He has an aggressive, impulsive disorder, which may continue to endanger the lives of the Broberg family. His compulsive-obsessive behavior toward their daughter is extreme, as has been demonstrated in the past two kidnappings. Miss Broberg is not safe from Berchtold, and he is capable of taking her again if he has access to her."

"Do you feel it is in the best interest of Miss Broberg if Mr. Berchtold is placed in a locked facility?" Pincock questioned.

"I recommend placement in a state psychiatric hospital and that he be allowed to receive medical treatment, but it should be a locked facility," Dr. Anderson stated.

Following the testimony of Dr. Anderson, Bob, and I were both called to testify. Bob expressed concern for his safety and well-being, explaining the times and places where Berchtold had threatened his life.

I told Berchtold's plan to kill Bob and how he told me he had pointed a loaded gun at Bob but had changed his mind. The defense attorney was on his feet continually, voicing objections. Other instances of Berchtold's threats to others were mentioned, but because they were considered hearsay, and no reports had been filed against him by law enforcement, they were not considered relevant to this hearing.

Jan had not been subpoenaed to appear.

Mr. Pincock decided not to contest the mental defect in lieu of a trial. He felt Berchtold would be placed in secure confinement for a long period of time, which would serve us well and hasten his lockup. Judge Beebe signed a commitment order to send Berchtold to the Idaho Security Medical Facility in Boise. He was expected to be taken there on June 27, 1977.

We were ecstatic. It had been three years of pure hell, but at last we might be able to turn our lives in a new direction. Other than a blurb in the newspaper, there was nothing eventful about his departure. With Berchtold's transfer from Bannock County Jail to the Idaho Security Medical Facility in Boise, we took on a whole new attitude about our approaching summer.

Can Life begin Again

Completing junior high school was a milestone for Jan. Watching her celebrate graduation festivities in her little size-one dress, fully aware of the fact that my daughter was still a little girl, I became deeply sad and had to hide in the shadows so my tears wouldn't cause her to be embarrassed.

Driver's training began the following week. This fourteen-year-old girl, who hadn't yet grown tall enough to see over the steering wheel, but who met the minimum age requirement for driving in the state of Idaho, began worrying other motorists—just like the rest of her peers. At last, she was in full swing with teen activities, and from our perspective, life was looking normal again.

Dr. Smith discontinued our visits. Jan was still not ready to disclose the trauma she had experienced or discuss whether she had been sexually molested. He emphasized patience, believing that she would talk when she felt safe. He coached me to look for signs that would indicate her willingness to disclose her feelings and experiences. With the perpetrator out of her life, he expected her to transition back into her familiar surroundings quickly and learn to trust again. Should there be a concern, Jan had earned top priority on his list of patients. Jan expressed relief. Her complaints about the tedious trips to Salt Lake City had persisted for several months, and she had considered the visits a waste of our money.

Back at home, often after we answered the phone, the caller would remain silent, but would stay on the line until we hung up. Although B was in a locked facility, we blamed these annoying calls on him or his associates. On one occasion, Jan answered, and it became evident by the manner in which she was responding that this was not a friendly call. Determined that Berchtold would not get to her again, I went to an extension and heard an unfamiliar voice speaking. I suppose raising the receiver tipped off the female caller and she hung up.

I questioned Jan. "I don't know who it was," she responded, appearing agitated.

"What did they want?" I asked.

"I don't know. It was a wrong number."

Her nervous behavior caused me to doubt the truth of her reply. Trying to be nonthreatening, I asked, "Jan, has B been trying to contact you?"

"No. I told you and Dad I would let you know if he did."

"I know. I just have to be sure."

I called Mr. Pincock and related the incident. He was keeping a log of all unidentified calls.

Jan's Diary, August 29, 1977:

It's been two months since B left, and I haven't heard from anybody except the lady who called to tell me he's okay. She works at the place where B was sent, and she said not to worry because he is doing well and thinks about me every day. Since he can't tell me himself, she is passing his thoughts on. "Tell her she is still my special angel and I love her with all my heart."

B used to worry that if he ever went to a mental hospital, the doctors would operate on him like they did Jack Nicholson in that movie about the cuckoo nest. I miss B, and no matter what happens, I love him. I wish he wouldn't call me at home because he's going to get himself in a bunch of trouble.

Jan, now fifteen, began her Sophomore year at Pocatello High School in September. She complained about being so small and thought she deserved to look older than Susan. She was also concerned about her late maturation. "Why haven't I started having periods?" she asked me. "All my friends have. I must be some kind of dork."

"It will happen," I reassured her, "I didn't start until I was sixteen, and I was a little shrimp too. It must be in your genes. Don't be so anxious."

Jan and her girlfriends attended a kickoff dance at the school's tennis courts to celebrate the beginning of school. Her excitement was refreshing as she burst into the house with an announcement, "I met this cute guy who's Caroline's friend and he wants to take me to the homecoming dance. What am I going to tell him? I'm only fifteen; you said said that's not old enough to date."

"Well, if it's a group date and you're with Caroline, we would consider letting you go," Bob said.

"But, Dad, I can't," Jan snapped back. "It isn't right."

"Okay. Just tell him you'll have to wait until you're sixteen," Bob said, reinforcing her decision.

"That's not it at all. You don't understand!" Jan said as she fled the room, clearly upset.

Turning to me with a disgruntled look on his face, Bob said, "Women. I don't understand them, and I live with a houseful. Even the dogs are female."

"But it's a relief to see Jan enjoying normal attention from boys her own age," I replied. "She's always so standoffish when guys are around."

"What did I say that made her think I didn't understand?" Bob asked. "I was just agreeing with her."

"Oh, she's still trying to feel okay about herself. At least she's sharing her feelings with us again," I said.

Against Belief, B is Released

The temporary tranquility of our lives was brought to an abrupt halt at the end of September, when we heard that Berchtold could be released right away. The news was harrowing.

We met with the prosecutor, Mr. Pincock, who was more than distressed—he was angry. "This is nothing short of ludicrous. An order of release is being filed in district court. It's only been three months."

"How could this happen?" Bob questioned. "I thought we had years before he was out terrorizing us again."

"Can you believe he's been declared non-dangerous to himself and others by two psychiatrists? How absurd," Pincock growled.

"What can we do to stop it?" I asked.

"Write letters to your congressmen—Health and Welfare too. We'll do what we can from our office to stop it. I'm appealing to Judge Beebe, requesting that Dr. Anderson reexamine him. After all, the court relied upon his expertise when they declared Berchtold had a mental illness. That guy is not ready to be let out on the street."

It was appalling that two experts had found him to be perfectly well and in need of no further care. The prosecutor stated to the press, "If the Court is now willing to rely upon the opinion of staff members from the Department of Health and Welfare, surely it would be incumbent upon that person or persons to read and consider the evidence introduced at the hearing, whereby the Court found Berchtold to be both mentally ill and dangerous." The prosecutor emphasized that "Mr. Berchtold is continuing to contact Miss Broberg, either himself or through a third party, which indicates he has not changed." Included in his bold statement, Pincock declared, "I am convinced that there will be bloodshed if Berchtold is released and allowed to return to this community."

Letters were sent to several influential individuals and agencies in an effort to stop his release. An editorial in the local newspaper mentioned that the criteria of mental defect was being used too often and was being manipulated by defense attorneys for accused criminals:

The game consists of convincing the psychiatrist and jury that you were crazy when you [committed the crime]; then you're home free. Unfortunately, there are too many persons taking advantage of that tactic—at the expense of our legal system. Mr. Berchtold, who was acquitted on a charge of kidnapping of a Pocatello youth by reason of mental defect, has been deemed sane following mental evaluation by the Idaho Department of Health and Welfare, and the department now recommends that he be freed.

Despite efforts to block Berchtold's release, a Sixth Judicial District Court judge signed a court order:

In this case, the defendant, R. E. Berchtold, was acquitted on the grounds of mental illness and committed to the custody of the Director of Health and Welfare. On October 13, 1977, a report, including psychiatric evaluations, requesting the discharge of R. E. Berchtold from the custody of the Department of Health and Welfare upon the grounds that Berchtold may be discharged or released on condition without danger to himself or to others; and the court being satisfied by the report, . . . such conditions being reasonably necessary and required to control the pedophilia or pedophilia tendencies, existing or heretofore manifested, relative to Jan Broberg, a female minor, and conduct related thereto and directed toward said female minor and her parents, it is: Hereby ordered that R. E. Berchtold be conditionally released from the Department of Health and Welfare upon the conditions that said R. E. Berchtold not voluntarily be physically present during the next three (3) years in Bannock County, Idaho, so long as Jan Broberg or her parents or any of them are residents therein.

There was nothing for us to do except live with the order and pray he would stay away. Jan had nothing to say. We were not able to detect her feelings. Discussing the conditions of his release, we pled with her to tell us if he tried to see her or contact her in any way. We became extremely cautious about where our children went, and we wanted to know every detail of their time away from us. Our involvement in every activity our children participated in, whether at school, church, or in the community, was considered by some to be extreme.

Jan's Diary, November 30, 1977:

Today I got a note at school to call a number. I about dropped dead when I heard B's voice. He got released from the hospital and needs to see me, but he can't come to Pocatello, so I had to drive out to Fort

Hall. I had play practice, so I told Belinda I was sick. I almost got lost since it's been so long since B took me out there. When I saw him, he looked good and was very happy. He said being in the hospital he had to convince them that he wasn't crazy. B asked if I was still doing everything I was supposed to and not going out with any guys. I hadn't heard from "Z" for a long time. B said I'm following the plan, so they don't need to contact me. Time was short, and he didn't want to get caught, so later we will figure things out. Nobody can find out I saw him, or he'll get sent back to Boise. He's not supposed to see me until I'm eighteen.

Chapter 21
THEATER CAMP

Summer 1978

Jan had been acting since the age of seven, and at the age of eight, she announced to us that acting was her life's dream. She was hooked. Although concerned, Bob and I realized that the summer theater workshop might be the best medicine for her overall confidence. Doing what she loved in a new environment with new people might truly help her.

Jan heard in her High School drama class about a Summer theater workshop at Brigham Young University for the youth. She expressed excitement about going as she waved the application in front of us. "I'll learn everything about acting, and we get to do costumes, design sets, lighting, and participate in all kinds of production stuff. Plus do a final student written play! It really sounds cool."

Housing would be at a girls' dorm, and each attendee would have to adhere to strict rules. The environment appeared safe.

I watched Bob's eyebrows rise while savoring her enthusiasm. Turning to me, he smiled and winked. "There's no question about it. You're going. Just call us collect every other day so we know you're okay."

"Please," Jan begged, "don't tell anyone about what happened. I don't want them to think I'm some weirdo."

Prior to her departure, a teenage boy called our home and asked to speak with Jan. I told him she wasn't home, but I would have her call him if he would leave his number. The boy identified himself as a friend and said he would call back.

I enlisted Karen's help to take the call if the boy called back and to try to find out who he was.

"If it's Berchtold, I need to know so we can report him," I said.

A couple of hours later, the phone rang. Karen answered and pretended to be Jan. After a few brief moments, she handed me the phone. In a high-pitched, falsetto voice, the caller babbled something strange that didn't make any sense. With no response on our end, the caller hung up.

After I related the incident to Jan, she was furious, "Don't anyone ever do that again!"

"Well, Jan, it wasn't any big deal. Probably some kid sitting home bored." I concluded she was out of sorts only because her privacy had been invaded.

B's Not So Subtle Reminder

When Jan was in the third week of the theater workshop, our poodle went into convulsions. We rushed the dog to the vet and learned that she had been poisoned. Tiff had been such a wonderful comfort to all the girls during the worst of times. Karen and Susan were in tears. A day later, Tiff's puppy, Bandit, was found in the front yard having convulsions. We rushed her to the vet and learned that she had also been poisoned.

Following our instructions, Jan called home every day. On the day of Bandit's poisoning, she fell to pieces. "Oh no!" she shrieked. Her outburst was reminiscent of the night the store had burned. "Mom, who did it? How did it happen?"

"I don't know."

Jan was bawling, "Oh, I just feel like . . . I don't know. If they die . . . They can't die, Mom! Should I come home?"

"Jan, the vet said Tiff is doing better. I think she'll come home to-morrow. It's too early to talk about Bandit." I handed Karen the phone, and she explained every excruciating movement of the dog's convulsions. Jan was nearly hysterical. Her affection for the dogs was strong, but this was way beyond sorrow. It was a cry of helplessness, and there was a sense that Jan somehow felt responsible. We understood that this unexplainable emotion from Jan needed to be scrutinized.

"Bob, something's wrong. Jan's overreacting. She's too emotional about this," I said. "I know she doesn't want us talking about her past, but I think somebody at BYU needs to know about Berchtold. I've had a feeling that he knows she is there." We contacted the workshop director and drove to the campus the following day.

The counselor assured us that there had been no suspicious persons sighted.

I explained that Berchtold would fit naturally into any setting. We requested that they keep Jan's past from her peers since she was extremely sensitive about it.

Jan would be celebrating her sixteenth birthday during the five-week workshop. With permission, we bought party decorations and ordered birthday treats to be delivered to her dorm for a Gala Event. After being assured that her birthday would be a fun surprise, we apprehensively returned home.

When I called the day after her birthday, a counselor reported, "The birthday was a huge success, except Jan was very emotional. Before we put the party together, Jan came running into the dorm crying. I asked if there was something wrong, but she brushed me off and went to her room. I listened at the door and could hear her sobbing. I talked to another staff member, and we decided to give her some time before insisting she talk to us. After decorating the reception room, I went up, and she seemed to be okay."

We didn't know what Berchtold had meant in his letter from jail about "having time" before she turned sixteen, but we suspected Jan might be upset about something he meant by that now that she was turning sixteen.

Ice Cream Miracle

Jan's Diary, July 31, 1978:

This has been the worst day since I came here. I was at the Student Union standing in line to get a drink when Curtis came over and wished me Happy Birthday. Somebody told him that it was my birthday, so he wanted to buy me ice cream to celebrate. I know he likes me, and we've had lots of fun doing our drama classes. I said I didn't want one, and he just kept saying he wanted to and asked what my favorite flavor was. I kept telling him no, but he did it anyway and brought it over and gave it to me. I didn't know what to do. I was so upset that I don't think I even said thanks. I just took it and left. I know I can't talk to boys or have any boys who are friends. What's going to happen? The dogs almost died. What next? Is something going to happen to my sisters or dad? Or maybe me! I'm 16 today and I haven't had the baby. Does that mean I'm going to vaporize, and they will take Susan? I can't stand to think about it. I need to tell her about the mission. If she doesn't want to do it, I will take that gun hidden under Dad's bed and kill her and then I'll kill myself. I wish I could talk to B. He wanted to meet me while I was here, but it hasn't worked out. I haven't heard from any of them since I came here. I know they are watching me. Everybody here has been so nice, but I can't talk to anybody about my life.

As Jan neared the end of five weeks, we traveled to Provo, Utah, to attend two days of theatrical presentations by students of the drama workshop. Observing a jubilant, excited, and outgoing daughter, we felt the experience was one worth celebrating with her fully.

Caroline came to stay overnight after Jan returned home. We listened to Jan's jubilant voice as she reiterated the "blast" that had taken place.

"Oh, this cute guy from California said that he was in love with me," Jan giggled. "You guys saw what he did when we were getting ready to leave; he knelt down on the hot pavement in front of all my family, took my hand like he was proposing, and said how much he would miss me. Then he said, "Please grow up and wait for me." He was really dramatic. He was always fun and crazy."

The girls erupted in laughter.

"Oh, the drama. It's more than I can take," Bob said, picking up the newspaper and heading for the patio to enjoy the beautiful August evening.

All three girls retreated to the basement, where they could talk privately without parents listening in. As they headed downstairs, Caroline asked Jan, "What do you think of your bedroom?"

Because Jan was sleeping upstairs, Karen and Cousin David had decided to change the room by hanging new posters, introducing new colors, and even taking the wallpaper off the walls. Karen longed to have Jan's company again in the basement. I told them I was doubtful it would make any difference because Jan disliked the room so intensely.

Jan, though grateful for the kind attempt, firmly reiterated that she would never sleep in her old room in the basement again. We didn't know exactly how yet, but the joyful bond between these sisters and their best friend would be at the heart of Jan's healing.

Chapter 22
WILL WE EVER GET BACK TO NORMAL?

Fall 1978

Caroline's update on her latest boyfriend raised Karen's eyebrows. "Of course, my parents are having a fit about me dating Ricky. My dad says, 'That kid doesn't seem to have much sense.'"

Caroline draped herself over most of the bed while Jan happily sat on the floor. Karen bounced up onto the big blue velvet hanging chair—the one we bought from B's shop years before when their rooms were first divided. The matching pillow provided a good headrest. Karen noticed the zipper was partially down, and she began to zip it closed, but it got stuck. She noticed a piece of paper wedged alongside the foam cushion and pulled the paper out.

Laughing, Jan said, "Your dad hasn't ever liked any of your boyfriends, Caroline."

"Jan, what's this?" Karen asked, holding up the crumpled piece of paper she had pulled from the cushion. "Who's Zada?"

"Zada?" Caroline said, laughing.

Jan sat up with a startled look. The color drained from her face. "What did you say?"

"This note. I found it in here," she said, pointing to the cushion, "It says, 'Call this number and Zada will—'"

"Give me that!" Jan screamed as she jumped to her feet.

Karen held her hand above Jan's reach and continued reading, ignoring Jan's protests, "'. . . will tell you what's next. There's still time!' Time? For what?" Karen asked.

Frantically, Jan attempted to grab the paper from Karen's hand. With one final lunge, shrieking at the top of her lungs, Jan grabbed the paper and shredded it into small bits.

Caroline shouted, "Jan, what's wrong with you? You're acting crazy! Karen, stop it!"

"Tell her, Caroline. Tell her what we found!" Karen hollered.

"When we were working on your room, your cousin David found some notes B wrote to you, but we took them away from him, and now I've got them!" Caroline exclaimed.

Jan stared in disbelief at Caroline. "What? Did you read them?" she shouted.

"Yeah! And now you've got to tell us what's going on."

"I can't—besides, nothing is going on! You guys need to get out of my room and leave me alone," Jan screamed. "You aren't supposed to take or read those—they're private. Just get out. I don't want to be interrogated by the two of you. You wouldn't understand anyway!"

"Karen, let's go," Caroline snapped back as she and Karen quickly exited. "Jan needs to calm down, unpack, and stop being such a jerk. She obviously doesn't want us in here. We were just trying to be nice, redecorating your room so you'd like it more. You can be so rude!"

Jan sat on her bed and stared into space. Big tears rolled down her inexpressive face. Thoughts raced through her confused mind:

Why had the dogs been sick? Why didn't they die? What happens now? I'm sixteen—I don't think I'm pregnant with the special baby. Where is B? When Curtis bought me the ice cream, I was so scared. I figured that was it, that I'd be vaporized, but I'm still here. What about Susan? Before I kill her, I need to know for sure. Are they real?

Are you watching me? Reading my mind? Wait, I'm just kidding. I know you're real, watching me, reading my mind. Don't worry—I'll do whatever you tell me to do. Just please don't hurt my family.

For the past four years, Jan had never doubted or questioned the reality of Zada, Zethra, or the mission with B—her male companion. But on that day, for about ten seconds, she had a brief moment where, in her mind, she questioned everything.

Testing the Water

As school started, Jan made up her mind to carefully begin "testing the water" with small and simple things, such as talking to a boy at school and letting herself speak civilly to her father. Even hanging out with her friend Jan Hull, who had a boyfriend and who always seemed to have various friends to talk to at lunch, was a risk. After testing the water, she would wait to see if anything bad happened. The weight of the mission was becoming a burden she could hardly bear. Killing herself began to seem like an escape, almost a fantasy she longed for. But first, before she hurt her sister or herself, she had to know for sure.

***

Homecoming season was approaching, with its many school activities, including, football tournaments, bonfires and the dance. Jan was playing the piano for a church fireside when a boy she barely knew approached her and asked her to the dance. She gulped hard, searching for the answer. She blurted out the words almost involuntarily, "Yes, I'll go!" Then, realizing what she had said, she immediately felt lightheaded and excused herself.

The day of the dance was coming quickly. This was her first time buying a special gunnysack dress, like her friends had. I was elated that she wanted me to take her and Caroline to pick it out. She found one with pretty cream lace and a square neck that tied behind at the waist. She was nervous, but there were four couples going together, and she was good friends with a few of the girls. This gave her some measure of comfort. They all met at our house to get the flowers situated. Bob had generously offered to provide boutonnieres for all the boys and wrist corsages for the girls. Jan seemed happy—nervous, but excited.

Jan knew that this was the biggest test of all. Going to a dance with a boy—so many things could go wrong. What if she came home and we had been harmed or killed? But on the other hand, if she came home and we were all intact, then she would know that the voices were not real.

She tried to enjoy her date, but as this was a first for her, and the constant barrage of horrible thoughts were persistent. She developed a bad headache. Her date was shorter than she was, so she took off her wedge sandals and tried to keep dancing. Having only picked at her dinner before the dance, she was beginning to feel a little sick. The snacks on the beautifully decorated tables in the gymnasium were unappealing to her, and the punch tasted like straight sugar. But even so, she wondered how it would feel to be a "normal" sixteen-year-old. She barely knew how to act, but she had her girlfriends with her who distracted her, joked with her, and secretly cheered her on, knowing this was her first real date. She had missed out on being a normal young preteen and teen at ages twelve, thirteen, fourteen, and fifteen.

As the date was coming to an end, she wondered, *What do "normal" girls do next? Surely, he will not try to kiss me, will he?* Terrified, but hiding it all behind her big, warm, sincere smile, she thanked the boy on the front porch of her home, gave him a quick, stiff hug, and said good night as she shivered and opened the door. The warmth of the living room on the other side gave her a moment of relief, but immediately her thoughts turned to fear as she wondered what destruction she might find. First, she peeked through the curtains of the dining room window to see the boy driving away. Then she turned off the porch light.

Turning toward the hallway, she took a few steps toward the bedrooms. She was startled when she heard a quick snort. "Jani, is that you?" Her heart stopped beating for just a moment when she realized her father had been dozing in his favorite chair—the big recliner at the edge of the living room. He had waited up for her.

She was overwhelmed with relief, "Yes, it's me."

"So, you made it home. Did you have a good time?" he said sleepily.

For the first time in such a long, long time, she sat on the arm of the recliner and looked in his eyes, fighting back tears of relief and joy. She simply said, "Yes, Dad, I did. I am home." She leaned in and they hugged—the first affection she had shown her father in almost two years.

"Well, I guess we better get to bed. I love you, Jani. I'm so glad you're home safe."

Jan walked down the upstairs hallway past our room and peeked in Susan's door. Seeing that Susan was tucked in and sleeping safe and sound, she wandered to the last bedroom. In a state of shock, she wondered, *What do I do now? Would the consequences of breaking the rules already have happened? I hugged Dad; that's really bad. Would Karen wake up blind? Is there still a chance they will vaporize me? What about Mom?* Jan took off her shoes. The adrenaline from the fear and panic she had been dealing with for the past several days came crashing down on her exhausted body and mind. Lying on top of the bed in her new dress, she pulled the comforter up from the side and fell asleep.

Caroline came over the next day, Sunday, for a sleepover since there was no school on Monday in observance of Columbus Day. As the three best friends—Jan, Karen, and Caroline—made their way to the basement playroom to look for a game, I began to clear the dishes off the bar area and coffee table from the tomato soup and the toasted cheese sandwiches that we had as our Sunday evening meal tradition. Susan was watching the Disney Sunday night movie with Bob on the couch. The day had been peaceful.

The girls began playing Chinese Checkers in the middle of the family room floor around the coffee table. Bob detested "parlor games," but encouraged the rest of us to play. "Have fun," Bob said. "I'll play referee if Jan starts to lose." Jan was not a good loser. She and Karen had always been competitive when it came to games, friends, singing, and most other things, but Karen was not a sore loser like Jan. Caroline's good nature was a plus. She was always firing quips and remarks to keep everyone laughing. She tried to keep things from getting too serious. Jan won that round.

Caroline suggested they play rummy next. Jan began to lose, and the playful chiding from Caroline began. "Okay, rummy dummy, it's your turn. Go ahead, rummy dummy—what's your next move? We're waiting—just put a card down, rummy dummy!" As Jan became more and more upset, the rest of us tried to laugh our way out of an explosion, but the explosion came. Jan suddenly slid her arm across the table, clearing the table of all the cards. Then she ran screaming out of the room. She slammed her bedroom door shut—a startling reminder of her still-fragile state. "We'll go apologize. We can talk to her. Come on, Karen," Caroline suggested as she and Karen stood up to go to Jan's room.

Susan, Bob, and I headed upstairs to get ready for bed.

Caroline knocked on Jan's door and said, "Jan, we are coming in." They opened the door and saw Jan lying face down on her flowery white-and-blue bedspread—the one I had hand-quilted for her. She did not respond or move. Caroline and Karen flanked Jan on either side at the bottom of her bed. Caroline finally broke in, "Jan, I'm sorry. I shouldn't have called you a rummy dummy. I didn't want you to get mad."

"I'm not mad," was Jan's muffled reply. "I just feel bad—about everything. You aren't supposed to . . ." Jan never finished the sentence. She turned over, and as she moved her head slowly and mechanically, the girls could see that the life had drained from her body. Bringing herself to a sitting position, she became transfixed on some item sitting on her dresser.

"Jan, what's wrong?" Caroline asked. Jan continued staring at the dresser.

Karen snapped at her, "Come on, Jan. Quit it!"

Jan's head moved slowly toward Karen. The blank expression on her face was strange. Her eyes became fixed—trancelike. Within a few moments, her persona changed dramatically as she started talking incoherently and began brushing her arms frantically, as if she were trying to brush something off her body. Her tongue thickened. She was forming words, but they were jumbled and strange. Without warning, Jan's knees buckled under her and she fell to the floor.

Karen thought Jan was staging a scene, which she had done before as a way to tease her sisters. Jan's face was buried in the carpet, and her piteous groan became a painful wail. Her body was still, and she began hyperventilating. They thought she was going to pass out.

Caroline and Karen glanced at each other wide-eyed, and then they stared at Jan as she continued the mournful cries.

When the groans turned to gagging, Caroline scolded, "If you're going to throw up, go to the bathroom, for heaven's sake!" As the contortions continued, Caroline cried out, "Karen, something's wrong. Jan's sick! Get your mom!"

Ignoring Caroline's plea, Karen stood over her sister's contorted body and demanded, "Get up and stop it!" Jan continued to groan as she rocked her body from side to side, pulling at the carpet with her fists. She continued to babble incoherently. Anxious and scared, Karen said, "Jan, quit acting this way. Tell us what's wrong!"

The gyrations continued as Jan's eyes widened and she sat up. She stared into space and began mumbling indecipherable words. Again, she started brushing off the imaginary creatures as if they were crawling on her body. "Get off!" she cried out and again fell into a heap on the floor, mourning painfully as she pulled at the carpet. "Oh! You can't," Jan groaned. "No, you can't know."

Caroline knelt down by Jan and said, "Jan, you're scaring me to death. What's wrong?"

Jan's face was ashen and she responded with another wail. "I'm going to get Mom!" Karen reported.

"No! Karen! Don't! Don't," Jan cried out. "You're . . ." she started, but again her speech was garbled.

"Are you crazy? What's wrong?" Karen demanded.

Jan fell in a helpless stupor on the floor. Her face glistened with perspiration, and her skin was cold and clammy. Shaking and howling, she clawed at the floor. Jan was inclined to be dramatic, but Karen had never seen her sister contorting and thrashing about so violently. It terrified her.

"We need to do something," Karen announced, realizing things were getting out of hand.

Caroline clutched Karen's arm as she stared at Jan's feeble form. "What's wrong with her?"

Karen shrugged her shoulders. "I don't know, but that's B's writing," she said, looking at bits of tiny paper notes strewn around the floor. Had Jan thrown them there?

Whimpering sounds emerged from Jan's shaking, trembling body. With Karen and Caroline hovering over her, Jan slowly began to relax from the trance. She let go of the carpet and pulled her body into a fetal position.

Ferocious sobbing ensued. It seemed that four years of pent-up agony were being expelled, and once she had found an outlet, her sobs seemed unstoppable. Berchtold's carefully planned secret had been discovered. She didn't know what to do, and her cries were gut-wrenching.

With no knowledge of what had caused Jan's unexpected outburst, Caroline encircled her distraught friend in her arms while Karen patted her sister's limp hands, offering silent comfort.

***

It didn't surprise us that the girls were up late talking, but around 1:30 in the morning, Bob heard commotion coming from the basement. He got out of bed and walked to the top of the stairs.

"Are you girls ever going to turn it off?" he asked.

Karen stuck her head out of Jan's door and responded, "Sorry, Dad. We'll try to be quiet."

After the door closed quietly, we could still hear loud whispering. "It's late," Bob stated loudly. "You kids need to get to sleep. Now go to bed!"

When Karen heard her father's voice from the top of the stairs, she looked at Caroline and said, "I don't think Dad should come down here right now." Karen opened the door, spoke to her father, closed the door, and then whispered to Caroline, "Let's get Jan out of here."

Jan nodded her head in agreement and whispered, "It can't be in this room! Now I have to tell you, but it can't be in this room!"

The two girls supported Jan as they moved down the hall and into Karen's room next door. Jan instantly kneeled down on the floor and took deep breaths as if getting ready to start a marathon. Karen and Caroline sat on the side of the bed. For short periods of time, Jan seemed to be getting a grip, but then she would revert to her previous condition—crying, gasping, clawing at the carpet, and scratching her head, arms, and lower torso.

The Fear is Real Even if the Aliens Are Not

Karen and Caroline whispered to each other. Had Jan seen something in the room that had scared her? They both looked around but saw nothing unusual. The duo decided to wait out the ordeal until Jan could give them a sensible explanation.

Gradually, Jan's energy began to return. Between trying to speak and choking back sobs, she took a deep breath and said, "Here goes!" There was a long pause. "I have to tell somebody, but I can't. You don't get it. This will affect all of you. You're in danger. They might be listening," she whispered as her eyes darted around the room.

"What are you talking about?" Karen asked.

Jan blurted out, "I'm going to die! I failed!"

"Jan, you're not going to die," Caroline stated boldly.

Bawling, Jan repeated, "I'm going to die!"

"Why are you saying that?" Karen asked.

"She said so!" Jan cried out.

"Who said?" Karen asked.

"Zada!" Jan shrieked, her body trembling.

Karen and Caroline looked at each other with questioning faces.

"Who told you that you were going to die?" Caroline asked.

Jan exploded as she began rubbing her arms again. "You're not supposed to know!"

"Know what?" Karen asked. "That you're going to die?"

"About me having a baby!" Jan exclaimed, holding her hand to her mouth as tears gushed down her face.

"What?" Karen's mouth flew open as she stared at her sister in shock.

"You're going to have a baby?" Caroline questioned in disbelief.

"No—I mean I'm supposed to . . . to help them!" The words spewing from Jan sounded desperate but didn't make any sense.

"Help who?"

"People from this other world!" she blubbered, scratching her arms furiously.

The girls stared at each other.

Jan, what are you saying?" Caroline asked. "You're talking nonsense!"

"You've got to stop acting crazy and tell us what you're talking about," Karen declared.

"Awful things! I can't!" Jan's voice wavered between sobs.

"Like what?"

"Bad things that can happen to both of you!" Jan cried out.

Karen and Caroline looked at each other in disbelief. Prodding Jan to tell them about Zada, the girls softened their demeanor as they felt Jan's fear. In a trembling voice, Jan began recounting the traumatic experiences of her past.

Recalling the horrid account of waking up in the motorhome with her arms and feet strapped, Jan's body quivered. Goose bumps appeared on her arms, and her hair stood on end. Karen and Caroline looked at each other, amazed. With great emotion and long pauses, Jan related her encounter with Zada and Zethra, reliving each horrid episode. Relating each event brought her renewed terror. Only prodding from Karen and Caroline persuaded her to continue.

Dumbfounded, the two girls listened carefully to the incredible story. Though it had been nearly four years, Jan's memory about these events remained vivid. Jan frequently stopped and went through the peculiar antics of rubbing her skin and moaning before being comforted by her listeners. Jan concluded her unbelievable ordeal, and the girls simply stared, not knowing how to react.

"It's all so weird!" Caroline stated. Jan simply nodded.

"And you believed they were real? These people from another world?" Karen asked, doubting that her sister could actually believe such a thing.

Jan murmured emotionally, "They were real!"

"What did they mean when they said you wouldn't exist?" Caroline asked. "I don't get it."

"They told me I wouldn't . . . if my mission failed, I would be nothing. My body and spirit would be gone, just disappear, and I wouldn't exist in the next life. I'd vaporize."

"Did you always believe they were real?"

"Yes, there are so many of them," Jan replied, frustrated.

"Who are they?" Karen prodded.

"I don't know. Just a bunch of people who call me, or I've had to go meet them," she responded anxiously.

"Why?"

"Because I had to. I'd go on my bike—to Ross Park, down by the railroad tracks, once to the train station, once to a trailer park that was a long way out on Yellowstone when it was raining really hard. I'd get so scared." Jan wept.

"Are they real people? I mean, what do they look like?" Caroline asked.

Jan nodded her head, "They are like us."

"Maybe that's who they really are," Caroline said. "You know what I mean?"

Jan shrugged her shoulders and looked perplexed, "Do you remember the homecoming dance last year? I wasn't supposed to go anywhere with guys unless they said so. But you and Jan Hull begged me to go, and since it was a group, I thought I could get away with it."

"Yeah. My parents think you're so level-headed," Caroline said, laughing.

"Caroline, this isn't funny," Karen reprimanded.

Jan's voice was quivering. "Caroline, something bad is supposed to happen to you."

"Me? You're kidding! What?"

"A bad disease." Jan's voice drifted off as she began thinking about her failed assignment.

Caroline nudged Jan, bringing her back to the present.

In a trembling voice, Jan said, "Sometimes I hoped I'd die or get killed! Then it would all be over."

"Oh, Jan, you didn't!" Caroline responded.

"It's so awful." Jan broke into sobs. "One time I planned how I was going to kill myself because I hated all the things I was supposed to do, but I kept thinking about Susan. What if they took Susan?" Jan burst into another episode of crying and groaning as she thought about her little sister. She clawed and pulled at her skin.

"Don't do that," Caroline said, grabbing Jan's hands. "This is sick," she murmured.

Karen jumped up, got a roll of toilet paper from the bathroom, and handed it to Jan.

"When nothing happened after that dance," Jan explained, "I started thinking everything might be okay. B was in prison, so the plan wasn't working. They hadn't talked to me in a while. But then he got out and told me it was going to happen. When the dogs were poisoned while I was at the drama camp, I knew they'd seen me with Curtis, and I was in bad trouble."

Looking anxiously at her sister, Jan's voice rang with alarm. "Karen, if you went blind, it would've been my fault."

"What? Why?" Karen asked.

"They said! Look at all the things that happened," Jan replied. "All the time I was afraid somebody was going to give me a note or something. I got lots of messages at school until B went to prison. Before he got out, I got a note from the school office to call a long-distance number. I knew it was a message from one of them."

"Did you call?" Caroline asked.

"I had to," Jan said as she shuddered and then blew her nose. "The lady told me I needed to meet B and make a plan for when he got out, but he couldn't meet me in Pocatello because he'd get thrown back in prison. I had to drive out to the Indian reservation and meet him. I said that I was going to play practice, but I told them I was really sick; then I went to see him instead. B knew I was scared, and he felt bad. He said I should stay in school. We were supposed to work something out in the summer."

"What's going to happen now?"

"I don't know. What if they take Susan?" Jan asked with her eyes wide open in panic.

"You're going to tell. You have to," Karen said. "No matter what these people say, you're not supposed to marry B."

"But, they told me I had to!" Jan declared. "I don't think it's real, I guess, but I'm still so scared."

The Baby

"Karen and I think something else is going on," Caroline said firmly. "I mean, you said once that B really loves you, and—well, you know—you and I talked about sex and other stuff. Has he done bad things to you? Jan, just tell me."

Jan's face dropped.

Caroline's position as her best friend was at an advantage since they didn't keep secrets. Curious, she asked Jan pointed questions about the relationship. With Caroline's assertiveness, Jan disclosed small bits of information regarding Berchtold's sexual behavior toward her. As Caroline sought deeper explanations about the abuse, Jan protected her dignity by disassociating herself from the molested child, speaking about herself in third person.

"When it first happened, they were on a trip together. She was very frightened, but B said he would take care of her. He loved her so much that he promised he would do everything he could to save her."

Through the long, difficult night of confession, Jan revealed that the sexual assault had continued for more than three years. "B was only doing what he was told because she had to try and get prepared for the baby, and he had to protect her from other people who wanted to hurt her. Since nobody understood, it was really hard for both of them."

Caroline asked for details about the sex stuff. Jan was specific. Karen, who maintained the position as a silent listener, was shocked and pained as she tried to imagine the horrible defilement of her sister. Karen could sense how deep Jan's wounds were. She couldn't understand why Jan did not recognize herself as the victim.

"Did he ever try to do it for real?" Caroline probed.

"Yeah, but it hurt, and she cried. He didn't want to hurt her, so he had to be very careful."

Contemplating the admissions from Jan, Caroline tried to make sense out of everything she was hearing. Jan continued expressing details about her admitted abuse. Caroline asked pointed questions. Jan obliged as she openly and descriptively revealed the details of the abuse of this "little girl." At one point, Caroline asked how often this happened, and Jan painfully revealed, "The girl had to try several times a day. This little girl was supposed to be free from any impurities, you know—like, you know, not having periods."

"Girls have to if they are going to have babies," Caroline exclaimed.

"That's why this little girl was so special—because she could fulfill the plan. She wasn't all human. Her body was different, special."

"But it's not possible," Caroline said.

"They said not to worry, and it would happen when it was supposed to."

"You mean getting pregnant?" Caroline asked. "Is that why you've been so worried?"

Unwilling to share more, Jan stopped responding and withdrew into a small ball, pulling the blanket around her.

Caroline stared for a long time at her dearest friend before she spoke. "Jan, this has all been one big, fat lie."

Jan's eyes filled with tears again. In one last effort to make them understand her mission, she tried to explain. The two girls listened quietly while Jan dug at her arms again. "They said their planet was sterile and that the old people were dying. I want to be a mom someday. I don't want to die. I just want to go on with my life."

Caroline put her head back on the bed without responding. The silence brought welcome relief to the subdued group. Karen thought Caroline's interrogation had ended until she asked, "When was the last time you saw B?"

Yawning, Jan quietly confessed, "A long time ago." After a brief pause, she continued, "He called me before I went to the workshop. I was supposed to call him when I got there. He wanted to see me and talk about stuff."

"Oh, now that's scary," said Caroline.

"I wrote him a letter, but didn't mail it. It's in my suitcase in the closet."

"I want to see it," Karen said as she jumped up. She picked up the suitcase and rummaged through the unpacked bag. Unzipping the little side fabric pocket, she pulled out an envelope. It was addressed to "B Berchtold" and read:

Dear B,

Sorry that I can't be with you. I wish I could be. Please have a nice week. I'll try to be able to call you while I'm here. I love you. Please remember this all the time. I really long to be with you. I love you more and more every day!

Smile all the time because I love you. So, keep smiling today and always. Be happy because we are going to make it no matter how hard the road may be. So, keep in mind I'll always love you no matter what happens. I think you are Grrrreat.

I'll do my part and anything I can to help you. I love you so much that I couldn't show you. XOXOXOXO

I'm having a great time. Maybe I'll call you if I get the chance!

Love,

Your Dolly, Jan

After reading the note, Caroline asked, "Jan, remember when I'd come over and you would leave? You wouldn't tell Karen and me where you'd gone. When you got back, you were like a . . ."

Karen interrupted and said, "You acted like a zombie."

"Karen and I used to talk about it and get so mad because you wouldn't tell us, but you always had this strange look on your face," Caroline added.

"Before you left for the workshop, you left on your bike and came back with a new necklace. We knew it was from B. You can't hide it anymore," Karen spurted out, "B did all of this."

Jan put her head down and didn't answer.

"You've got to make it stop," Caroline remarked.

Jan replied, defending B, "They told me stuff that B didn't even know. That box was everywhere. It would just show up—like magic—in my bedroom. It just talked to me! I didn't dare touch it because it had some kind of power, and I thought I might die. It scared me to death." Her eyes darted fearfully.

The troubled look on her sister's face made Karen feel extremely sad. Why didn't Jan see that B had actually done this to her?

Drained from Jan's overwhelming disclosure, and with bloodshot, puffy eyes, Karen had heard all she could handle. "You guys, it's almost four o'clock."

"You can't tell anybody about this," Jan said pathetically.

"Oh, sure. So, what are we supposed to do? Let B come and get you?" Caroline said.

"Mom and Dad have to know," Karen said emphatically.

Caroline urged, "Jan, you've got to tell them."

"I just don't want people to think I'm crazy. They might lock me up like B and do bad things to me like what happened to him."

"Your parents won't let that happen," Caroline said.

"What if they make me go back to Dr. Smith? I know he thinks I'm crazy," Jan declared.

Caroline and Karen silently stared at Jan. Finally conceding, Jan said, "Okay, I'll tell them."

"Are you going to tell them about the bad things he did to you?" Caroline asked.

"I don't know."

"That would be awful. I'd never tell my parents," Caroline said.

Exhausted, Karen pulled a blanket onto the carpeted floor and wearily rolled up in it, saying, "Jan, you sleep in my bed; its big enough for two." Caroline spread out in the bed and welcomed Jan to crawl under the covers with her. Sleep did not come easily for the three since they could not turn off the thoughts that had been stirred up during their very difficult night.

Jan's thoughts, feelings, and dreams were a jumble the next morning as she drifted in and out of restless sleep. She was so relieved that Caroline and Karen finally knew, but she felt great apprehension about telling her parents. She told Caroline and Karen, and she hadn't died, but she was still so confused about what was real and what was not. Her mind bounced from one thought to another. *Wow! I told Caroline and Karen about Z, and they believed me. Mom and Dad will probably be mad at me for not telling them. Remember when Z talked to me here the first time? I was so scared that I ran out of my room and B was standing in the hall without his shoes on. I almost fainted. He isn't supposed to come here ever. Karen and Caroline said Zada and Zethra aren't real, for sure. But they've been in my room.*

Am I crazy? I can't stand to do it all alone anymore. If I die, they have to know about Susan and protect her. Can they protect her? Is Bob my real dad? They said he isn't, but I don't believe them anymore. Can they really read my mind? I hope they aren't real. I need to talk to Bob—Dad. Mom too.

Just Tell Them

The whirr of the lawn mower going past the window aroused the sleeping trio. Caroline stretched and yawned. "It's too early. I need more sleep," she groaned, as she pulled the blanket over her head. For the next fifteen minutes, the girls shifted positions, hoping they could miraculously fall back to sleep.

Eventually, Karen said, "Are you awake, Jan?"

"Uh-huh," she grunted.

"Did last night really happen or was it just a bad dream?" Caroline inquired.

Receiving no response, Karen urged Jan to get up. Karen prodded repeatedly, but received little response from her sister. Caroline, annoyed at the intrusion of her sleep, pulled the covers off her head and insisted, "Jan, just go upstairs and tell your parents!"

Jan nervously bit her fingernails. "I can't!" she said uneasily.

Karen stood up, untangled herself from her blanket, and made her way to the door. "Then I'll tell them!"

"Okay! I'll go!" Jan blurted out irritated. "Just give me five more minutes. I've got a splitting headache."

Caroline and Karen attempted to pump Jan full of confidence by offering support. Did she want them to go with her? Would it be easier if one of them told first? Still trying to recover from her difficult confession of the past night, Jan felt trapped. She knew that her parents needed to hear it from her. Finally conceding, she began her climb up the steps to find them.

Her heart began to pound furiously against her chest. Standing at the back door, she paused. Karen's presence at the foot of the stairs gave her confidence to keep going. Making certain that Jan carried through, Karen watched until Jan went out the door and she could hear Jan's voice on the back patio. Approaching her father was unexpected. She didn't think he would be home. His patience during the past year had been remarkable. He had never questioned why she had been so emotional or impulsive and why she had kept aloof and distant from him during these many months.

Chapter 23
FINALLY, THE TRUTH COMES OUT

This was the day that broke open all of the secrets for our family so that healing could really begin. That morning, Bob had gone to work early while I went for my morning jog. On my return, the house was still in sleep mode, with the exception of Susan, who was eating a bowl of cereal. "I can't go downstairs to the family room because the girls are in there sleeping," Susan explained.

"My bedroom is available, and if you want, turn on the TV for Saturday cartoons," I offered. "The girls didn't sleep much last night. I guess we can let them sleep in."

Bob returned from work later in the morning to take advantage of the beautiful fall day by tending to yard work and cleaning off the back patio. Brisk weather was coming soon, but today was perfect. It was cool, and a burst of color appeared in the Fall leaves of our many backyard trees. After Bob finished the yard work, he settled in a lawn chair on the patio to cool off. I needed to snap the mess of beans from Grandma's garden, so I took them out and joined him.

"Oh, MaryAnn," he stated. "Isn't it a beautiful day?"

"Yes," I replied, and in the fashion I had become accustomed to, Bob began to count his many blessings.

"Yes, this is a great day to give thanks for our wonderful country. We are so blessed to have such a beautiful earth and our family together under one roof. I am so very grateful."

"Yes, we certainly are blessed," I said. "The girls must have been up half the night. I didn't get much sleep, but you seem full of energy. It's nearly noon, and they're still sleeping."

"They were on some kind of marathon last night. I didn't think they would ever go to sleep," Bob commented as he put his head back and closed his eyes.

"Oh, the girls have all been riding high with the homecoming activities last week, some new friends, and their school classes. We are lucky that our girls all love school," I said, feeling a sense of peaceful satisfaction watching the squirrels jump from one tree to another. I continued to snap beans, tossing the ends onto the lawn, when Jan appeared at the patio door. She was ghostly white and trembling.

"Jan, what's the matter?" I asked in an alarming tone.

"Dad, can I talk to you?" she said in a quivering, soft voice.

I nodded my head at Bob and quickly left them alone.

A little over an hour later, Bob entered through the back door. He was wide-eyed, pale, and perspiring. He swallowed hard and said breathlessly, "You have to come and hear what Jan has been telling me. You won't believe it! Berchtold was trying to persuade Jan to leave the workshop with him, but that's only one small part of it. You won't believe what Jan's been through. Oh, MaryAnn, it's so awful—it's beyond my ability to understand."

We went to the patio. Jan was seated at the picnic table looking pale and forlorn. Her eyes were red and swollen. Bob asked me to listen and let Jan tell me what she had just told him. I sat across from her as she began disclosing her unbelievable story. Flabbergasted, I was stunned as she talked about waking up in the motorhome, hearing a startling alien voice, and all the other details.

"From the minute I heard her voice," Jan said, "I believed what she said. Her name was Zada and she was from another world. Sometimes there was another voice who said she was Zethra."

Trying to be a good listener and avoid questioning, I nodded and swallowed hard.

Jan's voice quivered as she related the afflictions that she was told would accompany her if she was unwilling or failed to follow the plan. How could she allow her sisters, or her dad, to be harmed? Although she had not known how her life was going to end if she told anyone, she had known she would be destroyed if she ever told. To think about placing Susan in the same circumstances was unthinkable.

"When B told me what they did to him, he was really scared and said he didn't know what to do. After we drove for a long time, B told me to change into some clothes and dress up like a boy. He said we were getting near the Mexican border, and he didn't know what they would do if they saw a girl with him. I was supposed to be Jerry."

"Did he say why?" I asked.

"No, he just thought we wouldn't have any trouble if I pretended to be his son. It was getting dark when we reached the border, and I was really scared."

"Why? Were you afraid they would find out who you were?"

"No, but B was afraid of those people—you know, the aliens. They told him this is what he was supposed to do—go to Mexico. He didn't know what would happen to us if things didn't work out right. I heard their voices a lot when I was in the motorhome. Sometimes B was with me, but when they started talking, he would go into a trance. Other times I was all alone. They kept repeating over and over again what I had to do, and they told me I was chosen to be the mother of a very special child."

Bob and I avoided each other's gaze as we concentrated on Jan. Her voice shook, there was a noticeable tremor in her body, and she continually pulled and scratched at her skin. Obviously traumatized, she repeated how important it was for her to fulfill her mission and not fail.

I wanted to rush around the table and hold her close, but I dared not interrupt her account of what had happened.

"Do you still believe these people are out there and are going to make you do these things?" Bob quizzed.

Jan shrugged her shoulders, "I don't know. I decided things would be okay after I went to the homecoming dance Saturday, and nothing happened. I wasn't supposed to have any relationships with boys, and when the dogs were poisoned, I knew they were watching me and Curtis at drama camp. But then the dogs didn't die. I wasn't sure what was real. I wondered if one of them saw me go to the dance with a boy. But I got home, and you were here, and so was Susan—and Karen was fine too," she sputtered, seemingly on the verge of hyperventilating. "I just don't know exactly who they are, or if they existed like real people, but not aliens, and I'm still scared–and maybe they aren't real."

"How many times have these people contacted you?" I asked, confused by her nonsequential rant.

Jan shook her head slowly. "I don't know, but a lot. Maybe a hundred times. Sister Charlotte was always watching me at Flintridge and I was afraid I'd do something wrong. She's supposed to be one of them, and I was scared of her."

"Jan, I know for a fact that these aliens are not real," her father said. "We know Berchtold planned and schemed all of this so he could control you. You may not believe it now, but you will."

Jan solemnly stared into space. She was trying not to cry, but her eyes looked pained, and her skin was ashen. Jan wanted to believe her father's statement. She wiped her nose with a wad of toilet paper.

Bob firmly stated, "Berchtold has been manipulating your life, lying to you, scaring you beyond all reason. He will continue to do anything he can because he only wants one thing, and that is you, my precious daughter. I can tell you are struggling with what is real and what isn't. He has made all of this up to control you, Jani."

Jan's eyes looked hurt and sad. She pursed her lips and sobbed desperately.

After she caught her breath and the sobbing subsided, I asked, "Does he still frighten you?"

Jan nodded and sobbed, "I don't want him or these people to do anything to any of us. I just want them to leave us all alone forever."

Hearing her statement brought me relief and caused my heart to leap. I could no longer hold back my tears. Confidently, I retorted, "The first step is for all of us to stay away from him and the whole family."

Bob added, "We want to protect you, and we will, no matter what the cost."

The more she willingly revealed, the more vigorously we questioned her. Finally, Jan heaved a sigh, not wanting to go into any more details. Her body was limp from exhaustion.

"Okay. That's enough, honey," Bob announced.

"I've been so scared for so long," Jan said between gasps that heaved through her body, as she continued to unload her deepest secrets. Her desperate eyes made my heart ache.

Bob extended his arms in invitation, and Jan folded into them and sobbed mightily. As he tenderly held his firstborn and comforted her, tears rolled down his face. It had been a long time since he had had the privilege of showering her with safe, loving affection. Seeing Jan in her dad's arms comforted me as well. After several minutes, Jan stood up and quietly whispered, "Thanks, Dad. I love you."

"I love you too," he replied.

I embraced Jan, acknowledging the lonely burden she had carried for so long. "I'm so sorry. I can't even begin to realize what you have gone through. Anytime you feel nervous or scared, talk to us. We are here. We are always going to listen and believe you and love you. We will do anything possible to help you cope with all of this!"

Nodding her head, she whispered, "I can't believe I told you and survived." Heading toward the back door, she turned around with a perplexed look. "You don't have to talk to anybody about this, do you?"

"Not right now," Bob replied.

After a few moments of studying Bob's anxious stare, I said, "Our Jan's a bright girl. She's a straight A student. How could she not have figured out that Berchtold was behind all of the voices. This story—how could he be so vile?"

"Why not?" Bob expressed. "Didn't we fall prey to his criminal mind? I think Jan has just scratched the surface. She didn't talk about being sexually abused, and I didn't have the heart to bring it up. I'm just in shock."

"It's bizarre! I can't wrap my head around it either. It's going to take some time to sort it out," I said.

With tears in his eyes, Bob whispered, "But I got my sweet Jani back today, and I can't explain how great and relieved I feel!"

The Long Road Ahead

We fell into a grateful silence, both of us trying to digest the unimaginable circumstances Jan had endured. We fully understood that Berchtold had taken her innocence, her kind, loving heart, and her vivacious personality, and had used each quality to twist, contort, and destroy her—and her entire family. Now that we knew the truth—what had actually been going on for the last four years of her life, what she had endured in silence, and the load she had been carrying—we could hopefully support her in the healing process. We did not yet know what we were to do or how, but we would listen and find counselors and talk. We would do our best to show her that she was still our Jani—our smart, empathetic, kind, perfect child—and maybe through enough love and time, we could help her.

We would try to help Karen and Susan heal too. *Had B done anything like this to them? I was praying they had been spared the worst. Would we ever completely heal from the web of deceit, lies, violations, and absolute incomprehensible harm this person had laid on our family?* The idea we previously held of loving and trusting this "good man" made me sick and angry. I was so sad for Jan and so mad at myself for not seeing through him sooner. I was angry at myself for not recognizing the signs, the dangerous pitfalls, and the slow game of enticement he was playing with Bob and me. Our precious girls were our lives.

I exclaimed, "Oh, Jan, how can we ever be forgiven? Your love for all of us is incredible! You were willing to save a planet and your entire family from doom and destruction." At that moment, she threw her arms around me and her father, and together we wept tears of gratitude, loss, anger, and fear. Her behavior made perfect sense given what she had experienced. I began to physically shake. I was raging inside. *Who could do this to a child? What more would be revealed, and how could I keep from killing him?*

I knew we had a long road ahead of us in helping our innocent daughter. How different things had looked from her perspective as compared to ours! Her concern for the safety of our family had been her prime motivation to continue to obey the purported mission and plan concocted by Berchtold. Her belief that her family would be harmed kept her in bondage. In her mind, she had been protecting us for the last four years. The threat that she would cease to exist if she told anyone was unfathomable. How cruel could this inhumane bastard be?

Now knowing that it was a lie, how would Jan grapple with unraveling the rest of the mind control she had experienced? How would this affect her confidence and ability to trust and love again?

For the moment, I focused on the image of Jan in her father's arms. We had survived as a family. I steeled my resolve that we could get through the years of healing. Jan was finally home!

AFTERWORD

MaryAnn Broberg

It was hard for Jan to pinpoint the time when she finally knew with absolute certainty that there were no aliens, there was no other planet depending on her for their survival, and no one was watching her or threatening any of us and our safety. Thankfully, within a few months, she fully recognized Berchtold as the deviant mind behind every painful thing she had suffered. It took time, professional counseling, and family support to help her let go of his control. He had kept her mind totally confused.

After Jan returned the first time, and I had eventually taken a stand against Berchtold, he hired strangers to deliver messages to her. Each contact had either given Jan specific instructions or an affirmation that had confirmed that everything was going as planned and that she would be told what to do at a later date. Berchtold's psychological maneuvering and manipulation had Jan completely resigned to follow the controlling authority. Her young mind coped by latching on to her absolute belief in a higher purpose—that of being a savior for another planet. Berchtold's calculating and carefully constructed story preyed upon her belief system. It was evil through and through.

With so many strangers interfering in her life, Jan was confused about what the truth was. She admitted to being extremely frightened of Berchtold after the fire but had dared not incriminate him for fear of retribution. B's deceptions continued to control her—mostly because Jan had feared for her life and for the fate of her family members. Since Berchtold's release from the Idaho State Medical Facility, he had sporadically contacted Jan to keep her enslaved. Thankfully, in a moment of clarity, Jan began to doubt the existence of the aliens; and finally revealed the secrets of her past to her sisters, to Caroline, and to us.

The Secret Agony of Sexual Abuse

Over the next few days, we asked every question we could think of, and Jan's response to our questions gave us incredible insight into her painful years of being groomed and deceived by B. Jan's anxiety became more extreme when pressed for details on any of her physical experiences with B, and we realized she needed professional help to unravel that twisted knot. Finding the right person was difficult since she resisted opening up to anyone. Dr. Cantril Nielsen, a child psychiatrist and lifelong family friend, suggested that a psychologist or therapist might be a better fit.

Jan agreed to meet with a local counselor, but she was concerned that anyone who knew her story would consider her crazy. Promising confidentiality, she tackled her experience with great courage and a desire to heal completely. Over time and throughout different stages of her life, various heartaches surfaced, but with many good therapists, the support and constant love of family and friends, and her ability to love and forgive—combined with the absolute belief that she could choose happiness and a full, productive life—she did indeed choose happiness and a full, productive life!

Although we knew that Jan's innocence had been robbed, for some time she refused to talk in detail about the sexual abuse. We, of course, now know that Berchtold's marriage demand was his cover-up for sexual molestation, and it was his only hope to avoid sexual abuse charges. But in the seventies, sexual abuse of children was hard to verify, and it remained mostly a quiet and personal issue. Few convictions against perpetrators were successful at that time. We were disappointed because her refusal to talk diminished any hope of bringing justice to Berchtold for those inexcusable acts.

Most children didn't talk with parents or adults about sexual matters in those days, and our children were no exception. The counselor told us children rarely disclose sex crimes committed against them, and will often keep them hidden because of shame, guilt, and demoralization. Perpetrators are skilled at making children feel responsible in some way for being abused. Many children who are abused become distrusting of adults in general as a result. Natural development is arrested, and moving into mature, adult relationships can be very difficult for them.

Children often carry guilt into adulthood in regard to the crimes committed against them until they experience a level of personal power and safety and are finally able to internalize the fact that they had little or no control over stopping the abuse. Many children remain embarrassed about their victimization and reject any thought of disclosing what they perceive as shameful secrets or weakness.

Jan chose not to tell others about her abuse for a period of time. When she was finally able to speak of it, she estimated that Berchtold had sexually abused or raped her approximately two hundred times from the time of her first kidnapping until the last time he saw her in the Summer of 1978. We know of at least six other victims whom Berchtold abused, both before and after Jan. Who knows how many other children he raped in his lifetime?

When we empower victims to speak up, not only can they begin to heal, but we can also help prevent perpetrators from continuing to abuse others. The hope remains that this book, Jan's story, can be the door, the pathway, through which victims begin to overcome their fear and misplaced shame, not only bringing healing to themselves, but also resulting in open conversations that warn others against the far too common friendly and familiar predators.

The Parents' Dilemma

Bob and I found it difficult to deal with our feelings of guilt, anger, resentment, and shock. It was not only Jan who had been groomed, manipulated, and brainwashed, but we had been as well. In the beginning of our relationship with Berchtold, we had been so taken by him that we had missed the subtle warning signs. He spent an inordinate amount of time at our home with us and with our daughters. He would give gifts that were often lavish. He made daily visits to our home in the mornings and often at bedtime. He initiated excessive activities that involved the girls. We should have seen his focus on Jan as a red flag, especially when he asked her to work part time at his furniture business when she was underage. The fact that he had been fun, loving, witty, charismatic, a big kid at heart, and a dad himself had distracted us from looking closely at his behavior and motivations.

An extremely trusting relationship had existed between our families for almost three years, and my absolute belief that Berchtold would never do anything to hurt my children had given him a privileged ground. We suffered much remorse for having been blind to Berchtold's long-term goal that caused our daughter so much pain. Parents are supposed to protect their children and we had somehow let the unthinkable occur. We grappled with so many questions:

- How could this have happened with the most trusted friend we had ever had?
- If others really saw through him, why didn't they say anything to us?
- What is our culpability in all this?
- How can we forgive ourselves for the terrible, immoral mistakes we made mistakes that created a pathway to blackmail and excruciating guilt?
- How do intelligent, loving parents not see or know more?

The Healing Journey Is Often Lonely

Our entire family faced the challenge of healing from those years of crisis. All of us handled our personal healing independently, and now that we know more about what it took to resolve our own pain, we encourage families to seek professional support for everyone. We see it as a long-term process and something that should be done both individually and as a family.

We each handled our pain differently. Bob soon closed the door on the past and refused to discuss any aspect of the trauma. He was not alone in feeling this solution was best. Many family members and friends felt the ordeal had intruded on their personal lives long enough, and they were tired of dealing with questions from outsiders—and they were tired of the whole ordeal. Trying to appease their feelings, I also felt compelled to stop discussing my feelings and to move on.

In the struggle to keep my emotional afflictions private, self-inspection became a priority. I educated myself about the problems that had nearly destroyed our family. I learned that survivors of trauma find comfort and healing in writing about their experiences. Writing the story of our family brought me satisfaction. I went back to school and graduated with a degree in social work. My studies and work in this field made me recognize that the comfortable, protected life I had lived before Berchtold invaded our family was no longer viable in our unkind and often brutal society. People had to know about threats and how to prevent harm with sophistication and personal power.

It appeared to us at the time that Jan's sisters, Karen and Susan, had escaped unscathed from physical trauma. Only years later did their deep feelings of anger emerge as a result of their grim ordeal. At the time, we hadn't realized how each family member was a victim in some way. We had given so much attention to Jan we were unaware that her sisters had kept their innermost feelings hidden. We also had not been informed that for years, Karen had been saddled with the burden of having detailed knowledge of Jan's sexual abuse. She had kept her thoughts and emotions to herself since the trauma seemed closed to discussion. It was unfair to her. Family counseling could have been a great healer and benefit to all of us, but because we didn't understand, it wasn't on our priority list at the time. It was also less common during those years for an entire family to seek and receive healing support together. We have done that work now, and our family is close and communicates well.

Jan and I chose to be as open and honest as we could in this book because we were convinced it is the key to helping other women, including mothers, grandmothers, daughters, and sisters, see the potential wolves in their lives—at least that is my hope. There are thousands of children, both girls and boys, who are targeted, and the first person the pedophile has to charm and win over to get to the child is the child's mother. People like Berchtold do this time and time again.

When we share our story, people are often horrified—not just by Berchtold's actions, but at our actions as a family. *After this man kidnapped our daughter, how could we have let him into our lives again for even a moment? How could we have been so naive? How could we have been so stupid? How could we have made mistake after mistake? How could we have acted against our best interests and against the best interests of the public?*

Understanding the Outrage

First, I take responsibility for my bad decisions and poor judgment. I was hungry for admiration and love in a way I didn't realize. Berchtold saw me as an opportunity and he manipulated me for his own purposes. Despite not being classically handsome, Berchtold had a dynamic personality that was particularly enticing to the female population of our community. He had a way of smiling, giving his undivided attention, and sharing an adoring look that caused many in our circle and congregation to blush. Many ladies whispered about his thoughtfulness, intelligence, sensitivity, and his "irresistible charm and charisma," while others even described him as a "tantalizing attraction."

Berchtold used every piece of information about me and our family to emotionally manipulate us. A couple of times, I had expressed to his wife, in confidence, that I was lonely because of my husband's long work hours at the business we owned, the many hours he spent with his identical twin brother, and the demands of his church calling, which took up a great deal of his time. She had likely shared my longing with her husband, so he knew where I was vulnerable. Berchtold's attentiveness to me, personally, was electrifying. I felt noticed and appreciated. Whenever he stood close to me or touched my arm, I had a feeling of giddiness. At first, I didn't think much about it. Sometimes I was irked with myself for acting like a teenager. I loved my husband, but I had a hunger for something that was being fed by B.

His manipulation of my feelings led to my very poor decision to visit him at the trailer park in Utah. Promises of information and his constant barrage of phone calls pleading with me to visit lured me to his motorhome that fateful afternoon. After our first meeting at the trailer park, our affair took place sporadically throughout the eight months that followed. Of the dozen times we met, only three or four were sexual encounters. The affair was more of an emotional boon for me since I had been shut out of my husband's confidence. Bob was rightfully upset and frustrated with me, but I was also hurting and confused. Instead of turning to each other as we should have done, Bob confided in Richard (Dick), his identical twin brother, and I stepped smack-dab into the trap Berchtold so carefully laid for me. The affair took place in between the kidnappings— when I wanted to forget the past and believe that nothing bad had really happened to my dear daughter. Perhaps somewhere in my subconscious mind, denial was easier than an otherwise far too painful reality.

The Berchtold Story Does Not End in the Seventies

On Thanksgiving Day in 1984, Berchtold called our house. I didn't recognize his voice at first. He laughed and said, "I can't believe you don't know who this is." A feeling of panic flooded my body at the frivolity in Berchtold's voice. He cheerfully explained that the phone call was not for him, but for his son Jimmy, who wanted to contact our daughter Karen. Mortified, I hung up.

A year later, while all three daughters were attending college and living together, Jan was called to the phone. She spoke with an unnamed caller who mentioned events in her recent life. Unable to put a face with the voice, she shared more about a personal matter before realizing she was speaking with Berchtold. Shocked, she made frantic gestures to Karen to pick up an extension and listen in. Berchtold had some of Jan's personal belongings and wanted to return them. He asked if he could see her. She was still enough of a people pleaser then to think that she always had to be polite to everyone, and so she said, "I don't think so." He gave her a Salt Lake City address and told her that he worked for a large auto dealer. Didn't she want to retrieve a home movie from her performance of *Amahl and the Night Visitors?* Unprepared to challenge him, she made no commitment and simply hung up.

Frantic, she and Karen called home. Fearful that he might interrupt her life again, we insisted that she and her sisters take protective measures by staying in the company of others whenever possible, never going home alone, keeping their doors locked, and carrying a protective repellent. Alerting Campus Police offered some protection, but it was important to be aware that Berchtold could show up anywhere unexpectedly.

Within the month, the following message came:

Dear Jan:

As I told you on the phone, I am engaged to be married in June. I had my attorney check in Mexico to see if you and I are still married, since your mother agreed to take care of this and apparently did not, so we are still legally married.

I have filed for divorce, and you will probably be required to attend a hearing. My attorney will notify you of the time and place. Since we haven't been together since the night on the reservation in Pocatello in 1977, there shouldn't be any problems getting a quick divorce.

B

Receiving no response, he mailed a second letter two months later, obviously determined:

Dear Jan,

The reason you haven't heard from anyone is that I changed my mind about any plans for marriage to anyone else. I am convinced that everyone is allowed one love per lifetime; I have had mine. If there is ever anything you need or if you just need someone, let me know. I will always be here for you.

All my love, B

Would Jan ever be free from his stalking? Two more phone calls to different apartments were made. He found her at an apartment she shared with her two sisters, and one day while her dear friend Jan Hull was watching, she answered a call, turned completely white, and began to sweat profusely. It was Berchtold. She hung up, trembling from the terror. She told Jan, her friend, that he had asked to meet her so she could sign some papers because he was going to get married again and he needed her to sign in order to be completely divorced from him. The second call came to the student apartment where she and her new husband, Duke, were living. B only got out a few words saying that he had changed his mind about getting married when she hung up on him. Jan collapsed into her husband's arms, crying out in anguish, "How does he know? How does he know? How does he know?"

Professionals have determined that personalities of his type do not shoulder the responsibility for their crimes. It is widely believed there is no cure for pedophilia. In some cases, treatment can be successful as long as the addict stays away from his addiction: children.

Even though Jan was no longer a child and should have been considered free from her molester, Berchtold had an obsessive-compulsive disorder, and she was apparently still his target.

Undisclosed sources have provided information to us regarding Berchtold's behavior throughout the years. In 1986, Berchtold was arrested on two counts of rape of a child in the state of Utah. He pled guilty to one count and was sentenced by the Third District Court of Salt Lake

City, Utah, to one year of probation in September 1987. After his probation was over, he moved to Nevada in 1989. Robert Berchtold should have been listed on every state's registry as a sex offender, but probably was not. More recently, another reliable individual confirmed that Berchtold became a drifter and had difficulties with employment, moving from one western state to another. Alcoholism became a problem. He suffered a severe heart attack at one point.

This same undisclosed source stated that Berchtold claimed responsibility for "ruining" the lives of two families, identifying ours as one. In that interview, Berchtold also stated that he had watched Jan in various TV movies and was surprised that she looked so beautiful and capable since he thought she had ended up in a Mental Hospital.

Approximately twenty-five years after the kidnappings, Jan started formally speaking to various groups about abuse and grooming. With this publicity, Berchtold resurfaced into our lives. He claimed that he was being defamed, and he accused us of spreading lies about him. Jan discovered that he had actually only been living about an hour from her current home, just across the Nevada state line. She felt sufficiently threatened to seek a stalking injunction against him in court. His objection to the injunction led to a dramatic face-to-face interaction in court between him and Jan.

Prior to Jan being granted a lifetime stalking injunction by the court, Berchtold confronted her about her goals in coming forward to tell the story. Jan's emphatic response was, "My goal, Mr. Berchtold, is to educate the public about predators like you." That exchange prompted Berchtold to give an empty apology, to which Jan stated, "If you want to apologize, you should stand up, tell the truth, and serve your time in jail, Mr. Berchtold!"

On March 6, 2004, Berchtold went so far as to show up to a conference where Jan and I were speaking. He had hoped to pass out flyers that told his version of the story. When those requests were rejected by the Bikers Against Child Abuse members who were standing guard outside of the conference, he brandished a gun and ran his van into one of the men, injuring him. In November, 2005, Berchtold stood trial for the incident in a Utah state court, and the jury found him guilty. After the trial, but before sentencing, Robert Berchtold headed to Bunkerville, Nevada, drank down a bottle of pills and died by suicide on November 11, 2005.

EPILOGUE

Jan Broberg with Judge Charles Gill

It has been my good fortune to have met a wealth of amazingly caring people who have helped me get ready to tell my story. It began with some of the very deep learning and personal work my mom did to heal herself. This lead me down the path of healing for myself. Telling this story is the first step. There have been many since we began to write it all down. I am on a journey of healing and am grateful to those wise ones, there have been many, along the way who have given me guidance and insights to the process. The whole story of healing has yet to unfold. It is coming. I am very much looking forward to telling the chapters of my life where I regained my happy memories and began to build new ones.

In one of my early speaking engagements, Mom and I had the pleasure of rubbing shoulders with Charles Gill. His wise and guiding counsel was among the first to give me the confidence I needed to begin to tell the rest of the story. I was the keynote speaker on the first day of an educational summit for teachers, school counselors, and administrators in Utah. Mom and I did an extensive Q and A session following the speech.

Charles Gill was the keynote speaker the second day. He was phenomenal as a speaker, but also clearly in his expert level of knowledge and understanding of the issues. Not only was he a Superior Court

Judge in Connecticut, but he had also been an attorney who spent his professional life advocating for child rights and other issues involving children. His primary focus was almost exclusively cases about abuse by pedophiles. He approached us at the end of our presentation, introduced himself, and asked if he could take us to dinner. We gratefully accepted, and we found ourselves in the company of a man who was a leading expert in the field of criminal pedophiles, the cofounder of the National Task Force for Children's Constitutional Rights, and a father to three children. He had been interviewed on every National News and talk show we could imagine.

He encouraged us to tell our story formally in a book—to take the writings both Mom and I had worked on and combine our efforts into a work that could be published. He said in his thirty years of experience, our family story encapsulated all of the cases he had ever been a part of. I said, "Charlie, I think that was a compliment in some strange way." He quickly added how sorry validating the fact that we had experienced every "trick in the book and suffered so many great losses." We could hardly eat the delicious spread in front of us so captivated were we by the stories he shared. At one point, he stopped us and said, "I'll write a foreword or an afterword or both for you, if you like—no charge." That was the beginning of what you have in your hands today!

Months later, after reviewing the manuscript, he contacted me and said, "Jan, I am not so sure you want me to do this after all since your family made every mistake in the book."

I said, "We're beyond that, Charlie. Go ahead and write. Maybe your insights will help someone else see what we did not. Maybe it can change the reality that millions of children are abused by someone they know, love, and most likely trust. Write it all, Charlie. Tell the truth. It's okay. We are ready for the backlash. The truth will set us all free.

Judge Charles Gill

It has been my experience as a Superior Court Judge for more than twenty years that for too many of our children, there exists not a childhood, but a "terrorhood."

Most of these terrorized children's stories are never made public and are carried as lethal secrets throughout their lives. These children come from families of all races, religions, and social standings. None is immune—not yours and not mine.

One impediment to stopping the terror is the public's inexperience in first recognizing and then dealing with the terrorist. This book is the encyclopedia of what adults should know about the particular terrorist called the pedophile. It is also a powerful handbook of all the things that loving and protective parents can do wrong when fate places them in these circumstances.

The Broberg's were and are a wonderful family with sound religious and ethical values. They instilled these values into their beloved daughter Jan. They were very trusting and naive. They were also an easy target.

I realize the mid-1970s were not particularly enlightened years for anybody on this subject. The Broberg's had the very best of intentions, but still made every mistake in the book.

Their first job as parents was to protect their daughter, not to create imaginary alibis for their "best friend." Upon Berchtold's release from jail, they should have immediately applied to a local court for a protective or restraining order, keeping this criminal from having contact with Jan.

Continuing a relationship with the Berchtold family was a tactical mistake. What would change in the world if the families stayed apart until the criminal matter was concluded? Their continued relationship benefited only one person—Robert Berchtold. This guy was still manipulating, and MaryAnn was the willing marionette.

Criminal trials are adversarial proceedings. The Broberg's should never have had a meeting with the criminal defense lawyer. The Broberg's never had a competent lawyer of their own to guide them through the foregoing legal actions.

MaryAnn should have stopped Jan when she was boarding that plane. It was her duty as the mother of a minor.

Law enforcement didn't provide adequate support, protection, or justice. The authorities failed to take action after the second kidnapping, when they had solid evidence that Berchtold again had control of the minor child. If the police had become involved sooner, they might have trailed the criminal upon his release instead of having the Broberg's do their own investigation.

Despite the multitude of crimes allegedly committed, Berchtold managed to escape any serious legal consequences. The plea bargain from the first kidnapping resulted in him only serving about fifteen days after he pled guilty. After the second kidnapping, Berchtold was released after only three months in a mental facility, and he never had to stand trial and answer for his crimes. Why was there no justice served for the multiple probation violations, arson, impersonating a government agent, and, of course, the repeated sexual abuse of a child?

Despite all of Jan's emotional and sexual involvement, along with the absolute misery it inflicted upon her family, one must feel relieved that there is a happy ending to this story.

I suppose the book has educated us, but beyond that it brings a message of hope to all who have ever been sexually abused or maltreated. As you know now, pedophiles are not one-time offenders.

I asked Jan, who is about as attractive and intelligent a person as one might meet, "How did you make a comeback after all of that?" She said, "Because of the absolute love and support of my family during the first twelve years of my life, and a bit of good counseling along the way."

Ironically, in the end, it was what the Broberg's did right for Jan that won the day: they loved her.

Judge Charles Gill
Connecticut Superior Court Judge and nationally recognized expert and adviser on children's issues. Cofounder of the National Task Force for Children's Constitutional Rights and a father of three children.

POSTSCRIPT

By Karen Broberg Campbell and Susan Broberg

We were there too.

As Jan's younger sisters, we think it is vital for the readers to under-stand that this type of terrible event inevitably involves all kinds of other "residual" victims. We sisters also experienced trauma, pain, and a life-time of effects from this experience. Being part of a horrific incident like this one, our family survived, and we recognize the abuse, grooming, and brainwashing that happened to all of us. Both of us want and deserve to be recognized and feel validated that our own experiences were important and meaningful. We still want that today, for ourselves, and for all of those who are within the orbit of any kind of trauma.

Jan's kidnapping and brainwashing affected us deeply. At the time of the kidnappings, our deep love and connection to our big sister was im-mense. We three sisters were connected at the hip, playing pretend school together daily, reading the Boxcar Children, making up performances for the neighborhood, riding our bikes to the park, or buying penny candy at the store. We were truly 'best friends' and had each other as our greatest allies.

During those terrible years, there was a significant impact on our own needs as children. We were at vulnerable and impressionable ages, developing ourselves and personalities, shaping our lives toward our future. Our sister was suddenly gone, and our parents were in shock, worry, and sadness. We lost our best friends. We were talked about in whispers by the other schoolchildren. We didn't fully understand what was happening except for when we knew more than children should know.

We developed our own coping methods. Karen, a naturally curious child, wanted to know the details of Jan's disappearance. She needed to be included in the investigation, to know everything that was going on, and yearned to be privy to every adult conversation. Susan, on the other hand, looked to find a way to fade into the background, to not cause any added stress or take any attention in an already unstable situation. These traits and individual traumas have stuck with us. They have unexpectedly shown up in our lives. At times they have shown up even in our children's lives. This undoubtedly affects our relationships with each other, spouses, family, and friends. As adults, we still must care for each other and the young, scared, vulnerable children we were. We want others to know the residual trauma they have been through, and survived, matters. Everyone's pain matters! All are deserving of help, healing, and joy.

Luckily for us, we have a family that rallied together and created bonds to see us through the difficult times, individually and collectively. By putting first the things that mattered most–family, faith, and unconditional love–we survived.

We all have healing to do; everyone must seek and find support from family, whether it's the one you're born to or the one you create of friends, colleagues, a trusted counselor, doctors, or others. A village of support is vital in helping all who survive such horrendous trauma. Many of those in the surrounding orbit of a sexual assault victim are forgotten. Having survived many subtle and insidious things, we often find ourselves dealing with shame, neglect, confusion, and significant emotional pain. We are much like those who survive war but witness friends die. Society falls short in recognizing how much the traumatic event affects the orbit of those left behind. This is a fundamental principle for which The Jan Broberg Foundation exists, to help survivors and those around them who are also affected. We want everyone to find the hope and pathway to healing that will assist them for the rest of their life's journey.

We must each seek the healing we need to resolve the ongoing effects of our own neglect, rejection, jealousy, fear, helplessness, or any other residual impact from trauma. It is a survivor's journey to find joy and thrive. We are ALL "thrivivors." We want that for YOU!

Healing is a lifelong journey. Finding support and love on that road is vital. Each one of us must be validated, heard, and understood. We matter. Each of you matter.

We See You!!!

– Karen Broberg Campbell and Susan Broberg.